SOCIAL REVIEW 1989–90

C000155781

Edited by

Nick Manning
Senior Lecturer in Social Policy, University of Kent

and

Clare Ungerson
Reader in Social Policy, University of Kent

Longman

In collaboration with the
Social Policy Association

SOCIAL POLICY REVIEW 1989–90

Published by Longman Group UK Limited, Longman Industry and
Public Service Management Publishing Division, 6th Floor,
Westgate House, The High, Harlow, Essex CM20 1YR.

First published 1990

British Library Cataloguing in Publication Data
Social policy review – [No. 2] –
    1. Great Britain. Social policies
    361.6'1'0941

0-582-06164-4

Printed in Great Britain by Bell and Bain Ltd., Glasgow

Contents

Contributors

Digby Anderson   Director, Social Affairs Unit.

Louie Burghes   Until recently, Deputy Director, Low Pay Unit; now a freelance researcher.

Crescy Cannan   Lecturer in Social Work and Social Administration, University of Sussex.

Bettina Cass   Assistant Professor of Social Policy, University of Sydney, and Consultant Director of the Australian Social Security Review.

Gary Craig   Research Fellow in Social Policy, University of Bradford.

Christopher M. Davis   Lecturer in Soviet Social Policy, Centre for Russian and East European Studies, University of Birmingham.

Judith Harwin   Lecturer in Social Work, London School of Economics.

Arthur Gould   Senior Lecturer in Social Policy, University of Loughborough

Stuart Lowe   Lecturer in Social Policy, University of York.

Calum Paton   Senior Lecturer, Centre for Health Planning and Management, University of Keele.

Raymond Plant   Professor of Politics, University of Southampton.

Gill Whitting   Until recently, Research Fellow, School of Social Sciences, University of Bath; now, Research Officer, Ecotec Research and Consulting Ltd, Birmingham.

1 Introduction

Nick Manning and Clare Ungerson

In social policy terms, 1989 has been a less eventful year than the watershed of 1988. While it is possible to review the outcome of some of the policies introduced and changes that have taken place in the past year for example, the NHS white paper, the 1989 Children Act, and the operation of the Social Fund – other initiatives, such as the introduction of the national curriculum and the start-up of the poll tax in Scotland, need more time for research and reflection. This year has thus been a welcome opportunity to raise our eyes beyond the immediate concerns of British social policy making to include two more general areas of interest. First is the state of social policy debate as we enter the final decade of the century which has seen the birth of various 'welfare states' across the world. Second is the question of international issues in social policy. Not only will British concerns increasingly be affected by European standards, such as the Social Charter, but there is emerging a truly international social policy community, through which ideas are frequently transmitted from one national context to another.

We begin this year, then, with a discussion of one of the most important developments in social policy in Britain since the middle of the century – the rise of New Right ideas and policies. The contributions by Plant and Anderson were foreshadowed in a unique conference in the summer of 1989, in which the platform and speakers were drawn equally from the left and the right of the social policy community. The consequent debate was a serious attempt to develop a dialogue about the questions that have been raised over the traditional operations of the welfare state. Plant sets out the arguments of the New Right in relation to freedom, justice, and poverty, and discusses the question of whether welfare rights provided by the state, and operated through the public sector can achieve these fundamental objectives. He provides a fair, indeed compelling, account only to combat it point by point in defence of the welfare state. Anderson approaches these issues tangentially, since his main focus is the subject of social policy itself, which he suggests has suffered fatally from repeated invasion by hostile ideas, with which it has failed to develop a productive dialogue. Hopefully the existence of collections such as this provide part of a response.

The present government has throughout its administration pursued the view that individuals – within families – should be responsible for their own welfare. This has underlain the great push towards the privatization of essential social services, particularly pensions and personal social services. In the case of housing, this view has been encapsulated in the government's very strong encouragement of owner-occupation while, at the same time, imposing severe financial constraints upon local housing authorities. As a result, during the 1980s, there has been a very sharp decline in council house building, and, due to the sale of council houses, a slight but steady decline in the stock of council houses. Stuart Lowe, in his article on the financial impact on households of the growth of owner-occupation, points out that the amount of personal capital generated by owner-occupation has been widely misinterpreted and underestimated. 'Equity withdrawal' that is, the actual money that owner-occupation puts into the pockets of owner-occupiers and their heirs is now, he argues, of enormous proportions amounting, in aggregate, to billions of pounds annually. So far, little is known about what owner-occupiers actually spend their gains on, but it has to be assumed that, in a world where social services are increasingly becoming private sector services, these gains will more and more be used by families, and individuals within them, to purchase caring and educational services in the market. In this sense, then, it would seem that the government's intentions are being neatly fulfilled. However, as Lowe points out, the position of those most likely to need services – namely, the elderly – is not an altogether straightforward one. The ability of elderly owner-occupiers to fund their own care depends very much on where they live, the type of property they occupy, and the way in which they choose to spend their withdrawn equity. There seems little doubt, however, that the recent great expansion in private residential care has been largely fuelled by equity withdrawal by elderly owner-occupiers. In general, though, the social and economic effects, on families and on the nation, of this great engine of wealth distribution remain to be fully examined and will no doubt be of perennial interest to social policy analysts and economists well into the next century.

As we have already suggested, the idea of family self-reliance permeates government thinking for the whole spectrum of social provision. This is equally true of services largely designed for families with severe problems. In her article on family centres, Crescy Cannan considers the provision of community and social services for poor families and the way in which the ideology of self-help has, particularly in recent years, been the basis for the strategy of prevention undertaken by family centres. However, Cannan argues that the ways in which family centres actually operate do not wholly reflect this aim, and that there are important conceptual differences of approach to the problems of mothers with children (by far and away the dominant 'client group' of family centres) even within single centres, let alone between them. The ideas and actions of the professionals who deliver services and the demands made by recipients of services, both, in complicated and subtle ways and at one and the same time, undermine and reinforce the regulatory nature of the activities of family centres.

A further example of changing expectations about the family is to be found in the area of child care law. Here the balance of rights and duties between parents and the state has been widely debated in recent years, both in terms of the failure of social and medical services to secure the lives of children neglected and battered by their parents, and in terms of the intrusion of those same services into the lives of families actually or potentially causing their children harm. Judith Harwin argues that, in addition to these very public concerns, account should be taken of research since the 1970s into the operation of both public and private law; these studies, combined with experience drawn from social work practice, have led to the important review of this area contained in the 1989 Children Act. A major thread in the act is to lay down a clear and consistent notion that parenthood means responsiveness to the child's interests, whether by parents, relatives or statutory authorities. The act then sets out greater limits to court intervention, tries to enhance support for parents to fulfil their responsibilities, and in general seeks to strengthen the family as the best place for child rearing. It also simplifies child protection law around the notion of harm to the child, but it is interesting to note there were heated debates at committee stage over whether the balance here was too far towards parents' rights. It is Judith Harwin's conclusion that although this act has resource implications markedly in excess of current funds, and is consistent with the government's general views on the self-reliance of the family, it nevertheless represents a major improvement on existing law.

The same conclusion cannot be reached about the Social Fund – which is the subject of Gary Craig's chapter. There has been widespread condemnation of this replacement for supplementary benefit introduced as part of the government's review of social security. However it amounts to less than half of one per cent of the total social security budget. Why has it generated so much debate? Gary Craig's answer is that it represents a particularly clear crystal-lization of the government's welfare ideology: for discretion, but away from rights, for expenditure constraint, for less dependency on benefits through the introduction of loans, and fewer and lower benefits. The reaction of welfare professionals and local authorities has been a universal determination to put pressure on the Fund through vigorous advocacy on behalf of claimants, and to maintain a very close watch on its operation. Gary Craig describes the three main projects that have been set up to monitor the operation of the Fund, and to keep its activities in the public eye.

The effects of resource constraint have also been a key element of the long running debate that finally led up to the government's review of the National Health Service. In his article on the important changes about to be enacted within the NHS, Calum Paton suggests that a new system of management has been produced in order to divert attention from chronic underfunding. This in itself is not an unusual reason for policy change, but in this case – the development of an internal market on the supply side – the new policy is made to look like a market while, Paton suggests, it retains, and indeed will further develop, centralized and politicized systems of control.

As Paton illustrates, there has been a notable tendency in recent years to refer to the experience of other countries in the course of discussing policy innovations. While American experience has been brought into the NHS Review, there has been a singular lack of interest in the experiences of what looks at first blush like a very similar system in the USSR. This lacuna is remedied in the detailed comparison of the two systems by Chris Davis. Since the 1960s the two health systems have faced a number of similar problems, particularly the growth of demand alongside tight budget constraints. However, the consequences and policy responses had less in common than might be expected. While UK health service expenditure has lagged by OECD standards, it has still risen from 4 per cent to 6 per cent of GNP since 1965; in contrast, USSR health expenditure has dropped from 2.7 per cent to 2.4 per cent in the same period. Consequently severe shortages of basic medical supplies such as medicines have occurred only in the USSR. Rationing by queuing on the other hand is pervasive in both systems, although high status and major city dwellers were better served in the USSR, and the young were similarly privileged in the UK. The effects of medical technology innovation, usually cited in the convergence thesis as the longrun engine of common development, have in particular not led to growing similarity, but rather the opposite. Chris Davis therefore concludes that the UK NHS has not been operating under nearly such severe resource constraints as the Soviet health service, and that technology is not as autonomous an effect on health care systems as is sometimes supposed.

The next three chapters all address in one way or another a complex policy area of growing importance in which the three elements of social security policy, women, and the labour market are closely connected. It is a feature of social policies in general that they are frequently gender-blind even though, in reality, particular policies largely address only one of the sexes. Louie Burghes' article shows that 'workfare' in America is one such policy where the efforts to persuade or coerce individuals to come off welfare and into paid work is, in practice, a policy to persuade mothers to enter the labour market. As she points out, inherent tensions about the purpose of 'workfare' programmes (and different views as to the appropriate role of mothers is one of those tensions) means that the legislation has been applied by different states of America in widely differing ways. In particular, the use of coercion to force people with different domestic circumstances on to a workfare programme, the operation of sanctions – i.e. the total withdrawal of benefits if individuals do not satisfactorily participate, the duration of the programmes, and the levels of pay available all vary widely between states. Hence it is difficult in itself to draw a 'lesson from abroad.' Perhaps the easiest lesson to take from this American legislation, should the present British administration be considering introducing such a policy (and there are indications that something like it is being considered), is that the purpose of such a policy has to be absolutely clear. Moreover, as Burghes points out, the success or otherwise of a 'workfare' scheme almost certainly stands or falls not by factors internal to the policy itself, but rather extraneous factors – in particular, local labour market conditions.

The labour market as an adjunct to social security policy is also an important connection that Bettina Cass makes in her discussion of the current Australian Social Security Review, of which she is the consultant director. She argues that the old distinctions between work and welfare must and will disappear, but that their reconnection made by workfare programmes does not address issues of the adequacy and equity of income, nor the rapid changes occurring in the labour market, particularly for women. She points out that a basic income scheme is not enough, and that these issues can only be satisfactorily addressed through significant regulation of the wage system in respect of low paid and part-time workers. In turn this can only be achieved, she argues, through the active support of a powerful labour movement, with the kind of major bargaining power that the Australian trade unions have and are using to this effect.

Of course this approach to social policy is premised upon national sovereignty. While this may be the case for Australia for the foreseeable future, it is less clearly the case in Europe. Gill Whitting's article outlines the legislation to which we will be subject after 1992, and the opportunities that might be contained within it for women. But, she suggests, it is most likely that some women will benefit – particularly those with skills in short supply – while for others the legislation will, at best, be an irrelevance and at worst, a disadvantage. The development of 'flexibility' in the labour market on a European wide basis may be very deleterious for women, particularly if they have lost out on the acquisition of skills, since 'flexibility' can and does often mean in effect part-time, temporary and unsocial. Unless social legislation designed to protect the rights of 'flexible' workers is introduced – and, at present, the British government is making strenuous efforts to prevent such legislation being enacted – then the prospects for women (especially migrant women) after 1992 look rather dismal.

Although the EC is now cast by many in the social policy community in the role of distant cavalry coming to the rescue of the embattled British welfare state, the most progressive social policies are generally anticipated not in Brussels but in Sweden. However Sweden is not necessarily progressive on all fronts, as Arthur Gould's comparative research demonstrates. Swedish attitudes towards alcohol and drug use are by English traditions quite puritanical. This stems partly from a long history of temperance activism, in addition to a modern effort to combat the damage that alcohol and drugs can cause. His evidence shows that, as a result, Swedish services in this area are much better resourced than those in the UK. Nevertheless in his conclusion he raises the question of whether the Swedes are setting themselves an impossible task in aiming for a drug-free society, and indeed whether they are not exacerbating the very problem they wish to solve. On the other hand, the liberal British approach which seems to be moving towards greater and greater tolerance of alcohol and drug consumption – may be storing up health and social problems for which we have still to pay.

Finally a word about this edition of the *Social Policy Review* which marks a further stage in the evolution of this annual. First, it is now produced in collaboration with the Social Policy Association in Britain. This will provide some continuity and connection with the interests and developments of the British social policy community, and, we hope, encourage a wider readership through sales to their members. Second, it has taken on a more overtly structured selection of topics and third, it marks the transition to a new editorial team. Clare Ungerson, after a five year stint, is retiring as co-editor. During her joint editorship, the *Review* changed its name twice, dropping – in 1987 – the two words 'in Britain'. This has turned out to be a very prescient alteration. As we move into the 1990s it is trends in Europe, both in the west and the east, that will no doubt increasingly pre-occupy the British social policy community. These influences will be reflected in future editions; at the same time, the policy innovations of the third term of office of the present government will continue to attract comment and analysis here.

2 The New Right and social policy: a critique

Raymond Plant

Since the mid 1970s the New Right in its neo-liberal form has dominated the debate about welfare and social policy. When properly presented, their arguments strike at the heart of the normative assumptions of the post-war welfare state and only if they are answered with the same vigour in terms of defending basic principles is it likely that the alternative view will recover the ground it has lost. The aim of this chapter is to consider the theoretical basis of New Right arguments, to identify their strengths – and there are strengths – and to go on to propose alternative arguments and principles. I shall be concerned with a number of things: with the relationship between welfare and freedom, social justice, the public choice critique of public sector interest groups, the status of welfare rights, the nature of poverty and the role of the state in social policy. First of all however, I shall discuss the neo-liberal approach to these issues.

New Right arguments

From the latter part of the nineteenth century with the growth of New or Social Liberalism the idea of welfare in Britain has been associated with the supposed link between welfare and liberty. The idealist philosophers such as T H Green, R B Haldane and Sir Henry Jones influenced the thinking of Social Liberals about the relation between freedom and the role of the state in welfare (Vincent and Plant, 1984). They argued that unrestricted *laissez faire* deprived the worst off of resources without which they could not act as free citizens. The state as the guarantor of equal liberty had to be concerned not just with civil and political liberties but also with the resources, opportunities and powers which individuals had to have if they were able to act as citizens and make a reality of the formal liberties which they possessed in terms of civil and political rights.

These ideas made an impact on liberalism and through the Social Liberals and the Fabians on the Labour Party. In this sense the link between freedom and welfare became central to the citizenship view of the welfare state that individuals needed not just civil and political rights, but also social and economic resources if they were to be able to realize the ideal of citizenship which equal civil and political rights embodied. The link however was not just with freedom, that poverty was a restriction on liberty, but also with the ideal of social justice and with rights. As this way of thinking developed, it was argued that welfare policy had to be governed by social justice, a just distribution of social resources so that the worst off could exercise to some degree the range of choice which the better placed in society had. It also brought in the idea of rights, that individuals had a right to resources without which they would not be really free and would not be fully citizens. This idea in turn assumed a doctrine about basic needs. That unless certain sorts of needs were fulfilled individuals could not live as autonomous citizens. In this sense needs underpinned the claim to social and economic rights. These ideas taken together also implied an idea of a modern form of community. Earlier, primitive forms of community such as may have prevailed in the Greek City state are irrecoverable, but the role of the welfare state is to be a surrogate form of community. The welfare state embodies the idea that individuals have responsibilities to one another. The political recognition of these responsibilities and the collective action to meet the needs of all members of society embody a viable idea of community in the modern world. It is not the immediate community of earlier and more primitive forms of society, but nevertheless it is an important form of which a sense of collective purpose and thus community can be achieved in the modern world.

These interrelated ideas are rejected by the neo-liberals and although their arguments on specific aspects of this vision may be well known, they are worth bringing together and assessing because, taken together, they do strike at the heart of the vision of the role of the welfare state which I have sketched above and which I would argue played an important animating role in sustaining the ideal of welfare in modern Britain.

The central issue, as I have suggested, is that of the nature of freedom in relation to citizenship. Lord Haldane once suggested that nineteenth century liberalism had played a crucial role in freeing individuals from all sorts of arbitrary and unjustified constraints on individual endeavour and initiative, but he also argued that by the 1880s it was necessary for liberalism to progress to secure to individuals not just freedom from coercion, but also freedom in what he called 'a more subtle sense', namely the powers, resources and opportunities which individuals needed in order to act effectively in the space secured to them by the increase in negative freedom, the freedom from coercion by government, or by the power of hereditary groups (Vincent and Plant, 1984, chapter 3). This new sense of liberty as power and opportunity came to be called positive liberty and the neo-liberals decisively reject this idea in favour of the earlier liberal idea of negative freedom. This change is put nowhere more starkly than in Sir Keith Joseph's book on equality where he argues that 'Poverty is not unfreedom' (Joseph and Sumption, 1979).

There are two arguments which are used by neo-liberals against this assimilation of freedom to act with ability to act. The first is that if freedom is assimilated to ability, then we are only fully free if we are omnipotent, that is to say if we are able to do all that we are free to do. However, this is absurd. It links freedom too closely with desire and means that individuals are differentially free depending on whether they can fulfil the desires which they happen to have. This leads to paradoxical results. The person with extravagant desires but few resources is less free than the individual with limited desires but with the resources to satisfy them. If we link freedom and desire in this way then the idea of freedom loses its objectivity. Whether someone is free will depend on that state of his desires and this cannot be right. If however we argue that freedom is diminished if we cannot fulfil our most important desires or perhaps needs, then we have to assume a moral consensus about what are the important desires or needs and this is rejected by the neo-liberals. While this argument may appear abstract, Hayek, for example, has drawn the political conclusion of linking freedom and ability in that once this assimilation is made it provides a strong case for the redistribution of resources to the worst off members of society just because increasing their resources increases their freedom:

> This confusion of liberty as power with liberty in its original meaning inevitably leads to the identification of liberty with wealth; and this makes it possible to exploit all the appeal which the word liberty carries in support for a demand for a redistribution of wealth. Yet though freedom and wealth are both good things which most of us desire and though we often need both to obtain what we wish, they still remain different (Hayek, 1960, p 17).

This confusion as Hayek sees it began to corrupt liberalism in the late nineteenth century transforming promarket, antistate classical liberalism into the social liberalism which led to the interventionist state and a central role for welfare as an important aspect of liberty.

It is therefore important in the neo-liberals' view to resist positive liberty, or liberty as power or capacity in favour of negative liberty which is seen as the freedom from the intentional interference of others. This is important because it allows the critic to block a further argument in favour of welfare and to clarify the role of the market in relation to liberty. The welfare case against the market in the context of liberty is that the distribution of resources which the free market will produce is in fact likely to restrict the freedom of the worst off, those who are made poor by the operation of the market mechanism. However, in the view of the critic, the market cannot restrict liberty if we understand liberty correctly as the absence of coercion because the outcomes of markets – the so called distribution of income and wealth – is not intended or foreseen by anyone. In a market people buy and sell for all the particular reasons which they have. The outcome of all this buying and selling is that some get more and some get less, but this outcome, although the outcome of all these intentional acts of buying and selling, is not itself intended. It is an unintended and undesigned consequence of human action. Given that liberty can only be restricted by intentional action, it follows that the free market cannot infringe liberty. At the same time the intervenionist welfare state which redistributes resources is a threat to liberty, because its actions and the outcomes which follow from such actions are foreseen and indeed intended. The market is an arena of negative liberty; the welfare state is the real threat to freedom, made more insidious because its actions are guided by a false conception of freedom as ability or power which as we have seen the neo-liberal rejects.

However, given this conception of liberty on the part of many welfare theorists there is a clear link to the idea of social justice. If freedom is to be understood as ability or power and the associated resources required to secure this capacity to individuals, it follows that we need a criterion for the distribution of resources and this will be provided by an appeal to social justice. However, in the view of the critic this appeal is purely rhetorical and illusory, or to use Hayek's own term a mirage (Hayek, 1976). The appeal to social justice is rhetorical because we cannot specify the meaning of social justice with sufficient precision to enable it to act as a guide to public policy and in any case the moral status of the appeal to social justice is misconceived.

Let us take this second point first because the argument here mirrors the argument about freedom and intentionality which I discussed earlier. Injustice can only be caused by intentional action on the neo-liberal view. If something happens to me as the result of an impersonal force, for example the weather, or as the result of the genetic lottery, for example if I lose my crops as the result of a drought or if I am born with spina bifida, these things are the result of an impersonal unintended process. As a result I do not suffer an injustice so much as a misfortune or bad luck. However, this is important because if I do suffer from injustice then there is at least a *prima facie* case for arguing that the state should seek to rectify or compensate me for my condition. However, if I suffer bad luck then the problem is much more one of an appeal to generosity, charity, benevolence or humanity. These are discretionary and private virtues which it is not the duty of the state to coerce. If we now return to the characterization of markets offered by the neo-liberal we can see that they are determined to say that poverty or the lack of resources cannot be seen as injustice so much as misfortune. The reader will recall the earlier argument that the outcomes of free markets are unintended and thus are not to be seen as producing intended or foreseeable outcomes for individuals and as such cannot produce injustice when injustice has to be produced by intentional acts rather than by impersonal forces. The outcomes of markets are like the weather in the sense that they are unintended and unforeseen and cannot therefore produce injustice. The moral demands of social justice therefore evaporate.

The second range of arguments about social justice concern the lack of specificity of the concept. There are many possible criteria of social justice. We can distribute resources according to need, merit, desert, entitlement, property rights and so on. In order to appeal to social justice as a guide to policy we need to specify the principle of distribution involved. In a free and morally pluralistic society, the critic will argue that this cannot be done. We have no consensus about the priority of one criterion of distribution over others. Even if we could agree let us say that needs should have precedence over others, the openendedness of the idea of needs and the incommensurability of different needs make distribution according to need a very poor guide to public policy. This gives rise to two very unfortunate political results in the view of the critic.

In the first place public policy charged with the duty to distribute resources according to socially just criteria will have to be arbitrary and discretionary just because we lack a clearly specified criterion of distribution. This will mean that at the very heart of the public policy of a welfare state will lie the arbitrary and discretionary power of welfare bureaucrats and experts charged with the impossible task of distributing resources according to intrinsically unspecific criteria. However, the idea of the rule of law is at the heart of liberal democracy, but there is no way in which the distribution of resources can follow a clear rule of law just because of the lack of specificity about the nature of human needs which is the obvious criterion of distribution in a welfare state.

The second political consequence is that if government seeks to distribute resources in the context of an ethical vacuum about the distributive principles involved, then it will follow that there will be a destructive kind of interest group competition for social resources. If government is in the business of distributing resources, then it is inevitable that there will arise interest groups seeking a share in the resources available for distribution. However, given the lack of moral consensus about distribution it will follow that government will be guided not by high sounding ethical ideals such as social justice but rather by the relative power of the interest groups to guide its allocation of resources. In such a situation social justice will turn into a camouflage for the rentseeking behaviour of the most powerful interest groups in society. In the view of the neo-liberals this destructive kind of interest group competition was the inevitable consequence of a welfare state seeking social justice and the politics of the late 1970s in their view bears out this diagnosis.

In their view therefore, the welfare state has become overmoralized in terms of dubious appeals to liberty and social justice and instead of seeking to secure to individuals powers and resources outside the market, when we lack a consensus about the nature of these resources, we should leave the market much more unfettered than it would be with a welfare state. The welfare state ideally should be concerned with providing a safety net for those who cannot make their own way in the market, rather than an attempt to secure a status of citizenship outside the market.

This argument is followed through in an attack on the idea of the welfare state as necessary to secure social and economic rights, an idea which received its classical articulation in T H Marshall's *Citizenship and Social Class* (1950), a book which has exercised a great deal of influence upon our thinking about the nature of the welfare state. In the view of the neo-liberals there is a clear and categorical distinction between genuine rights which are essentially traditional civil and political rights and postwar ideas of social and economic rights which are essentially dubious.

The argument against welfare rights depends crucially upon the issue of scarcity given that welfare rights are necessarily rights to resources. It is argued by critics that traditional civil and political rights imply little or nothing in the way of the commitment of resources. A right such as the freedom of expression is respected by other citizens and the government forbearing that is to say not interfering with my exercise of that right. Other civil rights are in the same category, they imply negative duties of forbearance, rather than the commitment of resources, a point put very clearly by Charles Fried in *Right and Wrong*:

> Positive rights are inevitably asserted to scarce goods and consequently scarcity implies a limit to the claim. Negative rights however do not appear to have such natural, such inevitable limitations. If I am let alone, the commodity I obtain does not appear of its nature to be a scarce or limited one. How can we run out of people not harming each other, not lying to each other, leaving each other alone? (Fried, 1981, p 110).

Scarcity implies a limit on the right which means that welfare rights cannot be considered as categorical and absolute in the way that it is possible on this argument to treat civil and political rights given that the latter imply duties of forbearance. Critics will point to recent cases like the Baby Barber case in Birmingham two years ago when parents sought to get an injunction to require the Birmingham Health Authority to perform an operation on their child. Their case was rejected by the courts on the grounds that they could not get involved in the rationing of scarce resources, thus showing that there was no categorical right to health care, as indeed there could not be given the fact of scarcity. The point is again well made by Fried:

> . . . it is logically possible to treat negative rights as categorical entities. It is logically possible to respect any number of negative rights without necessarily landing in an impossible and contradictory situation. . . . Positive rights, by contrast cannot be treated as categorical entities because of the scarcity limitation (Fried, 1981, p 113).

The political consequences of assuming that there can be rights to welfare mirror in the view of New Right critics the same political consequences as arise from the pursuit of social justice. Welfare rights would presumably be based upon a view about needs: that certain needs are so basic that they should be seen as implying rights to those resources necessary to satisfy them. Such needs would involve education, health, social security and income. However as we have already seen the neo-liberals take the view that such needs are intrinsically openended and thus the range of rights postulated on the basis of such needs could grow inexorably. With the idea of a right go assumptions and expectations about the extent to which society will seek to protect these rights. The facts of scarcity make this impossible and the failure to fulfil these dubious rights will lead to a social dynamic of frustration and resentment, a point well made long ago by Enoch Powell:

> The translation of a want or a need into a right is one of the most widespread and dangerous of modern heresies. . . . (it provides) unlimited fuel for dissatisfaction, it provides unlimited scope for the fostering of animosities between one section of potential recipients and another (Powell, 1972, p 27).

The assertion of rights to scarce resources therefore is a recipe for interest group competition with no clear way of regulating it.

In the view of the neo-liberal critics the concern with poverty on which these various welfare strategies are based is a misplaced concern. They tend to reject a relative view of poverty in which poverty is seen as a failure to attain some standard of living which is regarded as a norm in the society and is sometimes linked with the idea of citizenship: that citizenship requires the possession of a range of resources which will enable each individual citizen to act effectively in the society. This is rejected in favour of a more absolutist idea as for example Sir Keith Joseph argues:

An absolute standard of means is defined by reference to the actual
needs of the poor and not by reference to the expenditure of those
who are not poor. A family is poor if it cannot afford to eat. . . . A
person who enjoys a standard of living equal to that of a medieval
baron cannot be described as poor for the sole reason that he has
chanced to be born into a society where the great majority can live
like medieval kings. By any absolute standard there is very little poverty
in Britain today (Joseph, 1976, p 8).

This kind of point also informed some of the speeches of John
Moore in May 1989 when he was Secretary of State for Social
Security in which he rejected the relative view of poverty in favour
of an absolute standard which he refused to define. However, I
believe what lies behind the government's approach is the idea
that what matters to the poor is not their position relative to other
groups in society so much as whether their standard of living is
improving year by year whatever the degree of inequality involved.
This point is clearly revealed in the figures attached as an Appendix.
As can be seen from the figures on original and disposable income
(Table 1.1) the degree of inequality in households has increased
quite markedly since 1976, and particularly so in relation to original
incomes. However for the lowest decile of households of those
in work there has been a signficiant rise in real weekly earnings
(Table 1.2), an increase which is even more marked if one looks
at the position of the lowest quarter. Again the figures show a great
increase in inequality, but if one looks at these figures alongside
what Mr Moore and Sir Keith Joseph were arguing, then it can
be seen that at least for those in work the government's case has
some plausibility once the idea of relative poverty is abandoned. In
the view of the government, the market and the trickledown effect
of increasing real weekly earnings is the key to the problems of
poverty and deprivation and this mechanism will work far more
effectively than any set of regulations in terms of rights and greater
equality. The market rather than the state is the main instrument of
enablement, even though it leads to greater inequality.

Given this approach the role of the values of the enterprise culture
then become very important in social policy. The role of the market
has to be extended on this diagnosis and there is a need to try to
lock groups who are currently experiencing poverty and deprivation
into a more enterprising environment. There is growing interest in
work from the USA in this context, particularly in the writings of
Charles Murray such as *Losing Ground* (1984) and Lawrence Mead
in *Beyond Entitlement* (1986) along with the document produced by
the American Enterprise Culture *The Community of Self Reliance:
The New Consensus on Family Welfare.* One theme of this writing
is that poverty is not to be understood as just a lack of resources,
but rather a motivational and dispositional problem. Because the
way in which the welfare system works poor people have become

separated from the disciples of work and the market, they have become apathetic and alienated, dependent upon Giro cheques from the Social Security Office and upon the services of social workers. The growth of the culture of dependency is now a coming issue of the welfare agenda of the New Right. The welfare state which may have one of its central justifications in the attempt to eliminate dependency, particularly the dependency on private charity, has merely shifted the locus of dependency from private charity or voluntarily-organised charity to dependence on the state. It has not eliminated it, merely transferred it. The aim of the government now appears to be to create more a culture of enterprise among deprived groups to enable them to operate more effectively in the market, rather than seeing their problems purely in terms of the lack of resources. This point came out very clearly in Mrs Thatcher's warm endorsement of the Chief Rabbi's alternative to the Anglican report on inner cities, *Faith in the City* (1985). Lord Jacobovits had argued that the Jewish community had been able to escape from the ghetto and into prosperity by its own efforts and by the strength of the bonds of voluntary obligation, self help and communities (1986). The interesting philosophical issue here is whether dependency is endemic and is just to be shifted about between the market, the state and the voluntary sector, or whether for large numbers of people there are ways of eliminating it. If it is endemic then, as Robert Goodin has argued (Moon, 1988), the moral issue then becomes one of explaining how such dependency can be prevented from leading to exploitation. The neo-liberals, for reasons which I have given earlier, will deny that the market is exploitative and will argue that the welfare state can be; particularly in relation to the behaviour of welfare professionals and bureaucracies, and particularly if one accepts as many neo-liberal critics do the public choice critique of the behaviour of public officials and welfare professionals who are maximizing their utilities in the absence of market mechanisms which constrain the pursuit of their interests for the benefit of the consumer.

All of this adds up to quite a formidable critique of the post-1945 welfare state and aspects of this argument have made the running in academic discussions of welfare during the 1980s. Obviously in a short chapter I cannot hope to provide a fully developed critical response to the neo-liberal approach and nor would I wish to do so in all respects. Some of the arguments are powerful at both a moral and a practical level, but what I shall do is to try to indicate some of the lines of criticism which could be advanced.

Criticisms of the New Right

First of all I shall take the issue of liberty, partly because this has been quite important historically in the attempt to provide a moral foundation for the welfare state, partly because a good deal of recent thinking on the left has taken up the matter again and partly because the neo-liberals' argument about liberty reveals something both important and controversial about their characterization of the market and the possibility of providing a moral critique of the market.

As we saw earlier, there are several strands to the critique but primarily the argument turns on a very vigorous defence of negative liberty as the absence of intentional coercion which, when combined with the argument that the outcomes of markets are unintended, entails that market outcomes cannot restrict freedom, a point which also bears upon the question of whether market relations are exploitative.

Of course, it might be accepted that overall market outcomes are not intended, but they are clearly foreseeable. Indeed, if this were not so the neo-liberals would be at a very considerable disadvantage because surely their own arguments in favour of extending markets depend for their plausibility on the claim that market outcomes are in fact foreseeable, at least in some macro sense. So for example, when the neo-liberals argue in favour of extending the market in rented accommodation as a solution to the housing shortage, this assumes that we can make very good guesses about the outcomes which would arise from such a change, namely that the supply of accommodation would in fact be increased. Market outcomes are foreseeable therefore, but does this make any difference to the question of whether they can restrict the liberty of the worst off if such outcomes are not intended? In micro situations involving personal morality we can be held morally responsible for the foreseeable, although unintended consequences of our actions. This provides for instance the conceptual basis for a crime such as manslaughter. I can be held to restrict your freedom if I undertake an action which could reasonably be foreseen to restrict your ability to do something which you would otherwise do, even if such a restriction was not part of my intention in acting. However, can this tell us anything about the moral status of foreseeable market outcomes? The neo-liberal will argue that the issue at the level of personal morality cannot throw any moral light on the macro issue. The crucial difference is that at the micro level the outcome of the action can be reasonably foreseen in relation to individuals, but this does not hold at the macro level. It may well be that we can foresee that if we were to extend the role of markets against the background of existing inequalities, then those who enter the market with least are likely to leave it with least. However, this cannot be foreseen at the individual level and therefore the analogy does not hold. It is perhaps worth noting that most neo-liberals are in fact methodological individualists and this doctrine has an impact on this argument.

Nevertheless, if it is possible to foresee the outcome of the market for groups of individuals, that some will bear greater costs in the extension of markets than others, then there is a case for arguing that if there is a collective commitment to extend markets then we bear some responsibility for the poverty which some groups will experience as the result of this policy (Walker, 1987, p 8). So for example the issue would apply to Mr Prentice's assertion in 1979 when he was Minister of State in the Department of Social Security that 'If you believe economic salvation can only be achieved by rewarding success and the national income is not increasing, then you have no alternative but to make the unsuccessful poorer'. Does making the unsuccessful poorer by extending market mechanisms and market rewards mean that the freedom of those who are made poorer is infringed? The question might then turn on the issue of whether there is in fact an alternative. The reason for stressing this is that we might well want to argue that while the market is as Hayek argues in some respects like an impersonal force, it is nevertheless unlike impersonal forces in the sense that there are alternatives and the impact of markets on groups can be changed by mechanisms such as welfare states, transfer payments and the like. It could therefore be argued that if the losses of some groups are foreseeable and these losses will not be losses in terms of possible future opportunities, but restrictions on opportunities for action which are currently enjoyed as Mr Prentice's argument about making some groups poorer, rather than less rich than they might otherwise have been, seems to imply, and if there are alternatives to this, then it is arguable that the liberty of such disadvantaged groups is restricted by such policies. Furthermore it is interesting that an argument such as Prentice's also deals with groups, namely with the group of the successful and the unsuccessful. Given this it is not clear why the negative impact on unsuccessful groups cannot be an object of political concern when the impact on the successful group can be.

However, this argument still assumes something which the neo-liberal will wish to deny, namely that freedom has something to do with ability and the resources which the exercise of those abilities require. As we saw earlier this is a central argument. Hayek denies that freedom and ability are conceptually related and it is this denial that allows Keith Joseph to argue that 'poverty is not unfreedom'; it is rather, as he goes on to argue, a form of personal incapacity, but inability is not a restriction on freedom. However, can this case be maintained? First of all it is interesting to notice that Hayek in discussing monopoly in *The Constitution of Liberty* (1960) argues that a monopoly in essential goods is coercive, but it is unclear why this is so unless there is some conceptual link between freedom and the possession of essential goods such as food, housing and health. Second, it can be argued that we cannot understand the worth of negative liberty without linking it to an idea of ability and agency. If we ask the negative libertarian why liberty is valuable, then the obvious reply is that if we are free from the intentional coercion of others then we shall have space in which we can live a life shaped by our own projects and plans. However, if it is this which makes liberty valuable to us and worth struggling for, can freedom be seen as logically distinct from ability to act on our purposes and our projects? Can an understanding of the meaning of liberty be detached from an account of what makes liberty valuable? If not, and if what makes freedom valuable is in fact connected with enabling us to pursue our own projects, then a free society cannot be indifferent to the question of whether people actually possess the material goods which are necessary conditions of action.

At this point the neo-liberal will usually deploy two arguments. The first is that negative liberty can be detached from the idea of the worth of liberty, those qualities in human life which make liberty worthwhile, and second that in a morally pluralistic society we have no way of coming to an agreement on what are the necessary conditions of action, or those needs which have to be fulfilled for someone to be able to act as an agent. These two points are run together in the claim that, if we link liberty with the worth of liberty, then we are in the paradoxical position that liberty is linked with the fulfilment of our desires, which then means that the person with extensive desires but fewer resources to satisfy them is less free than the person with more limited desires, and indeed that freedom might then come via limiting our desires to match the resources which we have to fulfil them. The consequence of linking liberty to our ability to fulfil our desires will then mean that freedom becomes wholly subjective, turning as it does on our capacity to fulfil desire and this cannot be right.

However, I believe that there are plausible responses to each of these arguments. In the first case I would argue for reasons which have been well developed by Charles Taylor that we cannot detach an understanding of negative liberty from a conception of the good or human flourishing (Ryan, 1979). If we could, then the distribution of liberty would depend entirely on identifying all those examples of intentional coercion. However, this would have a very paradoxical outcome, namely that a society such as Albania, to take Taylor's example, may have very few regulations governing movement via traffic regulations and traffic lights. But if the existence of negative liberty is established by identifying the number of coercive acts rather than looking at the range of things and the quality of things which we are free to do, then it might be difficult to argue that Albania is less free than the UK or the USA. Liberty has to be connected with a notion of the value of liberty, with the type of actions which we are free to perform and not just with the incidence of coercion. If this is so, then there is a good argument for saying that freedom cannot be solely identified with the absence of coercion without reference to the kind of human flourishing which we believe a free society nourishes.

The second argument then depends on denying either that we have in a pluralistic society a conception of human flourishing which is sufficiently widely shared for us to be able to link an account of freedom to it, or that we have a sufficiently consensual account of the needs which would have to be satisfied in order for an agent to be able to act. I want to leave on one side the first form of this argument because it is not directly relevant to thinking about the role of the welfare state. The second version of the argument is much more central however. The defender of the welfare state will argue against the neo-liberal that freedom is linked not just with our ability to fulfil particular desires; if it were then the neo-liberal would be right in thinking that freedom would become wholly subjective, depending as it would open the particular desires that we have. Rather, liberty would be connected with the possession of those goods which are necessary conditions of action, not to particular desires but to the needs which would have to be satisfied in order for us to act to satisfy our desires at all.

Neo-liberals argue that in a pluralistic society we do not have sufficient agreement on what these necessary conditions of action would be as a basis for the welfare state. This is certainly the view which John Gray takes for example in his essay in *Dilemmas of Liberal Democracy: Essays on Fred Hirsch's Social Limits to Growth* (1983). There are however a couple of responses to be made to this. First of all it is not clear that there is any empirical evidence to suggest that it is true, and certainly none is advanced by thinkers such as Gray and Hayek. Is it really the case in the UK that there is no agreement that income, health, nourishment and housing are not part of basic needs, or the generic conditions of action? If it is so it would be interesting to see the empirical evidence on which such a claim is based.

Second it fits very badly with the neo-liberals, own account of poverty and the function of the welfare state. As I argued before, and this is a point explicitly made by Keith Joseph, the neo-liberal rejects a relative view of poverty in favour of an account of poverty based upon an idea of need rather than on the degree of inequality or relative deprivation. However, if this is so, then their position is paradoxical. How are we to arrive at a characterization of poverty as the basis for a depoliticized, absolute account, if we do not share a conception of basic needs?

The neo-liberal will then argue that the idea of need here is being used in a very limited sense as destitution, or in Joseph's view to characterize those who without assistance cannot afford to eat. They will then argue that they are in favour of a welfare state which meets these needs in this limited and residual way, but they are not in favour of a more extensive welfare state, based upon a more extended conception of needs. However, this claim is very dubious. Once needs are admitted as the neo-liberal view of poverty requires them to be admitted, it is not clear that there is a definate cut-off point in terms of satisfying the needs which they favour and more extensive needs which they do not. For example Gray argues about a need as basic as health as follows:

> . . . conflicts are endemic because, contrary to much social democratic wishful thinking, some basic needs, needs connected with the staving off of senescence for example are not satiable (Gray, 1984, p 73).

Here we are given a basic need which, in common with much neo-liberal thinking, is regarded as insatiable. However, it is precisely such basic needs that the neo-liberal invokes as a basis for a conception of poverty. However, such needs are capable of being bid up by political processes as much as any account given by wishful thinking social democrats. In sum therefore it seems to me that the neo-liberal has not in fact dented the claim that welfare has to do with freedom via the satisfaction of the basic needs of agency.

Social justice

I now want to consider the claim about social justice, that the welfare state is not to be seen as an instrument for securing social justice, which in their view, following Hayek, is a mirage. The basis for trying to answer this claim is implicit in what has already been argued. There are two aspects of the claim. The first as we saw is that injustice can only be caused by intentional action and the outcomes of markets are unintended. The second is that social justice cannot be a guide to public policy because there are no consensual norms of social justice in a modern complex society.

The answer to the first claim depends, as we saw in the case of the neo-liberal account of freedom and markets, upon the claim that we can bear moral responsibility for the foreseeable consequences of actions in relations to groups when such actions could have been different and are alterable. If this point is accepted in relation to freedom then it also goes through in relation to social justice too. However, there is a subsidiary way of making a parallel point. On the neo-liberal view, the question of injustice depends crucially upon the nature of the process which led to the alleged injustice. The action of the weather in destroying crops or of the genetic lottery in causing spina bifida is not an injustice because it is the result of an impersonal force, similarly the action of the market in perhaps lowering the standard of living of some groups is also not an injustice for the same reason. Leave aside for the moment the points already made about the foreseeability and the alterability of market outcomes, it is still worth asking whether this is in fact all that there is to identifying injustice. Does not injustice, as Rawls has argued, depend also on our response to a situation where it is alterable and not just on whether that situation was brought about by an impersonal force? Take again a micro example. Imagine that a toddler has been blown across a road by a high wind into a gutter full of water and that it is now lying face down and is unconscious and likely to drown. I am the only person in the vicinity who can save the child. Is the question of whether I act justly or not to be settled by reference to the impersonal force of the wind? If I choose not to save it, although it would be at no real cost to myself, have I caused an injustice to the child, or have I failed to perform a duty of benevolence? If we take the former view, that my failure to act would be an injustice to the child, then it cannot be that the question of justice is to be settled by identifying the nature of the process which led the child to be in that position and Rawls would be right to claim that justice is a matter of our response to an alterable or compensatable situation and not just a matter of how the situation arose. So again at the macro level, we could argue that if some people are made worse off by our actions and we fail to compensate them even if their being made worse off was not part of our intention, then we could argue that an injustice has occurred. Hence, my claim is that criteria relating to social justice are a salient basis for criticising market outcomes and these cannot be dismissed as irrelevant to the welfare state as the neo-liberal claims.

Of course, we have to meet the second criticism of social justice deployed by the neo-liberal, namely that there is no point in invoking the principle as a guide to public policy if we cannot formulate criteria of social justice. However, I have already argued in the case of need, which is the dimension of social justice of concern to the welfare state, that the neo-liberal has no consistent line here. Need is invoked as a basis for the claim about the absoluteness of poverty on the one hand and yet needs are regarded as open-ended on the other. If needs are indeterminate and open-ended, then they cannot be used as the neo-liberal wishes to use them to produce a depoliticized, absolute conception of poverty. Needs are always going to be a matter of political negotiation and bargaining and this is going to be true whether the role of government in welfare is to use the claims of need as an instrument of social justice, or whether it is to see welfare as a residual category. If neo-liberals were consistent in their strictures on needs then they would take Nozick's path and reject the idea of the welfare state altogether.

Rights

I turn now to the issue of rights. The neo-liberal rejects the idea of welfare rights and argues that they are fundamentally different from civil and political rights which can be defined in procedural terms which do not imply the commitment of resources. Again I think for the neo-liberal, but again not for a consistent libertarian like Nozick (1974), this is a very shaky argument. The discussion here is capable of endless ramification and I shall concentrate on just one point. The neo-liberal concentrates upon the problem of scarcity. There cannot be rights to welfare because of scarcity. However, the problem of scarcity is much more pervasive than the critic will allow. Negative rights, like positive rights, require resources once it is allowed that there is along with the idea of a right the idea of its enforceability, which after all is the idea which the liberal brings into play in trying to deny the legitimacy of positive rights. That is to say if I have a right to have my negative rights protected, then clearly this requires the state as the guarantor of rights to commit resources to its enforcement. These resources will include the police, courts', legislation, prisons and so on. This is because in the real world there is a scarcity not just in terms of material resources, but also in motivation relating to forbearance. Take two examples of paradigmatic negative rights such as the right to privacy and the right to security. The fact is that people do not forebear. They do infringe such rights and to prevent such infringements there is a need for such safeguards as the Data Protection Act, street lighting, or security checks at airports which go as far as possible to protect such rights. But these are rights to scarce resources and the demands embodied in such rights come up against this constraint. Debates about the appropriate level of resources to be committed to securing such rights become highly politicized – see for example the debate about the number of inspectors needed under the new Airport Security Bill. Recall the argument that the duties relating to such negative rights are supposed to be clear and categorical. Obviously this claim does not hold in the sense that securing the implementation of such rights is going to involve highly political disputes. We cannot say therefore, as some neo-liberals argue, that civil and political rights are depoliticized and not subject to political bargaining as welfare rights are. Bargaining about how to secure rights is a central feature of all these cases and we cannot therefore draw a hard and fast distinction between the two sorts of rights on this basis.

Several conclusions follow from this. The first is that the argument that positive rights involve open ended commitments in the way that securing negative rights do not is fatally flawed. For example in the medical case it is argued that there can be no right to medical care because of the open-ended nature of medical need which grows with technological change. But the same is true of the rights to privacy and security. There was no need for the Data Protection Act before the computer; there was no need for elaborate security at airports before the invention of plastic explosive. The enforceability of such rights is therefore always changing and open-ended, subject to technological change in exactly the same way as welfare rights. However, this is not seen as an insuperable objection to continuing to claim such rights. We are assured for example that there is no such thing as absolute security, but it is still thought worthwhile for the state to do what it can to ensure that travel can occur as safely as possible. Why cannot the same be true for social and economic rights? Clearly there cannot be thought to be a right to some kind of absolute level of medical provision, but why is this thought to be a fatal argument against the idea that there can be a right to health care and not the right to security?

The obvious point to make is that we can, through the normal processes of political bargaining, arrive at some kind of consensus about what at a particular time is an adequate level of public provision to protect rights such as privacy and security. If we can do this with those rights why cannot we do the same for rights such as health care and education?

However, there is still an important issue to be faced in thinking about rights in the context of the welfare state. It is argued correctly that such rights are not individually enforceable. This became apparent in the Baby Barber case mentioned earlier. The courts rejected the case on the grounds that it could not get involved in rationing disputes against a background of scarce resources. The critic will claim that if rights are not individually enforceable, then they are not rights. This is a central issue if we are to continue talking about rights. The idea of welfare rights has been a popular idea since Marshall but it has been assumed that talk of welfare rights just meant that the state had to provide an adequate level of resources for welfare, not that rights could be asserted by the individual to specific resources, except in the social security field. If we cannot enforce such rights as individuals, is it sensible to continue talking about rights? Or should we be considering ways in which these rights could be made enforceable by individuals?

The first thing to notice, however, is that rights to the enforce-ability of negative rights are also in the same boat. As an individual I do not have a right to the services of a policeman or a security official at an airport. And in a case brought in the 1960s the Law Lords ruled that an individual citizen does not have a right to the protection of the state. If we argue that welfare rights are not individually enforceable we cannot treat that as being fatal to the claim that there are welfare rights unless we also say the same abut the enforceability of negative rights. I believe that there is a way forward in trying to define rights to resources at an individualized level but to attempt that here would be too extensive a task but I can refer interested readers to two papers to be published in early 1990 by the Institute of Economic Affairs in which I try to see what mileage there is in this argument. One other benefit of the approach would be that individually enforceable rights in welfare would also meet one of the other objections of the neo-liberals to the welfare state, namely, drawing upon the Public Choice School, their strictures on the power of producer interest groups within welfare bureaucracies. In their view this power will be constrained if more of welfare is made over to the market. The idea of individually enforceable rights would be one way in which there could be a non-market alternative solution to what I believe is a genuine issue.

As things stand therefore, I do not believe that the neo-liberal case against the moral basis of what might loosely be called the social democratic project in relation to the welfare state can in fact be sustained. However, there is one strand of the neo-liberal argument which still needs to be examined, namely the claim that in practice an extensive welfare state is unnecessary because the trickle-down effect of the free market economy will in fact empower most of the worst off groups more effectively than welfare states. This is partly an empirical thesis and partly a moral one. The empirical claim rests upon the sorts of facts about increases in real income which I discussed earlier in this chapter; the moral case rests upon two things. First of all that welfare creates the problem of dependency and second that inequality is not a problem, in fact it is a necessary condition of the free market empowering the poor through the trickle-down effect. Obviously these are very large issues which I have tried to deal with elsewhere, but I would like to take the opportunity to sketch in the main features of an answer to these claims.

I shall not, for the purposes of this chapter, dispute the figures which were quoted earlier, but on the purely empirical issue it is worth remembering that they illustrate the trickle-down effect only to those in work. For those out of work and for other categories of the worst off the picture is far less rosy. Perhaps it is worth noting two points here. Even if we accept the government's own view of poverty, which was not defined by Mr Moore when he made his speeches in the spring of 1989 but nevertheless seems to imply a kind of absolutist approach and certainly involved rejecting the idea of relative poverty in favour of the kind of view enunciated by Sir Keith Joseph, there are still major problems of poverty. First of all the numbers of homeless have risen substantially in the past ten years. In 1970 just over 56,000 families were homeless; by 1985 this had risen to 100,000 and has increased since then. By even the Joseph view of poverty it would be difficult to deny that homelessness is not an important indicator of poverty and here the trickle-down effect is not working. Obviously the neo-liberal reply will be that this is in turn a reflection of the over-regulated market for private accommodation and the trickle-down effect is not working for that reason. However, it is certainly the case that the trickle-down effect has not worked here and shows no sign of doing so. Against this neo-liberal claim could be advanced the idea that homelessness is at least to some extent the result of the privatization of large sectors of the public housing stock rather than the over-regulation of the private market in rented accommodation.

Second, it can be argued that the trickle-down effect is in fact drawing more people into poverty if we accept that Supplementary Benefits are thought to be an indicator of poverty, which is a view from which ministers have not dissented. In 1978 three million people were in receipt of Supplementary Benefit; in 1987 five million were in receipt of such benefits. If we add to this those who are dependent upon the actual recipients of the benefit then again the figures are alarming, having risen by two million between 1979 and 1984. Second the level of Supplementary Benefits has declined. In 1978 Benefits were set at 61 per cent of disposable income; in 1987 this level had declined to 53 per cent. If this is a consequence of the liberalization of the market then it would be difficult to sustain the argument that the trickle-down effect is working in relation to the worst off groups.

It is at this point that the more moralistic arguments are usually employed by the neo-liberal, that apart from the disabled and the elderly this increase is in part the result of a lack of motivation in the worst off groups to latch onto the enterprise culture. They have become locked into a culture of dependency and this can only be changed by either trying to lock them into something like the disciplines of work through schemes like workfare, linking benefits to a more stringent interpretation of being available for work or being prepared to take a place in an Employment Training (ET) scheme. This approach is already in place, although it is not called workfare for the 16–18 year old group. The other more stringent approach would be to argue that benefits should actually be reduced in order to create a more effective incentive to take any job, however low paid, as a way of getting onto the employment ladder. I believe that these ideas about remoralizing the poor may well loom larger in future debates about the welfare state largely because of the influence of American welfare theorists such as Charles Murray, who favours cutting back on benefits, or Larry Mead, who is a strong advocate of workfare as part of the obligation of citizenship, that the receipt of a benefit as a right should be conditional on discharging a concomitant obligation. The Mead approach raises some deep issues about the nature of citizenship which again I think turn upon the idea that there is a categorical difference between civil and political rights on the one hand and social and economic rights on the other. We do not regard civil and political rights as conditional on discharging particular obligations or having a particular kind of moral character, and it is unclear why we should regard welfare benefits in the same way, unless we assume that the rights in question are fundamentally different. However, I have given reasons for thinking that this is not the case.

Indeed, the argument about dependency could be turned on its head. It could be argued that dependency and vulnerability are endemic features of the human condition and the question then is how these dependencies are to be handled, whether through the state or more through private charity and voluntary sector provision. It is at least arguable that dependency on private charity and voluntary provision is more likely to keep a person locked into a sense of dependency in the sense that the recipient of charity cannot claim a resource from these sources as a right. However, if it is possible to define individual entitlements in the welfare field as I suggested earlier then having such rights may well limit dependency more effectively than a greater role for the private sector.

The second point to be made is that the argument for the remoralization of the poor fits very badly with some other aspects of the neo-liberal case. As we saw in the context of both their account of freedom and social justice, they wish to rebut the claim that we can agree on a set of necessary goods of agency in the case of liberty and they reject the view that we can get to consensual norms of social justice. Both of these arguments are rooted in the idea that we live in a diverse morally pluralistic society and we do not have a sufficient sense of *Sittlichkeit* or agreed morality for that state to act in these fields. However, when it comes to claiming that the poor need to be remoralized this claim appears to be overlooked. This links up with two aspects of the neo-liberal view of the role of the state. First of all it is argued that because of moral diversity it is necessary for the state to be neutral between different conceptions of the good, a claim which cannot be sustained if part of the job of the state is to remoralize the poor. Second it is argued that the state has a very limited capacity. Collective action always gives rise to unintended consequences and it is better for the state to stay its hand when tempted to intervene in the lives of citizens. However, this argument seems not to apply when it comes to claims about using workfare or changing the incentives of the social security system to remoralize the poor. We know very little about individual motivation, and for the state to try to inculcate a particular set of attitudes towards the economy and individual motivation within it is fraught with difficulties, difficulties which in other contexts neo-liberals are only too keen to recognize.

Empowerment

I want now to turn to the final issue which is about empowerment and to sketch in an answer to the question of whether the free market can in fact empower the worst off even though it increases inequality. I have already discussed the directly empirical aspect of this claim, but there is a conceptual issue at stake here as well about the nature of empowerment. Can an individual or a group be empowered effectively without taking into account the relationship between that group and other groups in society? Is power a relative notion so that the power of X can only be increased if the power of Y is decreased? The neo-liberal has to reject this because if it turned out that power is relative then the claim that the trickle-down effect can empower the worst off alongside increasing inequality would be disingenuous. There are various ways in which one might try to tackle the question of whether power is relative. One way is to link it to the idea of positional goods pioneered by Fred Hirsch in *The Social Limits to Growth* (1977). A positional good is a good the instrumental value of which diminishes the more widely it is distributed. Unlike material goods such as washing machines, positional goods cannot be subject to the trickle-down effect. Washing machines can be distributed more and more widely without this affecting their capacity to wash clothes; positional goods lose their value the more widely they are dispersed. Standing on tiptoe to watch a procession is a paradigm case of a positional good in that if I stand on tiptoe I gain an advantage, but the more people in front of me do the same, the less valuable my doing it becomes and when everyone does it the advantage is lost altogether. Is power more like a good which can be indefinitely expanded without losing value, or is it more like standing on tiptoe? If we accepted a definition of power such as A exercises power over B when he is in a position to get B to do something which B would not otherwise do, then it seems to me that if power were to be distributed equally it would disappear in exactly the same way as the advantage of standing on tiptoe disappears when everyone does it. If this is so, then there is a good reason for thinking that power is a positional good, which in turn implies that empowerment cannot come about through the trickle-down effect. The trickle-down effect assumes that power is indefinitely expandable and therefore can be expanded alongside inequality. However, if power is positional, then competition for it becomes a zero-sum game in which some groups can be empowered only at the expense of others. On this view therefore again the social democratic intuition was correct, that inequality does matter and that the free market cannot distribute this kind of good in a painless way. Empowerment is essentially competitive and must have a close link to inequality. The neo-liberal claim that the freemarket is the best instrument for empowerment turns out to be flawed.

Overall then, my strategy has been to take the neo-liberal approach to welfare issues, which has provided much of the current agenda of welfare policy for the past ten years, and criticize it internally. There are other ways of trying to defend a commitment to the welfare state but to show that the agenda with which we have been presented is conceptually and morally flawed is a way of trying to make a defence of the welfare state link with current political preoccupations.

Appendix

Table 1.1 Distribution of household income in percentages

	Bottom fifth	Middle fifth	Top fifth
Original income			
1976	0.8	18.8	44.4
1981	0.6	18.0	46.4
1985	0.3	17.2	49.2
Disposable income*			
1976	7.0	18.2	38.1
1981	6.7	17.7	39.4
1985	6.5	17.3	40.6

*After tax and cash benefits
Source: *Social Trends* CSo 1988.

Table 1.2 Real weekly earnings (married man with two children * after tax, national insurance and child benefit)

	Percentage increase		Actual £
	1971–81	1981–86	1986
Lowest 10th	8.0	9.5	103.45
Lowest quarter	7.9	11.2	122.30
Middle	8.7	13.7	149.15
Upper quarter	10.1	14.7	185.48
Highest 10th	11.9	17.0	236.50

*Aged under 11 years
Sources: *Social Trends* CSo 1988.

References

Faith In the City (1985) Archbishop of Canterbury's Commission on Urban Priority Areas.

Fried, C (1981) *Right and Wrong* Harvard University Press.
Goodin, R (1988) Reasons for Welfare. In Moon, D J (ed) *Responsibility, Rights and Welfare: The Theory of the Welfare State.* Westview Press.
Gray, J (1983) Classical Liberalism, Positional Goods and the Politicisation of Poverty. In Ellis, A and Kumar, K (eds) *Dilemmas of Liberal Democracy.* Tavistock.
Gray, J (1984) *Hayek on Liberty.* Blackwell.
Hayek, F A von (1960) *The Constitution of Liberty.* Routledge.
Hayek, F A von (1976) *Law, Legislation and Liberty, 2.* Routledge.
Hirsch, F (1977) *The Social Limits to Growth.* Routledge.
Jacobovits, Lord (1986) article in *Jewish Chronicle, 24* Jan.
Joseph, Sir K (1976) *Stranded on the Middle Ground.* Centre for Policy Studies.
Joseph, Sir K and Sumption, J (1979) *Equality.* J. Murray.
Marshall, T H (1950) *Citizenship and Social Class.* Cambridge University Press.
Mead, L M (1986) *Beyond Entitlement.* Free Press.
Murray, C (1984) *Losing Ground.* Basic Books.
Nozick, R (1974) *Anarchy, State, and Utopia.* Blackwell.
Powell, E (Wood, J, ed) (1972) *Still to Decide.* Elliot Right Way Books.
Taylor, C (1979) What's Wrong with Negative Liberty? In Ryan, A (ed) *The Idea of Freedom: Essays in Honour of Isaiah Berlin.* Oxford University Press.
Vincent, A and Plant, R (1984) *Philosophy, Politics and Citizenship: The Life and Thought of the British Idealists.* Blackwell.
Walker, A and C (1987) *The Growing Divide: A Social Audit.* Child Poverty Action Group.

3 The state of the social policy debate

Digby Anderson

Introduction

'Social policy' refers, of course, to the policies followed by government in health, personal social services, social security and housing
and I would add, insofar as these are concerned with aims such
as engineering 'fairness' and 'equality' or alleviating hardship, also
those in education, transport or any other ministerial field.

It also refers to an academic discipline whose boundaries are
at least formally defined by degree curricula. This discipline is,
in part, an analysis of and comment on social policy in the first
governmental sense. Third, there is social policy to mean the
analysis and comments on government policies and the social
problems they address by academics from disciplines other than
that of social policy in sense two and by journalists, advisors,
voluntary bodies and many others.

This chapter is a review of certain ideas which have been
introduced into social policy in the second and third sense,
mostly the third, over the last decade. Some of them are
new; some, recycled old but hitherto neglected ideas. It also
contains an argument or speculation about the current state of
the social policy debate (Anderson, 1980, 1981, 1981, 1984).
The optimistic version of the argument is that the debate has
become more interesting, largely because social policy – certainly in the third sense and less certainly in the second –
has been widened to involve other disciplines. To give two
examples:

The analysis of social problems and policy by 'free-market'
economists has redirected attention to the more general links
between economics, whether free market or not, and social
policy; links scandalously neglected in the 1960s and 1970s when
many social policy undergraduates were permitted, perhaps even
encouraged to pass and end their studies economically illiterate.

And perhaps almost as important, the increasing intrusion of the churches into the public discussion of social affairs has, whatever the quality of those intrusions, re-awakened, if only in consequent contradiction, consideration of the links between social policies and ethics. In a sense, these changes take social policy back into political economy and indeed into the moral sciences.

More important than even these has been the stimulus of a government which has engaged in, listened to and occasionally even followed radical thinking about welfare services. Not only have its ideas and proposals stimulated debate but the fortunes of them as they have been translated into action have taught valuable lessons about the political feasibility of welfare reform.

There is, however, another way of looking at these changes, a way decidedly more pessimistic at least for some. This is that the widening, the new ideas and the observation of debate and government policy over the decade suggest that the discussion of social policy is now *out of hand,* in some way *out of control.* Only the most naive participants ever thought it was capable of resolution. But now it seems so wide as to be undisciplined. And it is not only the breadth of ideas, academic specialisms, methods and ideological frameworks: it is that some of the new ideas themselves introduce what are euphemistically called 'instabilities' into the discussion.

Sharrock *et al* (1985) recently argued that sociology should be considered not so much a science which provides answers and where questions are *settled* but a discipline akin to philosophy; an argumentative discipline in which the same questions are re-asked. They go further and describe it as a number of *games* asking different questions, games which cannot be aggregated into a single scalar comparison, games under different rules though each subject to its particular criteria of coherence, consistency and inventiveness.

Sociologists might be divided about accepting such a characterization. But to say the same thing about social policy would be even more controversial, threatening, as it seems to do, the reputation of a discipline with much more stake in being seen as *practical* and *instrumental* than sociology: it is, after all, about 'policies' and 'administration'. And if it does not provide 'answers', what does that do to the many social policy specialists employed, usually by the state, on the assumption that it does? Or to those who would turn the answers into politics?

Worse, the features of social policy which have emerged out of the developing debate may go even further. To continue the Sharrock game analogy, they suggest that social policy is not only developing into more and more games which are difficult to compare – indeed the comparison is itself a series of different games – but that in many of the individual games the rules are systematically broken, inoperative or have little to do with how the game is played in reality. Social policy considered as a debate may be not so much broken into different parts as anarchic, i.e. not a debate at all.

The body of this chapter is in two parts. First, following this introduction is a **Section A** which sets out briefly to list some of the ideas which have emerged in the debate and, where appropriate, to identify their intellectual origins. It is not intended to be complete – what on earth would be the criteria for judging it so? – and it reflects ideas I find interesting though I do not find them all convincing. Because it is a list, I have said about each item only enough for it to be identified. Items 1–7 are established ideas. Items 8–9 are ideas which may well prove controversial over the coming years. The list is followed in **Section B** by some speculations about what the items and the reactions they provoked tell us about the status of the social policy debate.

Most of the items are in some way involved in one particular debate, that about the worth of the welfare state. But I would emphasize that I am not here making an argument about the welfare state but describing one, or rather certain features of one, in order to see what they reveal about social policy as a debate.

A   The criticism of the welfare state

1   *Criticism on the grounds of ineffective or perverse redistribution*

It is alleged that the welfare state has failed substantially to shift wealth from rich to poor or to increase social mobility (via educational chances) or provide efficient services. In health the medical services do not accord to the poor resources in keeping with their greater morbidity. The criticism is, of course, an old one and one which originates on the left. But it has been taken up by new critics eager to emphasize the *continued* failure and hence to cast doubt on whether, even if redistribution is accepted as a goal, the institutions of the welfare state are up to the task. Old themes about the affluent and articulate playing the system have been developed. The liability of the welfare state to capture by producer or consumer interest groups (see below) is emphasized and the possibilities of alternatives which subsidize the poor directly, e.g. by voucher rather than by subsidy to welfare producers, have been investigated as have cash versus kind benefits.

The supposed failure of existing institutions has been one of the reasons given for investigating new arrangements and in particular the repeated simple observation that an obligation for the state to see that a service is provided or a standard reached in education, housing or whatever, does not mean the state itself has to provide it. What is misleadingly called privatization is often public provision via private organizations.

Not only is welfare said not to get to those in need but a significant part of this perverse welfare is funded by those in need. A consistent theme of criticism especially in the early 1980s is that those below official poverty levels are paying standard rate tax to pay for benefits to middle income groups (especially in higher education). Taxation, traditionally said to be the proper way of funding benefits to the poor, is itself causing poverty.

It is also charged that much welfare provision does not transfer income at all, returning benefits or services in similar proportions to the amount taxpayers have paid – minus freight charges in both directions. Frequently cited is the refusal to amalgamate social security and inland revenue calculations, a duplication of benefit neither to taxpayers or claimants but providing employment for civil servants.

2 Producer capture

At least one strand of socialist social policy thinking had indeed criticized the services for failing the clients especially in the early 1970s. The enemy were social workers who 'controlled' clients – remember 'Case-Con'? – and following Freidson, Illich and others, 'dominant' doctors. Customers – the word, of course was never used – were said to be alienated from the services allegedly set up for them.

But suddenly when the producers of welfare services came 'under attack' from Conservative 'cuts', the critics forgot their care for the consumers and rallied to 'defend essential services'. At that point their old themes, together with those of the deschoolers, were taken up and pressed into new service. The criticism that state services were run for the benefit of those who worked in them rather than those they were intended to serve and who paid for them became a persistent theme in discussion of school control in particular. Pupil power re-emerged as parent power.

It would be wrong to suggest that these arguments only came from adapted older leftist arguments. Economics provided good reasons why producer capture was likely given monopolistic state provision. But it is true that the virtual abandonment of consumers in favour of the solidarity with producers demanded by trade unionism dogma left the field open for others to take up the consumers' case.

3   The economics of politics

Producer capture was only one phenomenon to be analysed by
the economics of politics or public choice theory. This remains one
of the central disciplines of the modern critique of state welfare.
Its themes undermined the naive assumption of 'public service',
arguing that there is no reason to assume public bureaucrats will
comply with their organizations' explicit ends of public welfare.
What is curious in retrospect is that it took an economist's theory
of bureaucracy to challenge such naivete. Weber himself and
especially his revisers had long before provided a sociological
reason for wariness about the compliance of bureaucracies but it
was scarcely heeded by much academic social policy. Indeed one
fact which emerged was that social policy by the late 1970s was
not only unanchored in economics or ethics but was sociologically
naive. And still today there are calls for this or that state body to
cure this or that social problem based entirely on data about the
awfulness of the problem with next to no evidence that such a
body's members will indeed work towards the solution.

4   Economic versus electoral preferences

Also from work inspired by public choice as well as more general
market economics came the contrast between political and economic preference. Producers of goods sold in the market know
what their customers want by how they respond to goods offered
at a range of prices. Daily the shopkeeper is instructed by his sales
on which goods the customer values most and which more than
others – all at very precise intervals. Welfare goods, e.g. health, are
not sold in the market and their producers get no such detailed
information about their customers' preferences.

Two problems emerge. First, in the absence of prices and known
preferences, the producers decide how much of what goods are to
be provided. Rationing is done by the diktat of the producer – the
doctors, social services director, minister of health decide who is
to be helped and who not, who is to live and die – rather than
by price. Second, the information they do receive about customer
preferences is very crude. Customers vote but their votes do not
record their views of different departments, let alone of specific
services and they are unweighted – they give not the slightest hint
of how *much* the goods are valued. They simply endorse political
parties with packages of policies.

This failure of politically registered preference compared to
economically registered preference not only adds to producer
dominance but means that even a producer keen to serve the
customer is deprived of the information he needs. As Arthur
Seldon of the Institute of Economic Affairs remarked concerning

the appointment of a businessman to run the National Health Service (NHS), it is not being a successful businessman that is crucial. No businessman could run Marks and Spencer for example if the doors were opened, all the price labels removed and people helped themselves. It is the prices and sales which enable businesses to provide what people want.

Market registered preference also has another quality often absent from services subject to electoral accountability. The customer has a right of exit. Economists put against the numerous rights claimed by state welfarists as rights *to* health, education etc., the right to exit *from* e.g. a school a parent finds unacceptable. State monopoly welfare is thus liable to find itself coercing its customers.

5 The ignorance of social intervention

This ignorance of preferences is only one ignorance. State welfare is liable to others, ignorance of need, of solution, ignorance of practice and of evaluation. Social policy in the first sense, i.e. government policies, is founded on social policy in the second, social policy as an academic discipline. Put another way, a high view of social policy with ambitious goals in setting the problems of the world to rights implies a high view of social science especially social policy. Deprived of market information, policy formulation relies on the social scientific assessment of needs and their solutions.

What emerges are not so much questions of the adequacy of social scientific knowledge – do we know enough? – but questions about the suitability of such knowledge for intervention – does social science furnish the right sort of knowledge? The fact that the social world is orderly, and in part known by its members albeit it in an unexplicated and untheoretical way, does not necessarily mean that this knowledge is available to a central body or in a form necessary to plan intervention.

And both Austrian economics – especially Hayek in *The Counter Revolution in Science* (1979) and *The Fatal Conceit* (1988) and 'Austrian sociologists', notably Garfinkel, cast very basic doubts about the availability of what, interestingly, they both call praxeological knowledge beyond the interactions (market interactions for Hayek) which generate it. Such basic questions were commonplace in the sociology for the 1960s. Their implications for research were explored in Aaron Cicourel's *Method and Measurement* (1964). But, once again, social policy's comparative isolation from the basic disciplines on which it should be relying, meant that it largely ignored the 'knowledge question'.

The question does not just arise from epistemology. It is the natural question to ask of social intervention, not 'Is X intervention needed or desirable?' but 'Do we have the knowledge to do it?'

5(a)   A recent example

Consider a recent example (Anderson, 1988). One new departure in social policy has been the use of advertising techniques to engineer 'desirable' behaviour especially in regard to health – smoking, alcohol abuse, AIDS – and crime. To launch an AIDS information campaign with any chance of success, the campaigners need to know about the timings of the epidemics, both hetero- and homosexual, so as to time their campaigns. They need to know whether a heterosexual epidemic is likely: American heterosexual projections are increasingly being revised downward. They need to know what current sexual practices are, which of them need to change to prevent infection, why people engage in them and what might make them stop. They need to know how to assess, if change occurs, whether the campaign or some other factor is responsible for the change, whether the change will last after the campaign – in order to time repeats and developments. They need to be able to evaluate not only if the campaign has achieved its aims but if it has had other unintended effects. For example a campaign might increase condom use but lower standards of sexual morality.

At a government-funded seminar in 1987, the government department which initiates the campaigns had a Professor Healy sum up the proceedings and the state of knowledge. Of the heterosexual epidemic, where the numbers potentially involved are far greater

> we know almost nothing. Nobody can tell me whether such an epidemic exists or not . . . we have not got the necessary information (about) frequency of infection . . . varieties of sexual behaviour . . . our baseline data is drawn from the Kinsey report which relates to many years ago in a quite different society and which has been heavily criticized by statisticians . . . we know little about changes in behaviour or even about ways of measuring such changes.

We do not know how to avoid poverty and unemployment traps without creating other problems. We do not know how to reduce future lone parents without stigmatizing current ones. We certainly do not seem to have the knowledge to 'target' benefits. We know about the association of unemployment and ill-health but not the precise mechanisms or the solution. Drug policy is a sea of ignorance. Such are the allegations.

There are others. Brewer and Lait (1980) developed the ignorance theme to question whether a body of knowledge called social work existed and could constitute a course for learning. Anderson has drawn attention to the ways social intervention programmes are actually justified – by various rhetorical manoeuvres – rather than by evaluations proper to 'experiments' (Anderson, 1979). Saunders (1989) has questioned whether claims to know what the public thinks of services such as the NHS based on standard surveys and questionnaires are valid.

6 Formal and informal welfare

If governments do not know exactly who is poor, why, and what would counteract that individual poverty, who does? One theme has harked back to Spencer and emphasized the continuing capacity of informal institutions such as the family or neighbourhood to deliver more welfare in terms of quantity – more children and elderly looked after than the state or formal voluntary organizations ever could – and in terms of quality. One explanation is obviously that the family and neighbourhood has the rich, changing knowledge which the state lacks. Two developments have emerged. First, some commentators have concluded that the crucial question to ask of any state intervention, before asking whether it could be a success in its own terms, is to ask what effect it will have on the family, on the neighbourhood, on the values and institutions which provide this colossal informal welfare. Does the intervention undermine institutions more effective in welfare than itself?

Another rather different development has been to ask the state not to intervene itself but to support spontaneous informal welfare. Informal welfare, now unpleasantly retitled 'carers', are said to 'save' the government money by looking after e.g. chronically sick relatives or friends at home and therefore should be supported in what is a form of privatization or contracting out.

Some other important criticisms can be more briefly summarized:

7 Wealth creation, innovation effects, standardization, expansion and contraction

State welfare obstructs wealth creation which is the necessary condition for welfare. It does this by causing high taxes and interferences in market mechanisms, especially work incentives which reduce profitability especially at a time of world competition. It also does this because the ethic of welfare producers, especially that of social security, is inimical to the ethic of enterprise and risk taking.

The hand of the state is a dead hand which freezes institutions. Sometimes this is merely a reflection on the lack of innovation in certain state services. At others, it is a more analytical criticism which argues that the opportunity cost of years of state schooling and health is the countless changes which would have occurred under market conditions but have been foregone. Thus Green (1986) argues that one should not compare the NHS now with the situation in the nineteenth century or even the current situation in the USA. One should look at what might have been, in particular the developments in friendly societies, which were suppressed by state intervention.

Welfare is often discussed in terms of equality and a safety net but the theme of standardization is also a frequent goal, the theme that it should not matter who someone is or where they live, they ought to have standard services. The discovery that schools are not standard and that their results vary to the tune of 500 per cent within a Local Education Authority (LEA) from the best to the worst, or the more recent Department of Health assessment that, using a series of measures such as cost and length of stay and waiting list time, 'Some hospitals are 10 times more efficient than others' (*Daily Telegraph*, 1989), have proved to be ammunition not only for those asking for 'more resources' but for those criticizing the system. Their criticism is that the 'chance' of the market cannot be fairly contrasted with the standardization of the state system when 'chance' seems to play a significant role there too.

A final set of criticisms asks whether the welfare state can change rationally. We now have evidence of how it behaves in rapid expansion – the Robbins expansion of higher education or the post-Seebohm expansion of social services – and under contraction – university redundancy procedures or local government post-freezing in the early 1980s. The criticism is that neither were accomplished either rationally or with much view to the customers' welfare.

There are clearly many more criticisms that have been made, particularly by free market economists, but these are now well known. What are not so well known are some more recent ideas and developments which are by no means all targeted on the welfare state as such.

8   Ethics and social policy: some new fields of controversy, especially universalism and particularism

Elsewhere I have criticized the churches' intervention in social policy as ill-informed and relying on a sociologically naive model of a society. However, one very positive effect of these interventions – which the churches might well not regard as positive at all – is the revival of interest in ethical aspects of social policy.

Just one example to show how explosive this could prove. Until recently those who criticized state welfare criticized its performance. Apart from equality, most of its goals were accepted. Critics broadly accepted that we all have a responsibility to each other and should work for a fairer and compassionate society. Though they might have objected to certain benefits, they went along with the vaguer ethical universalism which underwrites state welfare.

Such a consensus was never total. Oakshott, for example, argued that the duties of the citizen, what we owe to all, are few and largely consist of civility. And throughout the last 25 years the widespread approving use of the term 'community' carried, despite the increasing meaninglessness of the word, the residual idea that we owe more to some than to others, more to family, friends and neighbours, than to those distant.

The stress on local obligations implicit in 'community' is certainly in tension with another revived popular term: 'citizenship' stresses the rights that all British people have and the obligations they all share to all others, especially through the central state. Those rights and obligations are universal and equal at least in opportunity. To find some schools doing more for their pupils than others, as discussed above is an affront against citizenship. If different areas will do better or worse out of the NHS reform, proponents of citizenship, at least the Labour version, are justified in being worried. Gross inequalities of wealth are difficult to reconcile with an extensive view of citizenship.

However, 'community's' ideas that we owe more to those near us, our family, neighbours and co-religionists, than to others is based on an ethical particularism which contrasts sharply with 'citizenship's' universalism. And though this idea offends certain Kantian philosophers, it is deeply embedded in popular moral intuitions. To fail to visit the man at No. 32 whose wife has just died or to ignore the child over the way who is tearfully trying to cross the busy road, or even more to neglect one's own father or mother is *worse,* much worse than not worrying about starving Ethiopians.

It is an idea central to both Judaism and Christianity. The rabbis, writes Rabbi Jonathan Sacks in a recent article (1988) were explicit:

> What does it profit a person if he saves the whole world and neglects those closest to him. The poor of your family take precedence over the poor of another family. The poor of your town take precedence over the poor of the next town.

Christianity, in addition to universal themes – loving all because all are in the image and after the likeness of God – also has its particularism. Christ is shown loving his mother, St John, the apostles, his own people with an especial love. The Good Samaritan's care, while explicitly transcending boundaries of race and religion is nevertheless not care for everyone but *anyone* whom he happens to meet, who is close. 'How absurd it is,' writes Newman, 'when writers talk magnificently about loving the whole human race. . . . The best preparation for loving the world at large . . . is to cultivate an intimate friendship and affection towards those immediately about us.'

The obligations of community and citizenship are not in total opposition. The first is meant to radiate to the second. Everyone fulfilling community obligations should 'trickle out' to satisfy some of the demands of universalism in a rough and unplanned way, but the web of welfare which the individual spontaneous threads weave will never be the comprehensive systematic welfare implied by citizenship. And the two are in tension because they lead to different policies. Emphasizing citizenship means a standardized, nationwide welfare system, services standardized to ensure citizen's equal rights are met, obligations standardized through taxation.

Community means allowing and encouraging more diffused sources to create the common good but each with more precise and very personal obligations. The 'good' member of the community does not just care for people but certain specified people because of who they are or where they are, or his relationship to them. Moreover a citizenship welfare which explicitly disregards who and what people are, and for which matrimonial state, address and other particulars are irrelevancies or even sources of stigma, will undermine the structures of family and locality which produce both the obligations of community and the means for discharging them.

9   More new fields of controversy: the re-moralization of social problems

Morality surfaces in a rather different way in another development. Recent American work has centred around the apparently common-place injunction to 'dis-aggregate' the poor. The poor are poor for different reasons and require different solutions. Many of these differences have moral or cultural implications. Some examples: one reason why the elderly poor are held to be different is that they are not reactive to benefits, i.e. the number of the elderly will not increase as the financial attractions of being elderly increase or the disattractions are reduced. Again, interest is shown in the different cultural factors which might explain why, of two persons, or indeed as the Chief Rabbi reminded us, two ethnic or religious groups or cultures, in similar economic circumstances, one manages to escape from poverty and the other does not. Yet again, with the feminization of poverty, increasing attention is being paid to divorced and never married single parents and the resemblances and differences between them. More generally, there is a renewed interest in 'the culture of poverty' and whether financial support helps or encourages dependency.

Murray (1984) in particular has looked at the role of self-esteem in dependency and it cannot be long before there is a re-evaluation of the role of the hitherto villains of social cement, stigma and exclusion. In health policy the point has been made that several of the major killing diseases are behaviour-related. Once the links between behaviour and social problems are admitted, especially when the cost of those problems is publicly borne, then morality is back in social policy in a substantial way. The policy implications of a view of poverty as cultural as well as economic are that benefits are made *conditional* on behavioural change of some sort such as presentation for work, education, detoxification.

The other main implication is that government should review those policies which might be encouraging poverty and dependency cultures, especially in divorce, single parent housing allocation, maintenance payment enforcement, and so on.

9(a) . . . and a consequence: conditionality and the individualization of welfare

A variation of this has been developed in a recent study by Segalman and Marsland (1989) which cites the Swiss welfare system's individualization of welfare in which locally based workers – acting as social workers and sources of social security – work with claimants to draw up individual contracts specifying what the claimant and the worker will do to get the claimant back to independence as quickly as possible. The authors also press for the abandonment of national rates of relief and the localization of welfare together with much stricter liability to maintain laws.

B The implications for the welfare debate and for social policy

We can now return to reflect on what the development of such ideas over the past decade tells us about the state of social policy both as a discipline and a debate. These and other criticisms of the welfare state have, of course, been responded to. Sometimes the respondents have argued directly with the ideas. At others, they have ignored the ideas and attacked the motives of the critics of state welfare – greed, grinding the poor – or even theorized the motives into an elaborate theory – noticeably the Stuart Hall thesis that reducing state control means increasing authoritarianism. At yet others, the respondents have merely got on with following ideas of their own. But what has not happened is an orderly intellectual debate according to common rules. The debate has not, for example, been progressive, that is conducted in a series of rounds which are cumulative. Rather each side continues to repeat opening manoeuvres which seem largely immune to any direct response.

The range of the battlefield I have described is now so wide, so many different academic disciplines, ideologies, values, examples, vocabularies and methods are deployed that a direct hit is highly unlikely. It is totally unclear what a direct hit would be anyway: what would constitute sufficient evidence or argument to make one of the critics or supporters of state welfare admit he was wrong and abandon a position?

Not only is the debate unprogressive, proponents simply ignore ideas or facts when it suits them. Thus the potential for state services to exploit or control their clients/customers has been recognized by left and right when it suited them – and ignored when it did not.

The debate is long on rhetoric: not just appeals to vague sentiment but different vocabularies – 'need', 'choice', 'tax payers' money' and other rhetorical manoeuvres. Consider for example, in how many of the arguments about welfare above, the same evidence can be used to justify more and less state welfare. The failure of the welfare state to ensure re-distribution, social mobility or whatever is adopted as evidence of its failure and as evidence that it has not been thorough enough. The importance of informal family welfare is ammunition against formal state welfare and the contrary – expand state welfare to support family carers. The same event can be interpreted by different ideologists differently: is putting hospital services out to tender while funding them via the state privatizing or making the socialist health system work more efficiently? Some arguments are more or less unanswerable: how would one prove that state welfare did or did not reduce enterprise culture?

The merits and demerits of more and less state welfare are almost impossible to *add up*. How does one quantify the value of the 'right to higher education' versus the 'right to exit from state health systems' or the worth of rationing by price versus rationing by bureaucratic diktat? And comparisons. With what should the NHS be compared and contrasted to see whether a private system would be better: the American system today, the pre-NHS system in the UK or what that system might have become?

And if the arguments about the ignorance of state intervention have any worth, then they mean that it will be difficult ever to establish with any finality whether this or that intervention is working. To prove it unsuccessful will be as difficult as proving it a success and the game will go to he who manages to shift the burden of proof onto the other.

It is not only the debate which is threatened by these instabilities. Insofar as state welfare is indeed characterized by ignorance or producer dominance, is insensitive to popular preference, incapable of rational expansion or reduction, then rational reform, even a rational reduction of the welfare state is unlikely. The very points on which state welfare is criticized are also barriers to its reform.

What is threatened by the emerging character not only of state welfare but the debate about the welfare state is a certain vision of the role of intellectual disciplines, especially social scientific disciplines and the role of 'debate' itself in parliamentary democracies. The vision, more usually expressed implicitly, is that the welfare state is the result of the application of principles, reasoned inquiry and popular preference. The system is administered by a compliant bureaucracy and updated and changed in the light of further reasoned inquiry, progressive academic scrutiny and popular debate.

Well, the last ten years just do not look anything like that. It is not just that interest groups often seem to count for more than ideas and principles. That is an old argument. It is that key elements in the supposed *rationality* of modern democratic states – voter preference, social scientific inquiry, intellectual values and most of all that great totem of intellectualism 'debate' do not work as implied by the vision.

If this thinking is correct then the conclusion for the welfare state is dismal indeed. It will remain, an unreduced and unreformed anachronism imprisoning its customers in its declining services.

Where does this leave 'social policy' as an academic discipline? If social policy as a government activity is uncontrolled by social policy as a coherent, orderly body of knowledge, then social policy as a discipline is left without its field of application and the status which derived from it. Worse, it seems that even as an intellectual inquiry it is maimed. For it has proved itself unable even to be an argumentative discipline such as the sociology envisaged by Sharrock *et al*. How long it can continue to be publicly subsidized is open to question.

References

Anderson, D (1979) *The Ignorance of Social Intervention.* Croom Helm.
Anderson, D (1980) Practical issues in Writing and Winning Sociological Arguments. Unpublished paper to the British Sociological Association.
Anderson, D (1981) *Breaking the Spell of the Welfare State.* Social Affairs Unit.
Anderson, D (1981) *Evaluating Curriculum Proposals.* Croom Helm.
Anderson, D (1984) *The Kindness that Kills.* SPCK.
Anderson, D (1988) *The Megaphone Solution.* Social Affairs Unit.
Brewer, D and Lait, J (1980) *Can Social Work Survive?* Temple Smith.
Chief Rabbi, From Doom to Hope. Chief Rabbi's Office, no date.
Cicourel, A V (1964) *Method and Measurement in Sociology.* Free Press.
Daily Telegraph, 28 July 1989.
D Green (1986) *Challenge to the NHS.* Institute of Economic Affairs.
Hayek, F A (1979) *The Counter-Revolution in Science; Studies on the Abuse of Reason.* Liberty Press.
Hayek, F A (1988) *The Fatal Conceit.* Routledge.
Murray, C (1984) *Losing Ground.* Basic Books.
Sacks, J (1988) The Moral Concerns We Share. *L'Eylah*, September.
Saunders, P and Harris, C (1989) *Popular Attitudes to State Welfare Services.* Social Affairs Unit.
Segalman, R and Marsland, D (1989) *From Cradle to Grave.* Macmillan/Social Affairs Unit.
Sharrock, W W, *et al* (1985) *The Sociology Game.* Longman.

4 Capital accumulation in home ownership and family welfare

Stuart Lowe

A family may gain more from the housing market in a few years than would be possible in savings from a lifetime of earnings (Pahl, 1975, p291).

In the fifteen years that have elapsed since Ray Pahl's observation his words have assumed almost prophetic proportions. The rate of capital accumulation in owner occupied housing has accelerated rapidly and the associated withdrawal of cash from this equity base began to increase rapidly in the late 1970s, and from the early 1980s has surged. Moreover, the trend in recent years is for these assets to impact on household budgets independently of earnings and social class position. This suggests that what Pahl recognized as a significant source of gain may now be so substantial and widespread that it has begun to have a significant effect on the nature of British society.

Such is the magnitude of this financial 'leakage' that it is already possible to identify important macro-economic and social consequences. The essence of this case arises from two features of owner occupation as it matures as the dominant housing tenure in the 1980s; first, that it is now the majority tenure, currently accounting for two-thirds of households, and is still growing relative to the rental sectors; and second, a gradually accelerating trend over 30 years for house prices to inflate more rapidly than retail prices as a whole, creating a rapid capital accumulation for most home owners through financial 'gearing'. The key here is the use of mortgage credit to sponsor access to the purchase of the house. This limits the household's financial liability but enables them to take all the profits from house price inflation if they sell the house. The wider availability of mortgage finance in the 1980s and the growth in the value of dwellings over several decades has created conditions in which households are able to extract some of this value by periodically re-establishing their gearing level in line with the growth in their incomes. A move of house commonly involves calculations about levels of debt and equity withdrawal. There is also a major and growing source of equity withdrawal from the housing market from the sales of houses acquired through inheritance. The gains from these types of equity withdrawal are not distributed evenly, either geographically or by social class, but their rapid growth at the apex of the recent house price inflation cycle is remarkable and may have contributed more than 2 per cent to disposable incomes in the mid-1980s. The downturn in house prices during 1989 does not alter the long-term logic of the processes which are involved.

In the past many commentators have doubted or simply opposed the idea that owner occupation could be a source of gain in the way outlined above. Kemeny (1981), for example, argues that '. . . the capital gains made in owner-occupied housing do not generally accrue to anyone: they are simply passed from one owner to another'. Ball (1983) also argues that the gains from owner occupied property are, in effect, unrealizable, while Forrest (1984) opposed them in principle and suggests that capital accumulation through housing will tend to intensify existing social divisions. Thorns (1981) also suggested that such accumulation would exacerbate existing inequalities, '. . . the process of accumulation transfers wealth to those who already have substantial assets, thus reinforcing rather than reducing existing social divisions'. All these points may well have been valid in the early 1980s, but increasingly the evidence shows that the wealth that is being generated by home ownership has filtered into a broad cross-section of society and, through the various opportunities for equity withdrawal, are net additions to the incomes of all social classes. Saunders and Harris (1988) conclude from a study of three towns that, '. . . working class people have secured high rates of return from home ownership and do not seem to have fared any worse than higher social classes'.

Privately owned dwellings now account for about half of all personal disposable assets compared with less than a quarter in the early 1960s, and have created a substantial group of moderate asset holders, whose wealth is mainly held in housing. Given that the expansion of owner occupation in the 1970s and 1980s has been particularly rapid in the skilled manual and middle range non-manual social strata, owner occupation has led to some levelling up in personal asset holdings within the class system. Two-thirds of skilled manual workers are home owners compared to only 30 per cent of unskilled manual households. Virtually all employers, managers and professionals are, if they choose to be, owners of at least one home.

At the other end of the wealth spectrum the growth of home ownership has opened a significant cleavage between these middle range assets holders and families with few assets of any type, who are almost all tenants. This social divide is underpinned by the role now played by council housing as a 'welfare' tenure which increasingly caters for newly-formed families and the elderly, and above all the poor. Nearly three quarters of households in the lowest income decile live in council houses, compared to 60 per cent in 1980. Existing divisions based on social class continue to be reinforced by housing processes, but it is now clear that the configuration of these divisions has been altered by the housing market and the new roles played by the rental tenures in recent years, and housing is of growing importance as an independent source of social change and life chances.

Among the most important changes in the housing market that have created the conditions for a higher rate of equity leakage are the new lending practices of the mortgage industry and the opportunity, which is partly related to the more competitive market for housing finance, for households' gearing ratios (the relationship between the current value of the dwelling and the outstanding mortgage debt) to decline rapidly under the impact of house price inflation. These processes lie behind the surge in the scale of equity leakage that began in 1981–82, the year when the high street banks entered the mortgage market on a big scale, and the building society monopoly ended. The banks took about 40 per cent of new lending in that year and the increasing competitiveness in the mortgage market meant that it was no longer possible for the building societies to operate as a cartel. These are endogenous processes constituted within the housing market and the lending institutions, and insofar as they have generated additions to income or access to new lending have an autonomous impact on the budgets of owner occupier households.

However, the growth of home ownership and the potential for financial gain arising from it in the 1980s and 1990s must be read in the context of the opportunities and problems of defending standards of welfare and consumption in an era increasingly dominated by private modes of service provision. Home ownership in this sense is not a 'certificate of entitlement to share in the fruits of capitalism' as Saunders and Harris claim, but an element in household budgeting which may help to sponsor access to private services when the cash limited public sector fails to sustain standards. The ability to trade against their housing in this way, particularly by moving more flexibly between the public and private sectors, provides options for home owners to defend welfare standards and general consumption, options which are unavailable to tenants. To the extent that this happens and is sponsored by autonomous housing market processes a consumption cleavage based on housing has opened up, and seems likely to widen during the 1990s.

Owner occupation is not, however, a homogeneous tenure and is subject to important patterns of unevenness in geographical and demographic distribution. These factors affect and complicate the patterns of gain, and in some cases loss, and in turn influence a household's ability to lock into housing generated wealth and cash. The chapter continues, therefore, with a brief profile of owner occupation and evidence of the scale and sources of equity withdrawal. Following this the effect of equity withdrawal and how cash leakage from housing is used at various stages in the family life-cycle is discussed. The inter-action between family life-cycles and housing careers are seen as being of growing significance.

A tenure profile

Owner occupation is not a homogeneous housing tenure and the pattern of capital accumulation and the potential for equity withdrawal are significantly influenced by a number of key elements, notably in the distribution of home ownership by age, social class, and region. All these factors also have to be read in the context of key identities within the structure of the housing market. There has been, during the recent period of expansion in the tenure, a much publicized disparity in house prices between the regions, and a house price inflation cycle which also has an important inter-regional dimension. Finally, the housing market has to be considered for its performance against other investments and a number of special qualities concerning the rate of return achieved in the last twenty years or so. These issues, on the rate and nature of the capital accumulation in home ownership, are at the root of Pahl's claim and it is necessary to account for them at the outset.

Home ownership is the housing tenure of over two-thirds of the population, and has grown by about 1 per cent per annum relative to the rental tenures, for the last 30 years. The reason for this rapid restructuring of the tenure system is very largely a consequence of the financial logic which underpins the 'popularity' of being a home owner (*see below*). This recent phase of growth, however, has not been evenly distributed across the age structure and there are significant differences in the owner occupancy rate among different age groups. Among the 30–60 year olds about three-quarters of households are home owners and are the cohorts in which the rate of increase has been particularly rapid, from less than 50 per cent in the late-1960s. At age 60 onwards the owner occupancy rate decreases with age, so that only about 40 per cent of the over-80 year olds own a house. It follows, of course, that this variation will wither away up to the middle of the next century, other things being equal. In the meantime important effects will be generated by this distribution, particularly in the growth in the quantity of housing inheritances.

Home owners are not evenly spread geographically or by the value of their property (either between regions or within them), and these factors also have an important bearing on how to interpret the social and economic consequences of mass home ownership. Thus the highest average prices for houses and the greatest density of owner occupiers are found in the south-east of England. Three-quarters of households there are home owners compared to only 50 per cent in the region covered by Cumbria and the north-east, while in Scotland owner occupation remains a minority tenure at about 40 per cent of households. The price differential between the 'North' and the 'South' is very substantial. Prices in London and the south-east have been between 25 and 50 per cent higher than national average prices, whereas the northern regions trend value has been 75 per cent of the national average. This is a stable pattern over the last 30 years or so and has not been changed by the surge in the southern markets during the summer of 1988. London 'drives' the market and price increases ripple out into the other regions. Overlying this inter-regional price gap is a house price cycle with prices rising and subsiding around the trend values. Thus when the southern market turns down the regions adjust by continuing an upward movement. Thus there is a significant price differential between London and the south-east and the other regions which is overlaid by the fluctuations in the house price cycle. The house price cycle is strongly associated with the period of expansion in home ownership from the late 1960s, and since then four quite distinct cycles can be identified.

One of the key features of the housing market during the last twenty years or so, and the underlying reason for the attractiveness of home ownership as an investment, is the pattern of inflation in the market. Evidence from the Halifax and the Nationwide Anglia building society data bases shows that owner occupied houses have inflated at about double the rate of the Retail Prices Index since the mid-1960s. As we have seen this has not been an even progression but the trend is clear. The reasons for this are complex and include factors such as interest rate instability, supply and demand factors in the market, and the increasing availability of mortgage finance. A number of advantageous tax changes were also very significant. Most notably the abolition of the schedule 'A' taxation of owner occupiers in 1963 (the tax on the imputed rental income enjoyed by home owners), and the absence of capital gains tax on housing transactions, in the context of the continuation of tax relief on mortgage interest payments, created an incentive for owner occupiers to treat their houses as investments as well as commodities. These tax changes in the mid-1960s in effect created a very large scale subsidy from the public purse for home owners, and these gradually became capitalized into house prices. Moreover, the 'real' rate of return on housing has been significantly better than almost all other forms of investment, while the costs involved over the life-cycle are lower on average than those for renters (Saunders and Harris, 1988; Lowe, 1990).

At the same time one of the key financial identities in this sector of housing, the ratio of average incomes to average house prices, has remained relatively stable as a trend across the period, with average house prices being at between three and a half to four and a half times earnings. 'Real' capital accumulation is thus achieved as a result of the market's rapid inflation in value in the context of the relatively stable trend in the earnings to house prices index.

The crucial factor which has secured the growth of the equity base of virtually all owner occupied households during the last two or three decades is the use of mortgage finance to purchase the properties. Currently about 80 per cent of the purchase price for first-time buyers and about 60 per cent for existing owners is financed by mortgages. Personal liability is thus minimized and the purchasers 'gear up' their investment, accumulating all the proceeds of inflation in the value of the dwelling and needing to redeem only the original loan when they sell. A household's gearing ratio (the ratio of current price to outstanding mortgage debt) is the key to the accumulation in home ownership and lies at the heart of Pahl's claim. For example, on an average price house, bought in 1970 for £5000, the ratio of outstanding mortgage debt to current value fell to less than 15 per cent within a decade, while the value of the house in 1989 had risen to about £60,000. The mortgage having been paid off after 25 years, and allowing for transaction costs if the owners now decided to move, and assuming a neutral figure for the long-term costs of renting an equivalent house compared to mortgage payments and maintenance costs, the capital gain is clearly considerable and compares favourably to all conventional forms of investment in the rate of return achieved.

Capital accumulation and equity withdrawal

The scale of the capital accumulating in owner occupied dwellings is of massive proportions. At the end of 1987 the Building Societies Association estimated that the value of personal sector dwellings was about £750,000 million, while outstanding mortgage debt was less than £180,000 million. The potential to withdraw some of this equity exists on a variety of occasions or circumstances. Very often the transactions involve the replacement of the equity in the dwelling being sold by new lending to the purchaser. There are two main sources of such 'leakage', through housing inheritances (when the house is passed in a bequest and then sold by the beneficiaries), and second, during a variety of types of moving. The main source of such leakage occurs when the movers increase their gearing during a move – by taking a bigger mortgage – and retain some of the proceeds from the sale of their previous house. Some owners simply 'trade down' to a cheaper house and either redeem the previous mortgage from the sale price or, if they are already outright owners of the house, retain the profit from the transaction, less any moving costs.

In a recent study Lowe and Watson made estimates of the scale of equity being withdrawn from the housing market using a model devised by A E Holmans, the Chief Economic Adviser in the Department of the Environment (Lowe and Watson, 1989; Holmans, 1986). Estimates were made of the flow of funds through the housing market using information on the number of moves taking place and the value of the transactions and mortgage funds. Despite some uncertainty about some of the accounting identities it was possible to arrive at figures which portrayed the magnitude of cash leakage from different sources in the housing market. Holmans' original report highlighted housing inheritances as the most important source of leakage, and there has been a spate of studies concerned with the consequences of housing inheritances (Hamnett, Harmer and Williams, 1989; Munroe, 1988; Forrest and Murie, 1989). The study by Lowe and Watson, however, drew attention to the accelerating trend in equity withdrawal in a variety of types of moving households. Table 4.1 compares the scale of 'leakage' from the housing market from inheritances and from movers (with and without mortgages).

These data show the gradually increasing amounts of cash released from housing inheritances and are sensitive primarily to average house prices, with fluctuations mainly associated with the house price cycle. There is some evidence of 'lag' in the timing of the sales with the beneficiaries delaying the sale until market

Table 4.1   Equity withdrawal from owner occupied dwellings 1982–1988 (£000,000)

	1982	1983	1984	1985	1986	1987	1988
Inheritances	2,988	2,998	3,965	3,562	4,304	5,545	5,545
Movers:							
with mortgage:	3,393	4,780	4,165	4,552	4,905	6,621	10,088
without mortgage	469	519	553	588	656	742	720
Total	6,850	8,297	8,683	8,702	9,865	12,548	16,353

Source: Lowe and Watson, Report to the Joseph Rowntree Memorial Trust, 1989.

conditions are favourable. As the figures show, movers within the market have in the 1980s always been a larger source of leakage and subject to greater fluctuations reflecting the number of transactions that take place and the house price cycle. The underlying trend is for movers to extract an increasing amount of cash, but in 1987 and 1988 the amounts released increased dramatically.

There are other sources of equity withdrawal such as the proceeds to private landlords of sales of their properties to sitting tenants or on vacant possession. So called 'last-time' sales are also a very substantial source of leakage, occuring when two existing owners get married and sell one of their houses, or when a household sells up prior to emigrating. In recent years there has been a spate of sales arising from moves made by elderly people into residential homes (where they are renters). Taken together Lowe and Watson calculate that a further £4000 million were released from the housing market in 1984 from these other sources, mainly moves involving households leaving owner occupation. Including a variety of re-financing packages, in which the house is used as collateral for a new loan or some additional borrowing, there may have been as much as £15,000 million entering the personal sector derived from direct leakage or new borrowing in 1984. It seems very likely that these forms of financial leakage feed into consumer expenditure through its effect in depressing the savings ratio, and the magnitude of finance involved suggests that personal disposable incomes may have been increased by as much as 2 per cent (based on the 1984 figures). There is very little direct evidence of what happens to this money but the availability of substantial home equity clearly does raise the possibility for families at various stages in their housing careers to extract cash or trade against the equity in some way.

It is a common view that it is only elderly owner occupiers who are affected by the issue of home equity, but there are a variety of issues and choices which confront households at various stages in their housing careers. There are major problems of access to the inflated market for first-time buyers, and once in the market, moving to another house at various stages in the family life-cycle creates a variety of choices of how to trade in the market, and problems of mobility in some circumstances. Later on elderly home owners face a diversity of problems, opportunities and judgements of timing about how to use or retain their home equity. Finally, as the owner occupation rate among the elderly increases so the scale of inter-generational wealth transfers is increasing, and there may be important interdependencies between these 'last-time' sellers and the new generations of first-time buyers, through lending within the family.

The uses of home equity

At the very outset of family formation there are major difficulties of access to the housing market. The 'affordability' of owner occupation, particularly for first-time buyers, is the key issue here, and there are a number of views about the nature of this problem. Bramley (1989), for example, has argued in a series of influential papers that the problems caused by the higher house prices in the south of England should be a major part of the indices of housing need which determine the allocation of subsidies for building social rented housing. He argues, *inter alia*, that the south should take a very much higher share of funds. Whether public subsidies should chase the market in this way is, however, very debatable and the recent rapid decline in house prices in London and the south-east suggests the need for caution. There is evidence that shows that incomes in the south are higher than the north, there are more two-earner households and less unemployment, and that the quality of the housing stock is better in the south than the north. The measurement of housing need is thus very complex and it is not self-evident that the higher prices in the southern housing market should necessarily cause a disproportionate share of subsidy to be allocated to the south, not least because the building costs per unit of accommodation are much higher in the south (so that the same amount of money used in the north builds more units). The problem of homelessness in London is a national disaster and should be treated as such from contingency funds, not the mainstream financial allocation to social housing, and certainly not at the expense of the more cost-effective investment programmes in the north. If subsidies chase the market in the way Bramley intends it is quite possible that the problems of homelessness and difficulty of access to the housing market in the capital will be made worse due to interference with market adjustments, with London attracting, for example, further influxes of young single people as accommodation becomes available. Bramley's work does not take sufficient account of these feedback effects (Barnett, Bradshaw and Lowe, 1989).

But whatever the merits of the debate on the north/south divide, it clearly is the case that many first-time buyers do not find access to the housing market easy. As we have seen they need to borrow a high proportion of the cost of their first house purchase (on average 80 per cent compared to about 60 per cent for movers already in the market), and this heavy 'front-loading' makes them especially vulnerable to mortgage defaulting and arrears. Thus the rapid inflation in the housing market in recent years and the resulting high level of equity stored in the form of housing is certainly a constraint on the immediate access to the market for many first-time buyers.

Once in the market the rapid decline in gearing ratios provides an early opportunity for families to trade against their housing equity. They may, for example, after a few years decide to trade up and re-establish their gearing by taking a bigger mortgage (because their earnings will have increased) and investing all the proceeds of the sale of the previous house into the new dwelling. Or they may trade down to a cheaper house and either reduce their level of mortgage debt or extract cash. The extent to which households consciously use their housing in this way is not known, but Nationwide Anglia building society data show that most moves are not related to job changes and in three-quarters of cases were short distances. This might suggest that households were trading in the market to improve their housing circumstances, and it is clear, whether trading up or down, that movers must adjust their living standards according to their debt and equity decisions. It seems very likely that families at different stages of the life-cycle and housing careers will respond differently with respect to the holding of debt and equity. For example, when children leave home or at the point of retirement a household will have different housing needs and may adjust by trading down. People moving on retirement represent a high proportion of equity withdrawn by movers without a mortgage because they are the outright owners of the property being sold and are trading down. Depending on the type of property being sold, its location and the price of the property being bought, a significant addition to post-retirement income can be made. A move from 'south' to 'north' during a change of job clearly offers scope for major adjustments to housing standards and size, and offers a range of possibilities on debt levels and equity withdrawal. There is, of course, a serious problem of labour mobility from north to south due to the disparity in house prices between the regions, and here other issues, particularly transport costs, are a significant part of the equation. The boom in house prices in East Anglia during 1987 and 1988 was largely associated with the overspill out of London. But the bidding up of prices by commuters was finally undermined by the 21 per cent increase in British Rail fares in January 1989, after which the cost of the season ticket was more than outweighed by the cost of new lending in the London housing market.

Home equity and elderly people

Elderly owner occupiers have a number of obvious advantages over their younger counterparts. First, a very high proportion of them (95 per cent of the over 60s) have paid off their mortgages, and so are the outright owners of the property. Second, they are very likely to have been in home ownership for a long time and will certainly have benefited from the rapid inflation in house prices in the 1970s and 1980s. However, there is plenty of survey evidence that households in retirement are less affluent than the economically active sections of the population. The 1981 English House Condition Survey (EHCS) found that 75 per cent of elderly home owners had low incomes, of only a little over £3000, compared to only 10 per cent of younger adult households. But precisely how elderly owner occupiers fare within this general picture of being 'equity rich but income poor' is not at all clear. The Family Expenditure Survey and the General Household Survey, two of the main data sources on income, do not cross-tabulate tenure and income or expenditure by age (Oldman, 1988). So far as the value of the properties of elderly home owners is concerned, the EHCS showed the somewhat older nature of the property and a worse state of repair than average, suggesting lower values. There is no direct evidence on this but the National Housing and Dwelling Survey (1978) found that the property of widows was worth 9 per cent less than average house prices.

The ability and willingness of elderly people to trade against these assets is a complex issue. Staying put is the norm and the vast majority of elderly people continue to live independent lives until frailty or illness drives them into hospital or nursing homes, from which they never return. In recent years there has been a tendency for some people to anticipate the consequences of ageing by moving into some form of sheltered accommodation. The rapid growth in private sector sheltered housing in the last five years shows the willingness of builders to intervene in specialist markets when evidence of an effective demand is apparent. Rapid inflation in the housing market combined with the example of public sheltered provision, from which the private sector learns the model, has generated a surge in this type of housing option. There are probably 50,000 units of private sector sheltered accommodation, the majority of which has been built in the last five years following the ideas of the developers Mcarthy and Stone, who are still the market leaders. The scale is such that about 5 per cent of all new house building has been of this type in recent years. The market has now become very sophisticated and specialized with a diverse range of products – retirement homes for 'empty nesters', retirement villages, second stage homes and homes for the very frail elderly (which are in effect nursing homes) and so on, and the industry has its own journal *Retirement Homes* which is full of glossy publicity.

The relationship between this form of provision and home equity can clearly be seen in the much greater density of private sector sheltered housing in the south than in the north, but developments are rippling out as the growth in housing equity spreads across the regions. One study of these residents, in York, suggests that they are not particularly affluent and were drawn from about the middle of the market (Oldman, 1989), but clearly the more recent up-market developments are targeted at the very well-off, and in general it seems likely to be an option mainly utilized by people with financial as well as housing assets (due partly to the necessity to pay service charges). Low income owner occupiers have to consider particularly carefully whether they will be any better off financially by moving into sheltered accommodation in the private sector. This is because the sale of the previous dwelling may produce an equity release (if they trade-down) which puts their capital above the level for entitlement to housing benefit (currently fixed at only £8000). It might be better to conserve their assets in 'bricks and mortar' for use at a later stage of life. Thus there are difficult decisions to be faced about the timing of a move, where in the limited market to buy, and how their income will be affected by equity withdrawal. Home equity is not easy to manage in old age and is not necessarily of financial benefit.

The home equity of elderly people has been used in a different way in sponsoring access to the burgeoning market in private residential care during the 1980s. This market grew rapidly between 1975 and 1984 from about 20,000 to over 60,000 places (DHSS, 1985). Low income elderly people were able to take advantage of changes in the supplementary benefit regulations in 1983 which enabled local DHSS offices to pay the costs. Owner occupiers, however, had to use up most of their equity from the sale of their house following a move to residential care. From Social Service statistics with adjustments for owner occupancy rates, Lowe and Watson (1989) estimated that in 1984 there were about 51,000 owner occupier movers into residential care. Assuming their houses were sold at 9 per cent below average house prices (an adjustment derived from the NHDS) these 'elderly households' dissolved released equity of over £1.3 billion. There is evidence that cash from the sale of the house is passed to relatives before entering the home, although this practice is illegal. It is, nevertheless, probable that substantial amounts of housing equity sponsor access to residential care, and are progressively used up on the fees until only a small amount of the original capital remains. Thereafter DSS support for the payments can be claimed. In this case it would seem that equity withdrawn from the housing market acted as a subvention for supporting the expansion of private residential care (Meacher, 1986).

Staying-put options for elderly home owners have received considerable publicity in recent years, but the evidence suggests that very few people have been able to avail themselves of these alternatives. There are a number of different schemes. The 'staying put' or care and repair schemes sought to use a combination of counselling, improvement grants and maturity loans using the house as collateral (Wheeler, 1985). But the 1986 Building Societies Act subjected the loan element to scrutiny under the Consumer Credit Act, and this, at one stroke, undermined the mortgage markets' confidence in this type of loan. The abolition of single payments and of tax relief on loans for home improvements further complicated the 'staying put' policy.

Home income plans and so called 'home reversion' plans have also been singularly unsuccessful as social policies which would enable owner occupiers of modest incomes to utilize their home equity. With home income plans, part of the equity is mortgaged and the proceeds used to buy an annuity to boost the owners' income during their life-time. With home reversion plans the whole of the house is sold and the pro-ceeds used to provide an income for life. There clearly is potential for such schemes but as yet they are used by very few people (Leather and Wheeler, 1989). The problem is that companies will only offer such deals to the over 70s or cou-ples whose combined ages is 150 years. It is also clear that the costs of providing the annuity are prohibitively high. In the case of home income plans tax relief on the loan is payable during the lifetime of the recipient and has to be paid out of the income received from the annuity. If these interest payments could be 'rolled up' and paid after death from the proceeds of the sale of the house they would be a more viable use of home equity. In addition, the notion of passing the property to heirs remains a staunchly entrenched social value.

It is clear from all this that the use of the huge quantities of home equity in old age is by no means simple or necessarily beneficial to the elderly owner occupiers themselves. In some cases its existence has stimulated the provision of private sector services which were formerly unavailable or were the prerogative of publicly subsidized and publicly provided services. But the consequences of these forms of provision are different. In the case of private sector sheltered housing the move does not use up the equity (apart from transaction costs) and may provide a net cash proceed to help bolster income. A move into a residential home often sees the equity rapidly consumed in paying the charges. The much publicized 'staying put' options have run into considerable problems and are not a commonly sought solution to the housing needs of elderly people. At this stage, therefore, it seems that the people most likely to benefit from the massive quantities of equity stored in the dwellings of elderly owner-occupiers are the beneficiaries of the will following their death.

Housing-based inheritances

Various studies and methods of calculation show that there are about 150,000 estates per annum passing at death which contain residential property (Morgan Grenfell, 1987; Hamnett, Harmer and Williams, 1989; Lowe and Watson, 1989). This figure will gradually increase as the younger cohorts of home owners, which contain a higher proportion of owner occupiers, age and die. The recent study by Hamnett, Harmer and Williams concludes that, '. . . we can expect to see the actual number of properties inherited due to property release to double within the next forty years' (Hamnett, Harmer and Williams, 1989, p76). The scale of equity currently being withdrawn from this source was described above in relation to Table 4.1. Housing inheritance has dominated the equity withdrawal issue, and a number of studies have begun to paint a picture of what happens to this cash and some of its possible social consequences. Munroe's research confirms that substantial sums of money are indeed passed within families, usually to people of the same or the following generation. At the time of the study Munroe (1988) concluded that these were people already well-established in their housing careers, and resulted in '. . . deeper wealth divisions in the longer term between those who own houses and those who do not'. Forrest and Murie (1989) make a similar point in their evaluation of this issue, which focuses on the uneven pattern of distribution of inheritances both by social class and region: '. . . wealth accumulation and inheritance through housing will be highly differentiated and may be more likely to accelerate rather than smooth out social divisions'. It might, however, be speculated that as the more recent cohorts of home owners, who are drawn from a wider social class spectrum, die out during the course of the next half century these conclusions will have to be modified. As to how these massive sums of cash are used, Hamnett, Harmer and Williams show that about half of all receipts is invested in financial assets, with a strong preference for building society deposit accounts. About a quarter was spent on general consumption, suggesting an addition to consumer spending of about £1400 million in 1988. A further 27 per cent was used on buying a first or second home and on home improvements. These are very interesting indicators of how money from inheritances is used, at least in the short term. It has to be remembered that inheritances mostly pass when the beneficiaries are already well-advanced in their own housing careers and are established in late-middle age. This pattern of use is unlikely, therefore, to be replicated in the case of other types of equity withdrawal, particularly movers. From this study it would appear that lending within the family from the proceeds of housing inheritances is marginal; only 2 per cent to assist children or grandchildren to buy a house and 1 per cent on helping sponsor private education.

Conclusion

The scale of equity withdrawal from the housing market reached an unprecedented magnitude in 1988. Moreover, this cash is derived from processes which are endogenous to the housing market. As time goes by financial leakage of this type is less tied to the dominant middle class home ownership model of the post-war era, and is spreading across the social class spectrum. This leads to some degree of levelling up of wealth. It also creates a significant social cleavage between owner occupiers and tenants. The inability of tenants to trade against the equity value of their dwellings cuts them off from this source of cash withdrawal. Given that welfare choices in the 1980s have been re-structured around private and individualized modes of provision, access to which is dependent on cash, there is a wider significance to these housing generated resources. Faced with cash limited and declining public services provision, millions of households have to defend their welfare standards by the purchase of marketed services. They are in effect compelled to opt for private services if they can afford the costs. It is this ability to move flexibly between the public and private sectors that is in part sponsored by decisions on debt and equity in home ownership (Lowe, 1987; Taylor-Gooby, 1986). In some cases, notably the growth of private sector sheltered housing, innovation in the market is directly related to effective demand generated by home equity. But the problems of being a home owner are for many elderly people very considerable, and there is as yet no satisfactory way of unlocking their equity in their life-times.

At an earlier stage in the life-cycle, particularly during a move, a range of options exist on how to trade against housing equity. A household can decide whether to re-establish their original level of mortgage debt or adjust to some other desired and lower level of mortgage liability. Equity from the sale of the previous dwelling can be leaked according to their decisions on their required or desired level of housing needs and ambitions, and, of course, this is influenced very significantly by moves between different regions of the country. Thus the place and point in time of entry to the market, the length of time within the market and the geographical direction of subsequent moves all influence the capital accumulation/equity leakage 'map'. Living standards and welfare choices for families are increasingly influenced by their housing options and choices;

housing careers and family life-cycles are subject to important interdependencies.

The financial gain to most owner occupiers from their housing over the last two decades or so can hardly be disputed. This has not created a bonanza as some observers imply or hope, although the impact of equity withdrawal *is* sufficiently great that the personal sector savings ratio has declined (Barnett and Lowe, 1990), and general consumption will certainly have been stimulated. Home ownership is unique because it is both one example of the gathering tide of privatization in the 1980s, but is also increasingly a sponsor of the wider shape and pace of welfare restructuring.

References

Ball, M (1983) *Housing Policy and Economic Power*. London, Methuen.

Barnett, R, Bradshaw, J and Lowe, S (1989) *Not Meeting Housing Needs*. Preston, Northern Group of Housing Associations.

Barnett, R and Lowe, R (1990) 'The Economic Consequences of Equity Withdrawal'. Forthcoming paper.

Bramley, G (1989) *Meeting Housing Needs*. London, The Association of District Councils.

DHSS (1985) *Residential Accommodation for the elderly and younger physically handicapped people at 31st. March 1984*. London, HMSO.

Forrest, R (1983) 'The Meaning of Homeownership'. *Space and Society*, 1.

Forrest, R and Murie, M (1989) 'Differential Accumulation: wealth, inheritance and housing policy reconsidered'. *Policy and Politics*. 17 No 1.

Hamnett, C, Harmer, M and Williams, P (1989) *Housing Inheritance and Wealth: A Pilot Study*. Report to the ESRC and Housing Research Foundation.

Holmans, A E (1986) 'Flows of Funds Associated with Purchase for Owner-Occupation in the United Kingdom 1977–1984 And Equity Withdrawal from House Purchase Finance'. *Government Economic Service Division Working Paper 92*, London, Departments of the Environment and Transport.

Leather, P and Wheeler, R (1989) *Making Use of Home Equity in Old Age*. Bristol, University of Bristol, School for Advanced Urban Studies.

Lowe, S (1987) 'New Patterns of Wealth: The Growth of Owner Occupation'. In Walker, R and Parker, G (eds) *Money Matters*. Sage.

Lowe, S and Watson, S (1989) *From First-time Buyers to Last-time Sellers: An Appraisal of the Social and Economic Consequences of Equity Withdrawal From the Housing Market 1982–1988*. Report to the Joseph Rowntree Memorial Trust, York, University of York.

Oldman, C (1989) Unpublished paper to Joseph Rowntree Memorial Trust. York, University of York, Department of Social Policy and Social Work.

Morgan Grenfell (1987) *Housing Inheritance and Wealth*. London, Morgan Grenfell Economic Review 45.

Munroe, M (1988) 'Housing Inheritance and Wealth'. *Journal of Social Policy* 17.

Pahl, R (1975) *Whose City?* (Second Edition). Harmondsworth, Penguin.

Saunders, P 'Beyond Housing Classes'. In *International Journal of Urban and Regional Research*, 8 (1984).

Saunders, P and Harris, C (1988) 'Home Ownership and Capital Gains'. Paper for the International Conference on Housing and Urban Innovation, Amsterdam.

Taylor-Gooby, P (1986) 'Consumption Cleavages and Welfare Politics'. *Political Studies*, 39.

Thorns, D (1981) 'The implications of differential rates of capital gain from owner occupation for the formation and development of housing classes'. *International Journal of Urban and Regional Research*, 5.

Wheeler, R (1985) *Don't Move: we've got you covered*. London, Institute of Housing.

5 Supporting the family? An assessment of family centres

Crescy Cannan

While recent inquiries into social workers' effectiveness in child protection have, by and large, focused their recommendations around *procedures* in such work (and while reassurances to the public are made in these terms) there have been developments in the conceptualization of *services* to children and families which have been less publicly debated. The rapid development of family centres, in both local authority and voluntary sectors, provides an example. The 1989 Children Act places a promotive duty on local authorities, following the proposal in the preceding White Paper (DHSS, 1987), for a broad

> 'umbrella' *power* to provide services to promote the care and upbringing of children, and to help prevent the breakdown of family relationships which might eventually lead to a court order committing the child to the local authority's care. Within this power the local authority will be able to provide services to a child *at home* . . . (para 18).

The White Paper noted the growth of family centres and identified them as one way in which local authorities meet their role in 'supporting the family in various ways especially where parents are under severe stress' (para 19).

Lord Mackay, the Lord Chancellor, has suggested that parental responsibility is the idea that runs through the Act 'like a golden thread': in speaking of 'parental responsibilities' rather than 'parental rights' the Act emphasizes the reason and justification for parental status, namely, he argues, the duty to raise the child to become a properly developed (morally and physically) adult. Further, he states that

> The government is anxious . . . to make it clear in the Bill that families should generally be left to sort out matters for themselves unless it is

shown that without an order the child's welfare will suffer (Mackay, 1989).

This chapter is based on research into the development, aims and nature of family centres. I shall argue that family centres exemplify broader issues and tensions in contemporary social welfare provision and in the relationship between the family and the state. They epitomize the view that 'supporting the family' means in reality the state's construction of a particular form of family characterized by women's economic dependence and informal caring (Land, 1979; Wilson, 1977; Pascall, 1986; Dalley, 1988). They also epitomize new developments in welfare policy, which I shall uncover by deconstructing the discourse on 'prevention', which in Britain in the 1980s has reaffirmed child welfare policies based on family (rather than public) responsibility, and which castigates welfare 'dependency'. I want also, however, to argue that while family centres embody elements of new right policies, they *also* reveal agency by professionals and organizations in shaping the discourse on family problems and in controlling the conditions of their work, so that their nature is plural, sometimes resistant to dominant policies, and possibly confusing to their (mainly female) users. Family centres reveal something of the ways in which women are regulated and their roles constructed by the linking of social resources to images of motherhood and family life. They also show how social provision can materially enhance the quality of life of individuals and communities, and how social welfare can empower rather than merely regulate its users.

The research

I began this research in 1982 when family centres were still relatively new. I collected documents on 49 family centres in both statutory and voluntary sectors, and during 1984–85 visited ten centres, and interviewed their managers. I sought a balance of urban and shire county authorities, and of Labour and Conservative councils. I interviewed middle managers with responsibility for developing family projects in both statutory and voluntary sectors, and I collected child care strategy documents and evaluative and descriptive papers from eleven local authority social services departments (having approached seventeen), and from the prominent voluntary child care organizations. I looked at the Young Family Day Care Association's data on 52 family centres, the British Association of Social Workers' Special Interest Group on Prevention survey of local authority strategy documents

(Tunstill 1985), at Phelan's (1983) and Holman's (1983) surveys for the Children's Society, Birchall's (1982) survey for the National Children's Bureau, and Wilmott and Mayne's (1983) report on the EEC-sponsored family projects in England.

The bulk of my information came from the professionals and organizations developing and evaluating this new approach; there was no social scientific research or discussion then available on family centres, but I have drawn on research on parental (maternal) involvement in health care, education, and playgroups (e.g. Finch, 1984; David, 1985; Graham, 1979) and on analyses of family policies and the state (e.g. Land, 1979; Dingwall *et al*, 1983; Donzelot, 1980; McIntosh, 1984) in forming my own assessment. I fed back some of my findings to family centre workers, and used these discussions to check my conclusions against the views of those in the field.

What are family centres?

Family centres are now established or planned in most English local authorities. Variously known as family centres, young family day care centres, community day care centres, or family projects they share a focus on the pre-school child and his or her parent(s). The centres are run by social services departments (occasionally with education or health also involved) and by voluntary child welfare agencies such as the Children's Society or Save the Children Fund. Some centres are former day nurseries which have gradually drawn parents into their sphere of work, some have grown from self-help projects such as playgroups, others are developments of community centres or children's homes. Some are open and accessible to all potential users in the neighbourhood (which might include teenagers, unemployed adults, elderly people), others have a strong boundary between themselves and the public and take only families referred by social workers or health visitors. All aim to prevent the reception of children into care (as under Section 1 of the 1980 Child Care Act, and preceding legislation), and to support families in their care of their children. Under the 1989 Children Act family centres will continue in their role as services provided to promote the welfare of children in need; unfortunately, however, neither the quality nor the extent of such provision is spelt out in the Act. The Act does away with the notion of 'voluntary' care, substituting the provision of accommodation to children whose parents retain responsibility; family centres will therefore retain their preventive role and their place at the interface between parental autonomy and state intervention.

Family centres are staffed by workers with backgrounds and varying levels of training in social work, family therapy, counselling, community work, psychology, teaching, nursery nursing or playgroup work. The sizes of the centres vary from, say, a small centre taking five referred families at one time, to larger centres with perhaps 50 children coming for day care, (though not all at the same time) and a large number of users coming to at least a dozen different activities. Such activities include play groups and day care for pre-school children, individually planned play, group and family therapy, parent education, counselling, and teaching on child development and care, womens' health groups, welfare rights, adult education, art and craft, keep-fit, sports, youth clubs and holiday schemes. A small number of centres take families on a residential basis; attendance on a daily or sessional basis is however more usual.

Family centres range from, or may combine, the forms of a community centre and a specialist therapeutic agency. While all family centres are situated in areas of social need (or take their families from such areas) some seek to offset the effects of poverty (whether of income, family relationships, or environment) by offering good compensatory play and social facilities and by avoiding social isolation and depression in mothers; others focus on children identified as 'at risk' by virtue of their own or their parents' behaviour or circumstances. In the latter type, which I shall refer to as the social work/child protection centre (in contrast to the community work centre) children and their families are likely to be found who have been referred for assessments of their parents' adequacy, for preparation for fostering or adoption, for the treatment of abuse or neglect, for family therapy, and for monitoring of 'risky' situations. Whereas in the community work centres most adults would choose their activities, in the social work/child protection centre there is strong professional surveillance of adults and direction as to how they spend their time at the centre. While all centre staff spoke of the need for gaining parents' consent and agreement in such programmes, some acknowledged the resentment this could cause, (confirmed by user research, e.g. Ely, 1984; Heiser and Godfrey, 1984). In such centres, strong sanctions may attach to noncompliance – loss of the services of the centre, perhaps loss of parental rights, or the shame of being labelled a 'bad' parent.

The apparent differences between the clients of the two forms of centres stem from *routes* to the centre and its services: *all* the centres I visited included families with severe social and personal problems. In order to gain access to the social work centres, they had to be defined as having children 'at risk' (of reception into care or of some form of abuse or of developmental delay). The centres construct parents' difficulties in personal and private terms: they may be understood as socially disadvantaged, but these tend to be individualized to become the *family's* deficits (Bernstein, 1971) rather than those of the environment or resources.

The two types of family centres are not pure and separate in practice: anxiety about child protection work means that there is pressure from social services departments on the community work centres to accept referred families, to monitor them and to provide a safe place for their children; at the same time financial restrictions limit the extent to which either the departments or the centres can provide a general service. Family centres are not a fixed 'thing', but consist of social practices in a space which is shaped by varied organizational (political) and professional interests. They illustrate well the ambivalences of care and control to be found throughout social welfare provision and the specific forms of regulation experienced by and directed at women. For example, a centre's leaflets given to the public might emphasize the practical help offered and the child-centred nature of the centre, while those aimed at other professionals might stress the centre's monitoring role and the close attention given to treating parents and to preventing child care problems. All such leaflets refer to 'parents' when the vast majority of parents attending are women, and a high proportion single. While many documents referred to abuse of children, they tend to be silent on the issue of abuse of women and indeed on gender issues *per se*.

While the public face of family centres shows some affinities with new right notions of the family as a single private unit, interviews with some centre workers showed considerable recognition of the conflicting interests at play within families and a commitment to helping women survive, to enhancing their lives and to addressing some of the consequences of their material deprivation (predominantly poverty and bad housing). These ambivalences reveal that social control in social welfare cannot be understood as stemming directly from the state, but that it also arises from organizational and professional enterprise and autonomy. Groups (segments of professions, welfare organizations) may express (for their advancement or desire to control a discourse, Manning, 1987; Parton, 1985) limited affinities with dominant ideologies, in this case, that of 'supporting the family'; social practices however, are never simple reflections of organizational or government policy and are often shaped, by front-line workers (Packman, 1986) and by the determined agency of women clients who assert their own interpretation of their problems and demand help based on this interpretation (Gordon, 1988). While such resistance and pluralism are strongly evident at the point of welfare delivery, a significant section of the policies on which they rest grows from conservative familist ideology; I now turn to the 'official' discourse (Burton and Carlen, 1979) on prevention and later return to social workers' views on the aims of their work.

Origins of family centres – the discourse on prevention

Family centres are described in local authority strategy documents as 'preventive' services, and from my brief description it can be seen that such prevention is understood as occurring at different levels and as addressing different problems. The two major things to be prevented are children entering care and the abuse and neglect of children within the family. Associated aims are the prevention of depression, low self-esteem and isolation in mothers, and the prevention of welfare dependency, habitual reliance on social workers and on services such as day care. Family centres then aim to affect the quality of family life, but they also and simultaneously seek to change the relationship of service users to the local state services, contrasting mutual aid in the 'natural' community with (pathological) reliance on formal services. Social services departments' documents gave many examples of this objective:

> The centre continually seeks to achieve a situation whereby the family is enabled to care supported by the facilities in their natural community. It must be recognized that in an ideal situation problems within the family would be met by support from the natural community . . . .

One centre aims

> . . . to help reduce the need for families with financial, domestic and child related problems becoming dependent clients of statutory welfare agencies.

And another aims

> . . . wherever possible to allow parents and children to become less dependent on the Centre through reduction of attendance.

Only London Boroughs with equal opportunities policies stressed the provision of a service, as a social benefit for their users. Conservative and traditional Labour controlled areas portrayed welfare dependance as a problem, and 'prevention' included diversion from child welfare services.

This deeper aim of family centres – to reduce reliance on formal services – is manifested in changing attitudes to public day care (and other public services such as those for the care of elderly or mentally ill people) over the last decade. Local authority day nurseries have been transformed from places which gave open-ended services to children and opportunities to working class women into centres specializing in short-term rehabilitative work with children *and* their parents (mothers) by insisting on parents' participation, involvement and ultimate self-reliance. One centre's documents put it this way:

A basic rule is that parents are always responsible for their children while they are with them in the centre. Activities and tasks are agreed between parents and staff. The latter act as resources for the parents, encouraging, challenging, supporting and confronting them in their care for their children. Our overall aim is to create an environment in which it is possible for families to change and acquire and practice new skills.

We find in family centres, then, an example of the 'new behaviourism' (Cohen, 1985: 139–155) which concentrates less on the mind than on action; mothers may only use the centres if they are working toward self-responsibility, which is understood in terms of traditional roles, rather than of educational and employment opportunities. It is notable, and I think a matter of concern, that family centres have broken away from the focus on the child, on giving the child a good environment, to drawing mothers into day nurseries in order to support, train or treat them as parents, as socializers of future school children, a practice which echoes the infant welfare movement at the turn of the century (Lewis, 1980).

During the early 1970s, with the mix of Conservative and Labour administrations, the concept of the 'cycle of deprivation' unified debates on the relationship between social and emotional deprivation, and on the origins and nature of child abuse and family breakdown. While a chorus of disapproval greeted Sir Keith Joseph's 1972 speech in which he implied that a hard core of inadequate families reproduce themselves through feckless socialization (Jordan, 1974; Townsend, 1979), and while the extensive SSRC/DHSS research concluded that there is 'a variety of pathways to deprivation (which) makes it essential to look beyond family history when assessing the life chances of individuals' (Madge, 1983, p201) nevertheless, in social services departments and in voluntary child care organizations the view persisted that a cycle of poor parenting and maternal deprivation reproduced social problems such as maladjustment, child abuse, delinquency and mental illness. This view is strongly reflected in family centres whose planning documents redefine day care as a method of serving children in need by teaching better parenting, and of preventing social problems by 'breaking the cycle'.

Such a view was underlined by 'experts' such as Kellmer Pringle, director of the National Children's Bureau, by Parker in the National Children's Bureau sponsored working party in 1975 on the needs of children separated from their families (Parker, 1980), together with those developing a discourse on parent education such as the paediatrician Dr Jolly, or Professor Whitfield, director of child care (UK) at the Save the Children Fund. The National Children's Bureau was acknowledged by Sir Keith Joseph as having provided him with new ideas and thinking (Joseph 1972), and the Bureau saw its funding increase under his Ministry when it was commissioned to develop and monitor projects on parent education (Pugh, 1980, 1981). Sir Keith Joseph also commissioned, for the purposes of developing new DHSS initiatives 'in connection with . . . (his) twin themes of breaking the "Cycle of Deprivation" and "Preparation for Parenthood"' (author's pre-face), Kellmer Pringle's book *The Needs of Children* (1975) which drew together current knowledge of child psychology. The book represents an attack on contemporary movements for parents' and for women's rights, arguing (effectively as it turns out in view of developments in child care law) that the 'politically fashionable emphasis on parental rights' needed to give way to a stress on parental responsibilities and duties (Kellmer Pringle, 1975, pp70, 139).

While the Labour Government went some way to note feminist concerns about women's rights, for instance setting up a Select Committee on Violence in Marriage (House of Commons, 1975), and grudgingly recognizing the need for womens' refuges, the Conservative push from the early 1970s was to stress the family as a basis for social care and service delivery, and thus to seek ways of 'strengthening the family'. Sir Keith Joseph and Margaret Thatcher embarked on a series of consultations between their departments (DHSS and Education) and interested academics and professionals on the theme of *Preparation for Parenthood* (DHSS, 1974a). A DHSS seminar on *Dimensions of Parenthood* (DHSS, 1974) was held at which parenthood and the family-in-crisis were debated, with contemporary campaigns on family poverty, domestic violence and abuse of women marginalized, a situation with parallels in the United States.

Some commentators (e.g. Nelson, 1984) have located this discourse on the family-in-crisis in the New Right's restructuring and reconceptualization of welfare, and its view that the 'crisis' reflects the so-called 'permissiveness' of the preceding decade. While the Conservatives *have* introduced a harder concept of parental responsibility into their social policies, a close look at social democratic thinking (closely allied to social work) reveals a similar, albeit softer, familist model of social pathology. Delinquency, for example has long been seen as generated by family problems (e.g. Longford, 1964; Home Office, 1965) as has educational failure (e.g. Plowden, 1967). Labour administrations have sought to tackle social problems by expanding family-based social work services and by taking quasi-psychoanalytical treatments to the residue who seemed not to benefit from greater opportunities and an expanded education system (Hall, 1976; Pitts, 1988). More recently the Short Report (1984) on *Children in Care* noted the link between family breakdown and poverty, reflecting the standpoint of pressure groups such as the Family Rights Group, the Child Poverty Action Group, and the British Association of Social Workers, and argued for more resources for families. The difference between the hard and soft versions is that the soft tends to view parents as themselves victims and as requiring welfare 'support', while the hard version sees such support as undermining responsibility and penalizes lack of responsibility by, for instance, fining parents of delinquents (Home Office, 1980). Both however have developed the view that targeting the most disadvantaged and 'strengthening' family life should be the core task of welfare services, albeit at very different levels of social provision.

The term prevention, then, has become associated with methods of strengthening family care and parental responsibilities. Primary prevention refers not to changing environmental conditions, but to changing parental behaviour. According to Kellmer Pringle:

> The driving force . . . must come from parents, aided by the skill and knowledge of paediatricians, psychologists and health visitors . . . (Kellmer Pringle 1978).

These professionals will

> . . . help families through periods of temporary strain and crisis . . . intervention should aim at enabling the child or family to cope independently as soon as possible (*ibid*).

This familist and diversionary notion of the prevention of delinquency, maladjustment, and child abuse underpinned and drew strength from the series of public inquiries into social workers' supervision of abused children. The Tunbridge Wells Study Group, formed of prominent paediatricians, NSPCC representatives and senior members of the social work profession and DHSS representatives in 1973, ensured that a psycho-medical model of child abuse, locating abuse in family dynamics, would be one that agencies such as the NSPCC could use for their subsequent expansion (Parton, 1985). Media interest in these inquiries meant that this model was widely disseminated, using a tone of authority, even 'audacity' according to its founder, Dr Franklin (1975). The anxiety generated by media interest meant that social services managers were open to being told by the DHSS, the NSPCC and eminent paediatricians that this model provided a foundation for effective child protection work, and for 'breaking the cycle of deprivation'.

The last decade has seen increasing threats to universal services and a redesignation of what could be understood as public or *social* services as targeted *family* services. I have concentrated on the new right in my description of this process because of its present political dominance, though I have noted the strength and influence of familist ideology in social democratic thinking and in the poverty lobby. Another strand of familism is found in left libertarianism which as Scull (1984) and Cohen (1985) have noted, has also developed views critical of state intervention into working class family life, views which have to some extent played into the dismantling of state welfare. Labelling theory, with its stress on stigma and career, provoked a view that the radical worker would strive to prevent welfare contamination of his or her clientele, and assertions were made that high rates of children in care represented an attack on vulnerable working class families (e.g. Geach and Szwed, 1983; Donzelot, 1980). While tempered by feminist research which has shown how this position romanticized family life and downplayed the victims of deviance, left libertarianism has been influential in social work and in some of the diversionary and the empowering strategies of family centres. 'Prevention' is thus not a single discourse, but composed of competing sub-discourses, the effect of which is a variability and instability in social practice. It is therefore to ideologies in social work that I shall now turn, in order to reveal the agency of the profession in the development and practice of family centres.

Social work ideologies: family therapy and community work

The family centre staff I interviewed and the documents I analysed confirmed left libertarianism to be a strand of social work thought: references to stigma, labelling, deviant careers were in evidence; keeping children out of care, and out of day nurseries, were seen by some social workers *sympathetic to the poor* as worthy objectives, echoing the 'rules of pessimism' noted by Packman (1986) in her research on decision-making in child care. Other staff were critical of families' or clients' 'dependence', seeing this as a result of psychological weakness and requiring paternalistic supervision, perhaps also reflecting the judgemental attitudes noted by Ferri (1981) in her research on nursery nurses who viewed mothers as dumping children in nurseries in order to evade their 'domestic responsibilities'. Others were committed to providing as good a service as possible to children, to empowering women, and to enriching local communities.

Just as the organizations in which social work is practised are diverse, so are the traditions and ideologies within social work (Harris and Webb, 1987). In family centres family therapy is a dominant form of practice, being both used as a technology of behaviour change and combined with some principles of community work, itself an important strand of social practice. The social workers interviewed saw family therapy as giving their clients more control over their lives, doing so by working on or with the significant others in the client's family. Critics have noted its strong focus on mothers (Dominelli, 1986), and its asocial assumption derived from systems theory that pathologies are symptomatic of individual family dynamics (Pearson, 1974; Poster, 1978). It is an example of the paradoxical social work attitude which, despite an explicit recognition of poverty as a major causal factor in social and psychological problems, in practice focuses on family relationships, a point recently demonstrated by Becker (1989).

Family therapy has grown enormously in size and influence over the last decade; the Association for Family Therapy was established in Britain in 1976 and includes clinical psychologists, psychotherapists, psychiatrists and social workers. Frankly eclectic in its roots and philosophies (Zawada, 1981; Walrond Skynner, 1979) there is a core assumption that childhood disturbance or abuse is symptomatic of parental 'malfunctioning', of parents' early childhood experiences or of 'system dysfunctions'. One root of the recent growth in family therapy must be sought in the child protection crises of the last two decades. Family therapy appears to offer a theoretically grounded, prestigious and medically legitimated technology of intervention, dissociating social work from its much-criticized basis in social casework. It is advocated and dominated by the 'big' (medical) names in the child protection field: Kempe, Bentovim, Franklin, Bowlby and Winnicott. It associates the mundane and anxiety-laden with multi-disciplinary work and world-famous hospitals and clinics: the Denver Centre, Great Ormond Street, the Tavistock, the Maudsley. Family therapy has transformed social work practice with its existing clientele: the prestige of this specialism has been used both to deflect public anxiety about child protection, and to legitimate targeted social work intervention with poor, needy and deviant families. Discourses on maternal deprivation have been reactivated, meshing with conservative themes of family responsibility, of the 'normal family' as the family who is private, self-contained, and not welfare dependent.

The success of family therapy as a segment of social work, in both creating some of the terms of the discourse on child abuse and in legitimating a family-based form of treatment, has accompanied something of a withdrawal in social work from the vision of broader social change. Community work struggles to keep this vision alive, but it suffers from crucial weaknesses, especially in its lack of academic prestige in England. While community work can and does draw on sociological and political analysis, it has never-theless eschewed high status by insisting on deprofessionalization and avoiding elitism.

While the community work family centres are based on sound evidence (e.g. on the link between poor care of children and isolation, ill-health and lack of opportunity (e.g. Holman, 1976; Madge, 1983; Coffield, 1981), and while they therefore seek to strengthen parents in caring for their children by increasing social and material resources available to them, the case for such intervention is usually made by emotive appeals to social justice (especially by the voluntary organizations, notably the Church of England Children's Society). The problem about all this, as Jordan

(1987/88) has noted, is that, in contrast to specialist family work, it is essentially practical:

> . . . there isn't much professional kudos in work which is essentially low key, pragmatic, often practical and quite humble, and where power is shared very equally not merely with other professionals, volunteers and lay people, but also with clients themselves (p9).

Holman's description of his own community work shows the accessible, 'resourceful friend' can make real changes in the balance of resources in a community and his work has strongly influenced Children's Society projects. He stresses deprofessionalization and public participation as inherent to community work. This aspect of community work however is what counts against it in bargaining for public resources, especially where social services managers are seeking effective and tightly monitored treatments for families 'at risk'. Hence, family centres find their (highly preventive) community work activities are underfunded, and often treated by local authorities as additional to the 'real' work of child protection. Social work/child protection centres also struggle to continue to offer, say, day care, as a service in its own right: while many social workers interviewed would have liked to have seen more opportunities for women to study and gain skills in order to be empowered by better employment prospects, pressure was always on the centres to reach more needy children and parents by offering care on a part-time basis, or to treat the need psychologically rather than as a matter of education or employment. All the social workers were acutely aware of their clients' poverty and of their need for better incomes and services; shortages of provision however forced them into a limited and perhaps not always desired method of social intervention. Where community work *does* appeal to the Conservatives is in its involvement of volunteers and its place in the self-help tradition; small scale projects, with fragile staffing arrangements, often in poorly-equipped buildings, tend to be the result (Finch, 1984). On the other hand, schemes like Home Start have received extensive government funding; these schemes use volunteer 'mums' to befriend mothers in difficulty, and (once again) are based on the notion of family normality as self-responsibility and independence from state services (van der Eyken, 1982).

Conclusion

While family centres have aspects which can be shown to mesh with new right ideas of the self-sufficient family, nevertheless I have been at pains to show how both ideological affinities *and* resistances are built into family centres. Local services are not ciphers of the local or national states, but develop their individuality through professional

organization, local politics, and the local welfare mix. Both ideological and opportunist assumptions about the 'best' forms of welfare
service compete in a small arena, while there is encouragement and
sponsorship offered to those with views akin to those in power (for
instance the DHSS Seminar and consultations in 1973 which gave
voice to familist segments of medicine and social work), rendering
such competition unequal. The old left and the old right have shared
a preference for family-based welfare; the new left and new right
have shared a dislike of professionals 'invading' families and argued
for liberation from welfare. Such diversity in the ideological roots
of provision produces a certain diversity in practice, especially as
other (currently marginalized) voices also struggle to be heard – the
poverty lobby, the women's aid movement, community action.

This diversity means that we cannot define the essence of family
centres, nor say whether they are centres of social control. While
they are strongly regulatory of women in some respects, in others
they are liberating and empowering; within the same centre we find
both aspects, and individual women may experience this confusing
mix. Ultimately however I would argue that there are two respects
in which family centres *are* strongly regulatory: first in their control
of images of good mothering, that is to say in an ideological sense;
second in their diversion of parents in need from (scarce) formal
sources of help and their castigation of welfare 'dependence'.
Because of these deeper aspects, family centres can be said to be
highly regulatory of women by forcing them back on to traditional
roles and the informal economy.

Family centres' services are offered in the name of children but it
is at women that they are targeted. Gordon's (1988) work on child
protection agencies in the United States shows just this: she argues
(from extensive reading of agencies' case records since 1900) that
children get little protection from such agencies, but that *women*
strive to use them to gain independence from abusive husbands,
sometimes gaining such help, sometimes being blamed for their
husbands' behaviour. She reveals, not the imposition of control,
but interaction and conflict between clients and social workers
as each seeks to establish their definition of the situation, and
as women clients try to render the agencies responsive to their
needs for support. While, she argues, child protection agencies
regulate women by extolling the virtues of the economically
independent family (thus keeping women down), they *also* help
some women to gain control of their lives and to care for their
children themselves.

Within this perspective, far more subtle than most social control
theories of social welfare, we can view family centres as offering
enormous potential to families, supplementing and strengthening
them, increasing the richness of the fabric of the community.
However, in a situation of scarcity of public services, or where their

workers hold a strong familist ideology, they become a means of turning families back in on themselves. Family centres demonstrate that the sociology of the family is in reality the sociology of the state, for family centres mediate the restructuring of welfare from the public and formal to the informal world of the family and female care.

In this realignment of the relationship of family to the state (of which family centres are in expression) we see a challenge to the demands of feminism and the equal opportunities movement. These movements would demand not less but *more* intervention in the family and *more* control. Self-realization and autonomy for women means public day care and services which make child care easier, more shared, less private. Recognizing the real problems from which families suffer, notably single parenthood and domestic violence (and family centre documents are remarkably silent on these except in relation to children), means sanctioning public intervention in families to protect women or children from other members of the family. Recent events in Cleveland have shown that media and government only tolerate such control and intervention when abuse (of children) is understood as exceptional and unusual. Family centres collude with this attitude by emphasizing images of 'normal' family life as their goal, thus running the risk of not addressing the needs which their users might express, and imposing deviant stereotypes on users as either dysfunctional or disadvantaged. Not all family centres do this though – some community work centres emphasize the strength of their users and seek to build on this, but as I have shown some of these centres find they are under pressure to narrow their scope.

Social control is not an adequate framework for understanding family centres: while family centres appear to be in the tradition of services which 'invade' working class families, current reality is more complex. The recognition of abuse of women and children in families necessarily contradicts an image of family unity which is somehow transgressed by the state or its agents. Control is not necessarily a 'bad' thing, indeed a worse thing may be failure to exercise control and leaving victims unprotected. Family centres could thus be seen (contemporarily) as representing social control by *refusal* to intervene in families, or by giving small amounts of aid conditional upon the social worker's interpretation of the problem and upon related behavioural change. In this sense family centres are highly regulatory of women, forcing them back into traditional roles and dependence, through the stigmatizing association of services with 'bad parenting', and the castigating of 'welfare dependency'. Regulation of maternal behaviour may therefore be increased by so-called preventive policies, which effectively *deny* a range of accessible support services to parents and children. It is to be hoped that services provided under the new Children Act will be sufficiently generous to change this, to extend the diversity I have noted and to offer choices to users such that they have the power to define their needs and to get them met. However, this would need yet further realignment of the relationship between family (women) and the state . . . .

References

Becker, S (1989) 'Keeping a poor woman down'. *Community Care*, 19 January, 1989, pp23–25.

Bernstein, B (1971) 'A critique of the concept of compensatory education'. In *Class, Codes and Control*, London, Routledge Kegan Paul.

Birchall, D (1982) 'Family centres'. *Concern*, National Children's Bureau, 43, Spring, pp16–20.

Burton, F and Carlen, P (1979) *Official Discourse*. London, Routledge.

Cohen, S (1985) *Visions of Social Control: Crime, Punishment and Classification*. Cambridge, Polity Press.

Dalley, G (1988) *Ideologies of Caring: Rethinking Community and Collectivism*. Basingstoke, Macmillan.

David, M (1985) 'Motherhood and social policy: a matter of education'. *Critical Social Policy* 12, pp28–43.

Dingwall, R; Eekelaar, J, and Murray, T (1983) *The Protection of Children: State Intervention and Family Life*. Oxford, Blackwell.

DHSS (1974) *The Family in Society: Dimensions of Parenthood*. A Report of a Seminar. London HMSO.

DHSS (1974a) *The Family in Society: Preparation for Parenthood*, an account of consultations. London HMSO.

DHSS (1987) *The Law on Child Care and Family Services*. London, HMSO.

Dominelli, L (1986) 'Father-daughter incest: patriarchy's shameful secret'. *Critical Social Policy* 16, pp8–22.

Donzelot, (1980) *The Policing of Families: Welfare versus the State*. London, Hutchinson.

Ely, D (1984) *Woodlands Evaluation*. Part of an unpublished M.Sc dissertation, University of Surrey.

Eyken, W van der (1982) *Home-Start – a four year evaluation*. Home-Start Consultancy, Leicester.

Ferri, E; Birchall, D; Gingell, V, and Gipps, C (1981) *Combined Nursery Centres: A New Approach to Education and Day Care*. London, Macmillan/National Children's Bureau.

Finch, J (1984) 'The deceit of self-help'. *Journal of Social Policy*, 13, no 1, pp1–20.

Franklin, A W (1975) *Concerning Child Abuse: Papers presented to the Tunbridge Wells Study Group on Non-Accidental Injury to Children*. London, Churchill Livingstone.

Geach, H and Szwed, E (1983) *Proving Civil Justice for Children*. London, Arnold.

Gordon, L (1988) *Heroes of their own Lives*. London, Viking Penguin.

Graham, H (1979) 'Prevention and health – every mother's business – a comment on child health policies in the 1970's. In Harris, C (ed) *The Sociology of the Family: New Directions for Britain*, Sociological Review Monograph 28, University of Keele.

Hall, P (1976) *Reforming the Welfare: the Politics of Change in the Personal Social Services*. London, Heinemann.

Harris, R and Webb, D (1987) *Welfare, Power and Juvenile Justice: the Social Control of Delinquent Youth*. London, Tavistock.

Heiser, B and Godfrey, M (1984) *Under-Fives in Camden: the parents' views*. Unpublished report, London Borough of Camden, Chief Executive/ Social Services Department.

Holman, R (1983) *Resourceful Friends: Skills in Community Work*. London, Children's Society.

Home Office (1965) *The Child, the Family, and the Young Offender*. Cmnd,2742, London, HMSO.

Home Office, Welsh Office, DHSS (1980) *Young Offenders*. Cmnd8045, London HMSO.

House of Commons (1975) Report of the Select Committee on *Violence in Marriage*. HMSO.

Jordan, B (1974) *Poor Parents: Social Policy and the Cycle of Deprivation*. London, Routledge.

Jordan, B (1987/8): 'Why is prevention neglected?' In *Family Rights Group Bulletin*, Winter 1987/88, pp7–11.

Joseph, Sir K (1972) 'The parental role'. Speech to the National Children's Bureau Conference, reprinted in *Concern*, Winter 1972–73, pp4–12.

Kellmer Pringle, M (1975) *The Needs of Children: a personal perspective prepared for the DHSS*. London, Hutchinson.

Kellmer Pringle, M (1978) 'Why prevention?'. In *Concern* (National Children's Bureau, 29.

Land, H (1979) 'The boundaries between the state and the family'. In Harris, C (ed) *The Sociology of the Family: new Directions for Britain*. Sociological Review Monograph 28, University of Keele.

Lewis, J (1980) *The Politics of Motherhood: Child and Maternal Welfare in England 1900–1939*. London, Croom Helm.

Longford Report (1964) *Crime: a Challenge to us all*. London, Labour Party Study Group.

Mackay, Lord (1989) 'Perceptions of the Children Bill and beyond'. *New Law Journal*, 14th April, 1989, pp505–6.

Madge, N (ed) (1983) *Families at Risk*. SSRC/DHSS Studies in Deprivation and Disadvantage, London, Heinemann.

Manning, N (1987) 'What is a social problem?' In Loney, M *et al* (eds) *The State or the Market: Politics and Welfare in Contemporary Britain*. London, Sage.

McIntosh, M (1984) 'The family, regulation and the public sphere'. In McLellan G (ed) *The State and Society in Contemporary Britain*. Cambridge, Polity Press.

Nelson, B (1984) *Making an Issue of Child Abuse: Political Agenda Setting and Social Problems*. University of Chicago Press.

Packman, J; Randall, J and Jacques, N (1986) *Who needs Care? Social Work Decisions about Children*. Oxford, Blackwell.

Parker, R (ed) (1980) *Caring for Separated Children: Plans, Procedures and Priorities*. London, Macmillan.

Parton, N (1985) *The Politics of Child Abuse*. London, Macmillan.

Pascall, G (1986) *Social Policy: A Feminist Analysis*. London, Tavistock.

Pearson, G (1974) 'Prisons of love: the reification of the family in family therapy'. In Armistead, N (ed) *Reconstructing Social Psychology*. Harmondsworth, Penguin.

Phelan, J (1983) *Family Centres – a study*. London, Children's Society.

Pitts, J (1988) *The Politics of Juvenile Crime*. London, Sage.

Poster, M (1978) *Critical Theory of the Family*. London, Pluto.

Pugh, G (ed) (1980) *Preparation for Parenthood: Some Current Initiatives*. London, National Children's Bureau.

Pugh, G (1981) *Parents as Partners*. London, National Children's Bureau.

Plowden Report (1967) *Children and their Primary Schools*. Report of the Central Advisory Council for Education, HMSO.

Scull, A (1984) *Decarceration: Community Treatment and the Deviant: a radical view*. Cambridge, Polity Press, 2nd ed.

Short Report (1984) Report of the House of Commons Select Committee on *Children in Care*. London, HMSO.

Townsend, P (1979) *Poverty in the United Kingdom*. Harmondsworth, Penguin.

Tunstill, J (1985) 'Aiming to prevent misunderstanding'. *Social Work Today*, 17 June 85.

Walrond Skynner, S (ed) (1979) *Family and Marital Therapy: a Critical Approach*. London, Routledge.

Wilson, E (1977) *Women and the Welfare State*. London, Tavistock.

Willmott, P and Mayne, S (1983) *Families at the Centre: a study of seven Action Projects*. London, Bedford Square Press/NCVO.

Zawada, A (1981) 'An outline of the history and current state of family therapy'. In Box, S *et al* (eds) *Psychotherapy with Families – an analytical approach*. London, Routledge.

6 Parental responsibilities in the Children Act 1989

Judith Harwin

Introduction

If the Children Act 1989 had confined itself exclusively to reform of the law governing the protection of children at risk of abuse, many members of the public would have been entirely happy. Indeed there are many people who believe that the new law is primarily a response to the 1987 Cleveland crisis when, in a five month period, a diagnosis of child sexual abuse was made on 121 children, most of whom were then forcibly separated from their parents by emergency proceedings (Butler-Sloss, 1988, p243). This view is entirely mistaken. The origins of the new Act go back much further than 1987 and incorporate the thinking of a wide range of reports dating from the 1970s onwards, covering many different aspects of child law and child care practice.

The first serious recommendation for a thorough-going review of child care legislation was put forward in 1984 as part of a Parliamentary Select Committee Report into the plight of children in care, known as the Short Report (House of Commons Social Services Committee, 1984). A year later an inter-departmental government report was produced, 'The Review of Child Care Law' (DHSS, 1985a) which provided the basis to the 1987 White Paper 'The law on child care and family services' (DHSS, 1987).

But the origins of the new law go back considerably further. In 1974, a much neglected report, the Harvie report, had drawn attention to the poor standard of care for mentally handicapped children, whose services were mainly provided by health and welfare law rather than by child care legislation (DHSS, 1974). The Harvie report had argued that the historically based administrative fragmentation of services for different categories of children had produced inequities in the quality of care which could only be overcome by comprehensive legal reform.

Research too has played a formative role in the new Act by providing valuable factual information on the operation of services and by highlighting particular weaknesses in the system. Finally, successive child abuse inquiries have contributed to the proposals for reform of law, procedure and practice.

All these investigations were focused on the operation of public child care law which deals with the relationships between state authorities and families. But the 1980s had also witnessed radical scrutiny of private law, which governs the legal relationships between individuals. The Law Commission had produced a steady series of reports calling for reform of custody law, guardianship and access arrangements (Law Commission, 1985 and 1986). For the first time ever, the new law fuses within a single Act the legal arrangements for children affected by both private family proceedings and public law.

Thus to appreciate the full scope of the 1989 Act several entirely separate strands need to be considered. The range of issues which are raised in the various reports underline clearly the extent and breadth of reform that is contained in the new Act. Indeed Lord McKay, the Lord Chancellor, has commented that the Children Act 1989 will provide the legal framework of service provision into the twenty first century (Lord Mackay, 1989, p505). The Act is therefore of considerable importance to an entire generation of children as well as for the many professionals who administer child care services. It is against this background that we must assess the impact of the Act and consider its potential contribution to the promotion of child welfare and the protection of children at risk.

In the confines of a short review, it is of course impossible to do justice to the full complement of reforms which the Act introduces. Instead this chapter will focus on the concept of 'parental responsibility' and its effects. This is a theme of major significance throughout the new law. For while the primary intention of the Act is to enhance and safeguard the welfare of the child, particular importance is attached to 'parental responsibility' as a vital means of achieving that end. Lord McKay has commented that this theme of parental responsibility 'runs like a golden thread' throughout the entire Act (Lord Mackay, 1989, p505). This chapter attempts to unravel this thread and to consider the way in which the notion of parental responsibilities influences the new law in both private family proceedings and public child care law.

The concept of parental responsibilities

The 1989 Act replaces the term 'parental rights and duties', which had been used in previous legislation, by the phrase 'parental responsibilities'. In so doing the Act articulates the philosophy which had been foreshadowed in the Short Report when it stated that 'the rights (of parents) have no absolute validity: they derive from the exercise of responsibilities' (House of Commons, 1984, pxiv). This view has long provided the actual basis for decision-making in child law in both the private and public arena. Parents have been unable to exercise their rights simply by virtue of parental status for many years. In recent years the child's welfare and the enhancement or protection of his interests has constituted the paramount consideration in decision-making by the courts. In operational terms therefore, prior to the new legislation, parental rights were perceived by the courts as part of a package. The exercise of rights was dependent on the way in which parental duties were discharged and these rights could be forfeited if duties were inadequately carried out. What the new Act does is to provide valuable clarification of this issue and lead us out of a blind alley which misleadingly implies a separation between rights and duties.

The new Act proceeds from the starting point that the defining characteristic of parenthood is responsibility to the child. It is important to appreciate that within the meaning of the Act parental responsibility is *not* synonomous with parenthood. In addition to parents, a range of other individuals may acquire parental responsibility via court orders, such as step-parents, relatives and other persons with a long-standing major involvement with the child. Furthermore, when a child is taken into care by the local authority, it too acquires parental responsibility for the child, as do any persons to whom the local authority delegates responsibility, such as foster-parents. It can be seen, therefore, that the term is deliberately used with identical meaning to cover the responsibilities of both private individuals and statutory authorities, thereby unifying the conceptual framework of both private and public child law.

The Act defines 'parental responsibilities' as 'all the rights, duties, powers and authority which by law a parent of a child has in relation to the child and his property'. (Section 3 [1]). Parental responsibility empowers the individual or local authority to take the majority of the major decisions in the child's life, subject to two key limitations which derive from criminal and civil law (DH, 1989, p9). Criminal law lays down the minimum acceptable standards of parental behaviour and civil law emphasizes that the age of the child is an important check on the exercise of unlimited parental freedom in decision-making. In line with the Gillick ruling (AC 112, 1986), the Act builds on the principle that parental responsibility 'itself diminishes as the child acquires sufficient understanding to make his own decisions' (DH, 1989, p9).

The acquisition of parental responsibility does not denote that the individual is placed under a statutory duty to maintain the child. Nor does the person acquire the right to inheritance. Finally, it is important to realize that when one person acquires parental responsibility this does *not per se* remove it from another individual. This is because the Act seeks whenever possible to promote the sharing of parental responsibility amongst the relevant individuals and authorities, rather than to exclude key figures in the child's life.

Indeed, the enhancement of parental responsibility is one of the primary intentions of the Act. From this flow several important developments. First the Act is concerned to limit intervention by the courts to those cases in which the welfare of the child will be promoted (Bracewell, 1989, p1). As will be seen, the courts will cease to routinely play a part in certain proceedings where hitherto, their involvement had been automatic. Second, a variety of social measures will be made available to families to enable them to carry out their responsibilities more effectively. Many of these directly correspond to the old notion of preventive services which local authorities were empowered to provide to families in their area to help reduce the risk of the need to receive a child into care. But the range of services has been extended as has the target population of potential beneficiaries. Third, in its attempt to strengthen the family, new administrative arrangements and legal orders will be available to help people acquire parental responsibility. More people will be able to share parental responsibility amongst themselves in family proceedings and parental responsibility will continue equally between parents after divorce.

These developments constitute the enabling aspects of the new legislation. They build on the view that the family is the best place in which to rear children and that social and legal measures must contribute to facilitate effective child-rearing. But the Act is equally concerned with clarifying the basis on which the State must protect children from harmful or inadequate parenting. In line with former legislation the new Act makes no attempt to define the content of parental responsibility. Nor does it disturb the definition of the minimum standards of care which derive from the criminal law. But it puts forward an entirely new set of criteria in civil law by which the state is empowered to intervene in family life to protect the child against the wishes of parents. At the same time the new Act is concerned to strengthen parental rights of representation and of appeal. That the Act should give priority to this issue is entirely appropriate. It reflects the view that the state's entitlement to intervene in family life must be balanced by the opportunity for parents to defend their position. Indeed, the Act claims that it has achieved a new balance between the protection of family privacy from unwarranted interference, child protection and intervention by state authorities. How far this has been achieved will be examined in the final section of this chapter. First however, the specific changes introduced by the Act need to be examined.

Measures to enhance parental responsibility in family proceedings

The new Act will greatly improve the position of unmarried fathers and significantly alter procedures for dealing with divorcing couples. It will be far easier for unmarried fathers to acquire parental responsibility than in the past. Previously, any unmarried father who wished to share responsibility for the child's upbringing with the mother had to obtain a court order. Now, provided that the mother consents, the couple will be able to draw up what is termed in the Act as a 'parental responsibility agreement'. This provision obviates the necessity to go to court and will constitute a 'simple and cheap' method of enabling joint care of the child (DH, 1989, p10). Its effect will be identical to a 'parental responsibility order' (PRO) reached via the courts – the remedy that will be available to unmarried fathers when the mother withholds her consent. The PRO will be similar to the Section 4 orders of the Family Law Reform Act 1987 and will confer parental rights and duties on the unmarried father. Both the court order and the administrative measure may only be terminated by court order, or by the child itself provided that he has sufficient understanding to make the application and obtains the court's consent to do so.

These provisions are important but undoubtedly the most far-reaching changes which the Act introduces in the sphere of private law relate to divorce. The new Act takes the standpoint that 'while divorce can sever the legal bond between husband and wife, the law in family disputes should do nothing that appears to sever the bond between parent and child. That bond is vital' (Mackay, 1989, p506). In adopting this view the Act draws on recent research into the effects of divorce on children's development. Longitudinal studies have shown that the child's wellbeing is best safeguarded when both parents continue to play a significant role in his life after the break-up of the marriage (Wallerstein & Kelly, 1980; Richards & Dyson, 1982; Wallerstein, 1987).

Yet until now the law itself has frequently intensified the fight between parents by enabling only one party to become the custodial parent. This runs counter to a major purpose of the new legislation, which is to ensure that parental responsibility will continue to be exercised by both parents after the break-up. To achieve this major aim, custody and access orders will be abolished and an entirely new arsenal of legal measures will be available to the courts to help resolve parental disputes.

Residence orders will give the courts powers to specify with which parent a child should live, but this direction will not affect the statutory right and duty of both parents to take equal part in decision-making in respect of the child. Residence orders will open up a brand new range of flexible permutations to the courts. First, it will be possible to make these orders in favour of more than one person. For example, an order could be made in favour of one parent and his new partner at the weekend and the other parent and her new partner during the week (Lowe, 1989). Second, as will be clear from the example just cited, residence orders are in effect 'time orders', enabling different arrangements to operate at different times and these could be particularly valuable for regularizing holiday periods.

Three other new orders have been created. 'Contact orders' will empower the courts to determine arrangements for access, and 'specific issue' and 'prohibited steps' orders will be introduced. The former of these empowers parents to obtain remedy from the courts when they are in dispute over a particular issue affecting their child. The latter order prevents any person with parental responsibility from taking particular action specified in the order without the prior consent of the courts. In function both orders are similar to existing provisions within wardship jurisdiction.

All these options undoubtedly give the courts wide discretion. But before any order can be made, the courts are instructed to satisfy themselves that 'doing so would be better for the child than making no order at all'. In keeping with this principle of restricting judicial intervention, courts will no longer be required to consider the arrangements for the child's future in *all* proceedings relating to divorce and nullity. Instead, only in certain highly specific circumstances will the courts be empowered to intervene.

In restricting the role of the courts in this way, the Act makes two statements. First, it assumes that parents can be encouraged to plan responsibly for their child without court surveillance. Second, it marks a significant shift away from 'the state knows best approach'. Whether the Act is over-optimistic in its expectations remains to be seen. Research has shown that parents may become so embroiled in their own emotions that they are unable to attend sufficiently to the child's needs and wishes (Mitchell, 1985). Confidence in the abolition of routine court surveillance of the arrangements for the children of divorcing couples would have been increased if the Act had provided a commensurate increase in the availability of conciliation services, which have proved so effective (Parkinson, 1986).

But in general the new provisions are to be warmly welcomed and are likely to ease considerably the situation of the 120,000 children whose parents annually get divorced (Timms, 1989, p13).

Services to help parents fulfil their parental responsibilities

Preventive support services to help families carry out their child-rearing responsibilities are not new. Under the Child Care Act 1980 the local authority had a specific duty to help diminish the need to receive a child into care, which itself derived from earlier legislation. The new Act considerably widens the preventive powers and duties of the local authorities and extends their scope to cover new categories of children. The rationale for these changes is expressed most clearly in the 1987 White Paper: 'the prime responsibility for the upbringing of children rests with parents. The state should be ready to help parents discharge that responsibility, especially where doing so lessens the risk of family breakdown' (DHSS, 1987, p2).

To achieve this objective, local authorities shall have a two-fold general duty: (a) 'to safeguard and promote the welfare of children within their area who are *in need*' (emphasis added) and (b) 'so far as is consistent with that duty, to promote the upbringing of such children by their families'. The term 'children in need' is new and is carefully defined within the Act. The definition is important and for this reason shall be quoted in full:

> (a) he is unlikely to achieve or maintain, or to have the opportunity of achieving or maintaining, a reasonable standard of health or development without the provision for him of services by a local authority . . . .
> (b) his health or development is likely to be significantly impaired, or further impaired without the provision for him of such services; or
> (c) he is disabled.

It can be seen that this definition is extremely wide-ranging. It extends to future as well as present development and covers all major areas of functioning. In principle, therefore, it gives the local authority powers to assist a very broad range of children and as such must be welcomed as a most positive step in promoting children's welfare. However it also leaves considerable room for the exercise of discretion. No guidelines are provided within the Act on how the term 'reasonable standard of health or development' is to be defined and it seems likely that individual practitioners and local authorities will vary considerably in the extent of support they will provide to families.

In principle, local authorities will be less able to exercise discretion in respect of support to families with a disabled child. For the first time ever all disabled children are brought under the umbrella of local authority preventive and support services. Moreover, in contrast to other types of children in need, disabled children are entitled to assistance purely by virtue of being disabled. Local authorities will be required to keep registers of disabled children in their area and to provide suitable services which will 'minimise the effect of their disabilities' (Children Act, 1989, Schedule 2[6]) and help normalize their lives as far as possible.

Local authorities are also under a far more active duty than in previous legislation to play a positive role in screening and early identification of children in need. They 'shall take reasonable steps' to identify the extent to which there are children in need within their area and, for the first time ever in law, 'shall take reasonable steps to prevent children . . . suffering ill-treatment or neglect' (Children Act, 1989, Schedule 2[4] p108).

Certain new services must now be provided on a statutory basis. All local authorities will be required to open family centres and for the first time, they will also be required to provide day care for children under the age of five who are in need. In addition, to meet the criticisms of narrow departmentalism raised by the Short Report (House of Commons Social Services Committee, 1984, pxxiii) the local authorities will be under a duty to cooperate with Education departments and to produce three annually published reviews of their provision in respect of day care and child-minding.

The scope of these powers and duties is admirable. What is unclear is how far adequate financial resources will be made available to finance the new preventive duties. A total of £4 million has been committed to the new legislation but it is unlikely that any central government funds will be released to assist local authorities resource preventive services. Nor do the local authorities have a particularly good track record of carrying out preventive work. In a frequently quoted observation, the Short Report stated in 1984 that 'if half the funds and intellectual effort had been put into what we can only lamely call "preventive work" there would be unquestionable advantage to all concerned' (House of Commons, 1984, pxix). Regrettably, the picture does not seem to have changed much since 1984. Figures from the DH show that in 1986/87 the total spent on preventive work in England and Wales was only £9.1 million. Over the same period a staggering £434.1 million was spent on fostering and residential care (Ryan, 1989, p17). The potential cost of the preventive services envisaged by the new Act is presently being calculated by the Association of Metropolitan Authorities, but there is widespread concern that the local authorities will have insufficient funds to finance the new schemes. This cannot be right. 'If the welfare of the child is paramount in law, it must receive equal priority in the allocation of resources' (Timms, 1989, p12).

Parental responsibility and local authority accommodation

The new emphasis given to enhancing and respecting parental responsibility in the Act has had major consequences on the redrafting of the 'voluntary care' arrangements found in former legislation. In the 1989 legislation an entirely new balance in the respective powers and rights of parents and local authorities is to be created in the use of accommodation services. In future, the aim is to create a partnership between parents and social services. Before examining this proposal in greater detail, the major changes in the former voluntary route into care need examination to help clarify the Act's intentions and thereby enable us to see how parental responsibility is to be enhanced.

The Act creates a potential revolution in thinking about voluntary care. First it abolishes the term itself and places local authorities under a duty to provide what is simply called accommodation for children in need. The new terminology deliberately breaks with longstanding tradition by dropping the word 'care'. In the new Act there is an attempt to recast entirely public and professional attitudes to local authority care when it is requested by parents and to view it in a positive light. In future, local authority accommodation for children in need is to be regarded simply as one of a range of support services for families under stress. In keeping with this philosophy, the former duty to 'diminish the need to receive children into care' (1963 CYPA) is abolished, although the local authority is still required to reduce the need to bring care proceedings.

These objectives build very closely on the findings of a range of important research studies carried out in the 1980s (DHSS, 1985b). The consequence of the former legal duty to diminish the need to receive a child into care has frequently led to considerable reluctance to admit children into care, a practice which has often been reinforced by departmental policies. Admission has been seen as 'failed prevention' and as a result families have often been 'put through hoops' to avoid care at all costs (DHSS, 1985b, p9).

It is striking that some research has shown that this negative view of care is not necessarily shared by the families themselves, who may see the offer of local authority care as a much-valued resource (Vernon & Fruin, 1985 and Fisher *et al*, 1986). The research indicates that real difficulties arose from this clash of perspective between parents and social workers, which in the final analysis was prejudicial to the child's welfare. For when the social workers rejected the family's request for admission to care, no alternative facilities would be arranged (Fisher *et al*, 1986). This had a knock-on effect and led to a stark choice between 'no admission at all' or 'compulsion'.

The reasons for these kinds of social work practice are complex. They reflect the accumulating evidence documenting the deficiencies in the care system (Berridge & Cleaver, 1988) as well as the real lack of resources to provide helpful alternatives to care. They indicate that an immense amount of work faces many local authorities if admission to their accommodation is to be seen as a constructive opportunity to provide short-term relief to a wide range of families under stress. If successful it will mean that the traditional boundaries which exist at present between being 'in care' or 'out of care' will be broken down.

The new criteria which the local authority must adhere to in the provision of accommodation are as broadly drawn as in previous legislation. As before, the local authority must provide it (a) for a child who has been lost or abandoned, (b) if 'the person who has been caring for him (is) prevented (whether or not permanently, and for whatever reason) from providing him with suitable accommodation or care' and (c) if there is no person with parental responsibility for him. The local authorities are under an additional duty to provide accommodation for sixteen year olds in need if the local authority considers their welfare is threatened. Also included is a further very broad power to extend this facility to *any* child within their area.

Certain conditions govern the local authority's actions. It cannot provide accommodation if any person with parental responsibility is willing to provide or make arrangements for alternative accommodation; nor can it retain a child in its accommodation if the parent, or person with parental responsibility decides to remove the child. This last measure has caused considerable controversy. For the local authority has now lost two powers previously at its disposal – the so-called parental rights resolutions and the 28 day rule, whereby parents whose child has been in voluntary care for six months or more were obliged to give 28 days notice of their intention to remove him.

The loss of the parental rights resolutions will probably be less significant than the loss of the 28 day notice rule. The parental rights resolutions empowered local authorities to convert admissions to voluntary care into compulsory orders if the parental behaviour was causing grave concern to the local authority. In fact, many local authorities had already ceased to use this power by the late 1980s and instead would channel cases through the courts via care proceedings. They had adopted this policy in recognition of the widespread criticism that no administrative body should be able to remove a child against parental wishes without the decision being tested out in a court of law (National Council for One Parent Families, 1982).

The parental rights resolutions were also abolished because they are in contravention of the European Convention for the Protection of Human Rights and Fundamental Freedoms, in particular in respect of the codes laid down in Article 6. This states that (1) 'in the determination of his civil rights and obligations or of any criminal charge against him, everyone is entitled to a fair and public hearing within a reasonable time by an independent and impartial tribunal established by law.'

The abolition of the parental rights resolutions had therefore been widely anticipated, but the termination of the 28 day notice rule was fought to the last through parliamentary amendment. Its loss has been criticized for placing parental freedom above child protection (R. White, 1989, p515). It has been argued that some parents may abuse their new right by, for example, removing their child from foster parents in the middle of the night (Pierson, 1989, p24). While the local authority will be able to invoke emergency protection proceedings if, for example, the parent is drunk, or alternatively to begin care proceedings, both of these actions can only increase the sense of crisis to child, parents and foster parents alike. When the 28 day notice rule was introduced into the 1975 Act, the intention had been to enable careful planning for the child. Research suggests the provision has not been abused (see Review of Child Care Law, 1985, p59). Indeed, it was in recognition of this fact that the Review of Child Care Law recommended its retention, although the authors added the important proviso that it should be 'only for the purpose of a phased return home' (DHSS, 1985a, p60).

The legislators over-ruled this recommendation because of their commitment to enhancing the partnership philosophy, which itself derives from their concern to promote parental responsibility. This may be one of the few instances in the new Act where respect for parental rights has taken precedence over commitment to child welfare.

Child protection and parental responsibilities

Most of the proposals for reform of compulsory intervention into family life to protect children were already in place after the publication of the 1985 Review of Child Care Law. But it was the impact of the Cleveland crisis together with the deaths of Jasmine Beckford (Blom-Cooper, 1985) and Kimberley Carlile (Blom-Cooper, 1987) which gave the issues underlying compulsory intervention added urgency and provoked widespread public debate. The Cleveland crisis had demonstrated the consequences of excessive professional intrusion into family life while the death of Kimberley Carlile had revealed the converse, by exposing the weaknesses in existing provision to protect children in their own homes. Achieving a correct balance between the competing matters of respect for family autonomy, the protection of children and the use of state power is one of the hardest tasks in any society. How have the legislators attempted to balance matters in the new Act?

The Act introduces an entirely new set of criteria in civil law to empower statutory child care proceedings. Existing legislation had been widely criticized both because of the variety of statutes which at present enable children to be taken into care and also because the criteria and effects of the orders differ from one another. Henceforth, there will be only two compulsory public orders – the supervision order and the care order – and common criteria will underpin both provisions.

The new criteria greatly simplify existing statutes and turn on one dominant theme – the notion of harm. In adopting this conceptual framework the law builds directly on the philosophy of the Review of Child Care Law when it stated that 'in our view the primary justification for the state to initiate proceedings seeking compulsory powers is actual or likely harm to the child' (DHSS, 1985a, p102). To guard against unwarranted state intrusion two further conditions must be established. The harm must be significant in degree and it must be attributable to parental behaviour. To assess the parental behaviour, a legal test is introduced which centres on what the reasonable parent would provide for the particular child under consideration. In elaborating this principle, Judge Bracewell, who has been given a major responsibility for the implementation of the Act, explains that 'if a parent cannot cope through stress he or she would be unreasonable if help is not sought.' But she goes on to add a crucial *caveat*, 'However, within the limits laid down, it is not for the courts to disapprove of the life-style of the parents, nor to decide that the state can provide an improved standard and quality of life' (Bracewell, 1989, p5). In keeping with this philosophy, a finding of harm does not automatically empower removal, but only provides what have been described as the necessary or minimum 'threshold criteria' (R. White, 1989, p8). As elsewhere, the court must consider the likely benefits and disbenefits of making an order.

It was precisely to avoid the dangers of a 'state knows best' approach that the Review of Child Care Law rejected the adoption of a broad welfare criterion and instead put forward the framework of harm as the basis for compulsory intervention. This indeed is already the framework frequently used by practitioners in child assessment and its adoption by law will bring closer together the philosophy and language of law and social work.

The new criteria are an undoubted improvement on existing law. They redraw the boundaries specifying which children should be the subject of care proceedings by appropriately excluding both children who fail to attend school and those who commit offences. Henceforth, children with unsatisfactory school attendance records will be dealt with by entirely separate orders, entitled education supervision orders, and the widely criticized, but little used 'offence condition' of the 1969 CYPA will be formally abolished. It signifies the end of the attempt to link within one set of criteria 'depraved' and 'deprived' children, (Packman, 1975) by suggesting that the commission of offences was in itself a reflection of the need for care.

As well as redefining the potential beneficiaries of care, the scope of the local authorities to intervene effectively is considerably extended. In previous law, the SSD were only able to protect certain defined categories of children before harm had actually occurred. In the new Act the possibility of preventive intervention is extended to include all children who 'are likely to be' significantly harmed.

The SSD have also acquired new powers to protect children in their own homes. One important advantage of the new emergency protection orders (EPOs) is that they will enable an application to be made if the social workers' access to the child is being unreasonably refused when there is cause to believe that the child needs to be seen urgently. It was precisely this problem which lay at the heart of the Kimberley Carlile tragedy, because it was unclear what powers were available to the social worker to gain access to Kimberley in the face of hostile opposition from her stepfather (Blom-Cooper, 1987). The new law provides valuable clarification of this issue.

It also makes it quite clear that when an EPO is made, the SSD also acquire limited parental responsibility, thereby giving them the authority to carry out medical examinations. One of the most worrying aspects of the Cleveland crisis was that when place of safety orders were obtained, medical examinations were carried out on behalf of the Social Services without parental consent. This was an incorrect use of the order because it does not transfer parental powers to the local authority.

The child assessment orders are a further innovation which will widen the range of measures to protect children in their own homes. They will enable a multidisciplinary assessment of the child to be carried out in **non-emergency** situations for periods of up to seven days. They have been designed to cover the kinds of situation where attempts to carry out assessment of the child have failed and there is serious cause for concern over the child's health or development. As with EPOs, the criteria enabling legal intervention are the likelihood of significant harm and they also involve a limited transfer of parental responsibility to the SSD.

By all these means the options of the SSD to act sensitively to protect children have been considerably increased. For the new range of orders provides the SSD with different degrees of control to cover a range of situations with varying consequences on the preservation of the family home.

The new range of measures available to the SSD are offset by the introduction of new curbs on their present powers of discretion, which will in particular modify their relationships with parents and the courts. In future when SSDs apply for care proceedings they will be required to submit their plans for the child to the court for its scrutiny. In specifying this requirement the new law is undoubtedly attempting to upgrade the quality of care provided to children once they enter the care system. For the use of statutory powers does not of itself guarantee children access to high quality care once they become children of the state (DHSS, 1985b, pp9–13). A range of research studies commissioned by the DHSS have shown that planning on behalf of the child tends to diminish once the child is taken into care, even when compulsory powers are used (DHSS, 1985b, p7). Thus, through the scrutiny of SSD plans, the courts will undoubtedly be able to exercise greater influence over the crucial initial decision as to the potential value of a care order.

When this power is taken in conjunction with the increase in alternatives to care orders, the stronger role of the courts becomes even clearer. In future, the court will be able to consider the possibility of making a residence order in favour of a relative or other significant figure as an alternative to a care order. Placement with relatives or friends is possible under present law, but is at the discretion of the local authority after a care order has been made. Regrettably, no figures are collected specifically on placement with relatives, but figures on the combined category of relatives and parents show that this provision is rarely used. In 1985 only 17 per cent of all children placed went to live with relatives or parents, a proportion that was virtually unchanged from 1977 (Harris and Hopkins, 1989, p25). Other sources suggest that the trend in placement with relatives is actually downwards (Hansard, House of Lords, 17 Jan. 1989, col 128). Yet the little research that has been carried out into the benefits of placement with relatives has suggested that children fare better than when placed outside the family and that these placements can offer a non-stigmatizing secure alternative to placement with strangers (Rowe, 1988, p67). It will be particularly interesting to monitor the effect of this new court-led power to see how far it alters existing practices and helps achieve the government's intention of promoting care by and within the family.

The courts will also gain new powers to direct contact arrangements, which once again constitutes a check on the local authorities' present discretionary powers. It is a fundamental principle of the Act that when children are taken into care, their relationships with parents, guardians or persons holding residence orders should be preserved, unless the court directs otherwise. The SSD will have extremely limited rights to refuse contact without the making of a court order for periods of no more than seven days in an emergency. Otherwise, any refusal of contact sought by the SSD must be processed through the courts.

Some of the reasons behind this decision which strengthens parents' rights over local authority freedoms can be found in the research. The DHSS studies, quoted earlier, consistently found that children's links with their families were given insufficient attention by social workers (DHSS, 1985b). In one of the large scale studies 41 out of 170 children still in care at the two year point of inquiry had a mother who did not know their address (Millham *et al*, 1985). Furthermore the studies found a correlation between family links and the likelihood of discharge from care, noting that 'when links wither, chances of the child's return home are diminished' (DHSS, 1985b, p10). The legislators of the new Act are determined that children in care should not drift. What is less clear is whether court-led directions on contact are the solution. While the shortcomings of practice must be acknowledged, so too must be the serious shortages of social work resources as well as the fragility of the families from which children in care frequently come. In Packman's study, at the six month follow-up 'no less than one in seven of the children were still headed by the same parent figures as before' (Packman in DHSS, 1985b, p11). The difficulties faced by social work staff in maintaining family links should not be under-estimated, and raise issues which go well beyond the control of either the SSD or the courts.

The account thus far has highlighted the increase in court powers and simultaneously drawn attention to new checks on local authority decision-making. It should not be thought that the Act does not also reappraise the responsibilities of the courts. As noted earlier, in care proceedings as in all children's matters the court will have to satisfy itself that making an order is better than no order at all. Moreover, the court will be required to specify in writing the reasons for its decision and this new duty will undoubtedly increase its formal accountability. So too a child of sufficient understanding is given the power to overrule a court order requiring him to undergo a medical or psychiatric examination. But in general the Act will undoubtedly increase the significance of the court in the decision-making process over children in need of protection by extending the range of matters it should consider and increasing the number of options at its disposal. This signifies a shift in the legislation towards a more justice–oriented model which can also be linked into the wider move within child care policy away from the hegemony of the welfare model of practice of the early 1970s.

The greater emphasis on justice has led to the introduction of fairer procedures and the strengthening of the rights of all to challenge decision-making. Complaints procedures with an independent element must be established by local authorities which will be available to children, parents and foster-parents alike. Parents will also be able to challenge the making of an EPO and apply for its discharge after 72 hours, a possibility not available in the current place of safety orders. The complaints procedure is an important innovation. Local authorities have been singularly slow to establish any formal mechanisms for handling grievances and dissatisfactions. For example, surveys show that most do not at present have any complaints procedures for children in care (Lindsay, 1989, p23). The statutory introduction of complaints procedures will undoubtedly give all parties a new and important right to challenge and test out decision-making. Some have suggested the new procedure should be wholly independent of the local authorities, but what is needed is a proper mechanism within the SSD to open communication between users and providers of service as a first line of action before invoking external measures.

All the measures discussed so far will indeed alter the present balance in the delicate triangle of relationships between parents, children and state authorities. In general the Act undoubtedly strengthens the emphasis in law and practice on child protection and much of the detailed statute is devoted to reform and expansion of the child protection measures, while the local authorities' preventive duties are tucked away in schedules rather than appearing in the main body of the Act.

This focus on child protection may have serious consequences on the wider aims of enhancing relationships between SSD and parents in non-statutory work. Indeed, in comparison with earlier law, the gap may have now widened between the role of the SSD as a preventer of family breakdown and as an instrument of child protection enforcement. For, as has been shown, many of the preventive measures are permissive rather than statutory and many local authorities may not have the staff or financial resources to fully implement the reforms. But the gap may also widen because the local authorities have been given new instruments of child protection which may only increase the commonly held public perception of the social services as agents of statutory child care first and foremost. To create a genuine partnership between the local authorities and parents in this climate would be extremely difficult.

Conclusion

The Children Act 1989 is a clear improvement on existing law. It has achieved a better balance between the powers and responsibilities of state authorities and families. It should also lead to more open decision-making with greater parental involvement, fairer procedures to challenge decisions, as well as greater accountability by all.

But the Act will not please everyone. It has failed to set up family courts and left intact the adversarial system of dealing with child care proceedings which many believe are wholly inappropriate to the nature of the difficulties. Nor has it created an entirely independent service of guardians *ad litem* – the officers charged with representing the child's best interests in care and related proceedings in the juvenile courts. In this respect the Act missed an ideal opportunity for radical reappraisal of the position of the guardians and rejected the chance to create a new expanded child advocacy service amalgamating the services of divorce court welfare officers as well as guardians. Such a move would have given real

D

meaning to Butler-Sloss's reminder after Cleveland that 'children are people – not objects of concern' (Butler–Sloss, 1988).

Nor will the Act protect all children equally. Serious concern was raised in the parliamentary debates over the government's commitment to safeguard the position of children leaving care. This is a problem of some magnitude. In 1985, the last year for which figures are available, 7700 young people left care in England and Wales (T. White, 1989, p23). Of these, 70 per cent will go on to live on their own in contrast to the 0.02 per cent of their peers in the general population. These care leavers are an especially vulnerable group who are substantially over-represented in unemployment, homelessness and prison statistics (T. White, 1989, p23). Their financial position is also known to be especially precarious because of changes in social security benefits to the 16–25 age group. Yet the local authorities have not been placed under any statutory duty to offer financial assistance to care leavers. This decision, undoubtedly taken on the grounds of cost, seems extremely short-sighted. These young people are amongst the most vulnerable in the population.

More generally, as noted earlier, there is a widespread concern that the resource implications of the Act have been seriously underestimated and placed in jeopardy the proposals to widen the preventive powers of the local authorities. The Association of Metropolitan Authorities has carried out its own costings of these sections which are substantially in excess of those of the government (Stewart, 1989, p22).

How are LAs likely to deal with the anticipated shortfall in financial resources? One possible answer is suggested by the Act's own provisions. Parts VIII and X pave the way for the growth of the private sector, both in relation to day care and also to residential children's homes, by laying down guidelines for registration and inspection by LAs. The possibility of selling off its stock of children's homes is already under discussion in one local authority and there has been some speculation that privatization may become a popular option to ease pressure on other hard-pressed authorities or because it fits in with the political beliefs of the authority (Harris and Hopkins, 1989, p25). When the possibility of privatization is taken in conjunction with encouragement in the Act to delegate preventive services to voluntary agencies, an actual weakening of local authorities' role as providers of preventive services can be envisaged. This pessimistic view is given some further credence by the current acute difficulties in recruiting and retaining social work staff. Yet the adequacy of social work staffing, both in terms of the numbers and competence of the personnel, is vital if the Act is to achieve its stated intentions. For social workers occupy a key position in the legislation. They are the only professional group who are centrally involved in children's lives from the first efforts at the prevention of family breakdown to planning for the child's future when it can no longer remain at home. It is true that the government has made available a generous training support grant to local authorities of £7 million annually for a five year period for training in child protection. But government strategy must be directed at the comprehensive training of social workers in child care in **all** its aspects rather than being narrowly focused on the sharp end of child protection. Without this training support, there is further danger that the Act will be first and foremost a highly effective instrument of child protection but founder on the attainment of its wider purposes of promoting child welfare by strengthening family bonds.

References

Berridge, D and Cleaver, H (1987) *Foster Home Breakdown*. Oxford, Blackwell.

Blom-Cooper, L (1985) *A Child in Trust*. London, London Borough of Brent.

Blom-Cooper, L (1987) *A Child in Mind: Protection of Children in a Responsible Society*. London, London Borough of Greenwich.

Bracewell, J (1989) Children and the courts under the new Act. In Legal Studies and Services Ltd. *The Children Act 1989*. London.

Butler-Sloss, E (1988) *Report of the Inquiry into Child Abuse in Cleveland 1987*. London, HMSO.

Department of Health and Social Security (1974) *Mentally Handicapped Children in Residential Care*. London, HMSO.

Department of Health (1989) *An Introduction to the Children Act 1989*. London, HMSO.

Department of Health and Social Security (1985a) *Review of Child Care Law*. London, HMSO.

Department of Health and Social Security (1985b) *Social Work Decisions in Child Care*. London, HMSO.

Department of Health and Social Security (1987) *The Law on Child Care and Family Services*. London, HMSO.

Fisher, M, Marsh, P, Phillips, D with Sainsbury, E (1986) *In and Out of Care- The Experience of Children, Parents, and Social Workers*. London, Batsford/BAAF.

Gillick v West Norfolk and Wisbeck Area Health Authority (1986) AC 112.

Hansard, House of Lords (1989) 17 June, column 128.

Harris, J and Hopkins, T (1989) Potential for Control. *Community Care*, 22 June, pp24–5.

House of Commons (1984) Second Report from the Social Services Committee 1983–84. *Children in Care*, 1, London, HMSO.

Law Commission (1985) Working Paper No. 91, *Review of Child Law: Guardianship*. London, HMSO.

Law Commission (1986) Working Paper No. 96, *Review of Child Law: Custody*. London, HMSO.

Lindsay, M (1989) The Children's Advocate. *Community Care*, pp23–24.

Lowe, N (1989) Orders between parents or other individuals. In Legal Studies and Services Ltd *The Children Act 1989.* London.

Mackay, Lord (1989) Joseph Jackson Memorial Lecture, Perceptions of the Children Bill and Beyond. *New Law Journal*, April 14, pp505–7.

Millham, S, Bullock, R, Hosie, K, and Haak, M (1986) *Lost in Care – The Problems of Maintaining Links between Children in Care and Their Families.* Aldershot, Gower.

Mitchell, A (1985) *Children in the Middle.* London, Tavistock.

One Parent Families (1982) *Against Natural Justice: A Study of the Procedures used by Local Authorities in Taking Parental Rights Resolutions over Children in Voluntary Care.* London, National Council for One Parent Families.

Packman, J (1981) *The Child's Generation – Child Care Policy in Britain.* Oxford, Blackwell.

Parkinson, L (1986) *Conciliation in Separation and Divorce.* London, Croom Helm.

Pierson, J (1989) A new age of child welfare. *Community Care*, 23 May, pp23–4.

Richards, M and Dyson, M (1982) *Separation, Divorce and the Development of Children: A Review.* Cambridge, Child Care Development Group.

Ryan, M (1989) The Children Bill: implications for preventive work. *Adoption and Fostering*, 13, pp16–21.

Rowe, J (1988) Relatives as foster parents. In *Planning for Children*, London, Family Rights Group.

Timms, J (1989) Local authority responsibilities: the implications of the Act for the welfare of children. In Legal Studies and Services Ltd *The Children Act, 1989.* London.

Vernon, J and Fruin, D (1986) *In Care – a Study of Social Work Decision Making.* London, National Children's Bureau.

Wallerstein, J S and Kelly, J B (1980) *Surviving the Break-up- How Children and Parents Cope with Divorce.* London, Grant McIntyre.

Wallerstein, J S (1987) Children of Divorce: Report of a ten year follow up of early latency age children. *American Journal of Orthopsychiatry*, 572, pp199–212.

White, R (1989) Progress of the Children Bill. *New Law Journal*, April 14, pp515–6.

White, T (1989) A duty to help. *Community Care*, 1 June, pp23–4.

7 Watching the social fund

Gary Craig

Why the fuss?

A recent bibliography, comprising material written in the last four years about the social fund, contains more than 220 articles, papers and booklets (Craig and Coxall, 1989). Two major academically-based research projects working with social workers and advice workers have been established to monitor the social fund in addition to a DSS-funded research project; most major national voluntary organizations concerned with advice-giving and many small community groups and advice centres have some mechanism in place to check the impact of the fund on their organization and its users; and debates about the appropriate stance social workers and advisers should take towards the fund have, at times, been acrimonious with 'determined advocates' and 'non-cooperators' (*see below*) each distancing themselves from the other with mutual accusations, often in lurid language, of betraying claimants' interests. Yet at the centre of this activity is a piece of social policy with an annual budget of just £205 million, less, that is, than one half of one per cent of the UK annual social security expenditure.

Why should the social fund have triggered such a high level of interest, in relation, say, either to similarly small spending programmes or to single payments, the immediate precursor of the fund?

In this chapter, I propose to explore briefly the reasons for this and to go on to describe a particular phenomenon, monitoring the social fund, which has developed from the early debates on the social fund and which has raised issues central to a wider discussion of social policy. I look first at the significance of the fund in ideological terms, then review the arguments about the appropriate stance to be taken by social workers and advisers towards the fund (each of which laid some stress on the importance of monitoring). Finally,

I consider the major monitoring initiatives taken since the fund became operational in April 1988, touching briefly on some of the evidence which has emerged from that monitoring. Much of this evidence has been fully reported elsewhere and I do not propose to repeat it here. The interested reader is referred both to the bibliography mentioned above and, for example, to issues of the bulletin *Benefits Research* (*see below*).

The initial structure of the fund and the criticisms of it have been described by many commentators, including one in an earlier edition of this review. (For a discussion *see* e.g. Bradshaw, 1987; Berthoud, 1987; Lister and Lakhani, 1987; Ward, 1987). The consensus of these criticisms—included a wide range of commentators—highlighted four aspects of the fund. It was to be cash-limited; decision-making was to include, in a return to the pre-1980 system of exceptional needs payments, a large degree of officer discretion; most of the budget (almost 70 per cent in the first year) was to be in the form of repayable loans, reclaimed by direct deduction from claimants' benefit; and, for those claimants dissatisfied with decisions (of whom it was anticipated there would be increasing numbers), the right of access to an independent appeal tribunal was to be abolished and replaced by a process of (largely) internal administrative review.

The emphasis of the criticism placed on each of these features varied from one commentator to another: for example, many critics claimed that the impact of a cash limit of any kind was inimical to the objective of meeting needs which were unpredictable and unquantifiable in advance. The government-appointed Social Security Advisory Committee (SSAC), however, was prepared to accept that the social fund could work within a fixed budget, but only if either the cash limits were substantially increased from those initially proposed (the SSAC suggested a starting budget of £350 million, the single payments budget of 1985/86 adjusted for inflation) or if 'the basic income support rates (were) to be increased by a substantial amount to compensate for the virtual disappearance of lump-sum grants for the majority of claimants which is implied' (SSAC, 1987, para 7). However, most commentators were concerned about the impact of the package as a whole and the interrelationships between these features. Amongst this critical comment, observations on the conjunction of a fixed budget and the exercise of officer discretion in identifying and meeting need was perhaps most striking. Berthoud, for example, observed of the draft social fund manual (the book of guidance and directions for Social Fund Officers—SFOs—to follow) that '. . . many of the problems presented in the social fund proposals arise from the combination of very different activities under a single heading and all apparently to be handled by the same tool – discretion. The mixture is particularly inappropriate if the whole is subject to a single cash limit' (Berthoud,

1985, p114). He returned to this theme more emphatically when it was clear that the government would not be shifted from its ground. 'Many commentators have focused their primary anxieties on the social fund's cash limit rather than on the exercise of discretion as such. In practice, they are part and parcel of the same policy; . . . to the extent that officials have discretion, a budget is likely to be the only effective way by which the government can indicate where to draw the line between needs which should and should not attract a payment' (Berthoud, 1987, p11).

Mullen also laid considerable initial emphasis on the importance of the cash limit itself *and* the constraints it would place on the exercise of discretion. Commenting on the first year's local office allocations in relation to previous single payment expenditure, he pointed out that 'It is difficult to avoid the conclusion that total national expenditure has been reduced in an arbitrary fashion. The fund appears, therefore, to be born of parsimony' (Mullen, 1989, p78), and concluded 'The crucial features of (the fund) have been the decision to place an effective cash limit on the fund, the level of general funding for loans and grants, and the allocations to particular officers. These are likely to place severe financial pressures on local offices which will tend to skew the exercise of discretion towards the limiting of awards' (*ibid*, p91).

What the social fund is, how it operates on a day-to-day basis, and the everyday dilemmas it poses for claimants, may, however, in the long run be of less significance than what it represents implicitly and at an ideological level. The SSAC commented that the sums of money involved were small but that 'they act as an important symbol of the way in which we operate the safety net for the poorest members of society' (SSAC, *op.cit*, para 45). As it stood, and in terms of the initial cash allocations, that symbol would be seen, in SSAC's eyes, as 'unfair' and 'unworkable'.

Fran Bennett, of the Child Poverty Action Group, observed that the fund attracted so much criticism because 'those people affected are some of the poorest and most vulnerable. Whilst the rest of society is being encouraged to expect ever higher standards of living, basic necessities are being placed beyond the reach of many of these claimants' (Bennett, 1989, p1). At a broader ideological level, however, she pointed out that the fund 'represents a change in the *nature* of part of the benefits system, away from rights and entitlement, towards "needs" and desserts. . . . indicative of a broader, worrying shift in views about the role of the welfare state which are increasingly being reflected in government social policy' (*ibid*). She goes on to suggest that government statements about the function of the fund being, in part, to reduce the 'culture of dependency' of claimants on the state are, at best, disingenuous. Reducing dependency on the state was to be achieved by the simple expedient of reducing benefits; meanwhile, it was charities, trusts, voluntary organizations, local authorities and—at the end of the line—that most hallowed of government totems, the family, that would have to provide the 'safety net' for the poorest in society.

Need is thus increasingly removed from the public arena and hidden from view, a theme taken up by Lister in her contribution to the same booklet. 'The government's policy of "reducing dependency on the benefits culture", of which the social fund is a primary plank, will create a blanket of invisibility over the needs of millions of people existing on inadequate social security benefits' (Lister, 1989, p70). Indeed, the degree to which the social fund, in operation, is able to mask the extent of unmet need (which had been 'privatized' in this way) became both an argument for monitoring and one of the particular problems associated with monitoring initiatives, as we shall see below. This process, by which more of the poor become invisible, provides the government with a further line of defence against claims that poverty is increasing. Those amongst the poor who are unable to 'join in' the mainstream of society, are structured out and hidden from public view. By dismissing those applicants who are refused social fund money as 'ill-informed', the government is not only cash-limiting the supply of cash but the extent of need.

The government, in setting out its objectives for the 1985 social security review as a whole (which led to the 1986 Social Security Act and the bulk of the April 1988 changes, including the social fund) also insisted that changes in the system would have to be consistent with its overall economic objectives. The need to contain or, where possible, reduce public expenditure featured strongly amongst these objectives. This involved the shift of major parts of the public sector into the private sector (including, from 1979–81, perhaps two-thirds of the former state-owned industrial sector).

For those parts of the economy which were perceived as being inescapably bound to the public sector (and even parts of the social security system, such as the Livingston computer centre which processed income support claims, were transferred to privatized or quasi-privatized status), the technique of cash limits was to become a major instrument for controlling expenditure. Need, again, was to be defined in terms of supply (of cash) rather than by demand. The social fund was not to escape this management tool and for social fund managers, managing demand became *the* imperative amidst the thousands of paragraphs of directions and guidance in the Social Fund Manual. Above all else, managers were instructed, the cash-limited allocation for each local office was not to be exceeded at the end of the year (thus contradicting an earlier government assurance that the first year's budget was not the same as a fixed cash limit).

In the event, managers contained demand so effectively that the first year's budget was £35 million (or 18 per cent) underspent whilst over half a million applicants were refused any money at all and countless others had reduced awards. In the first year, over £370 million was applied for (close to the SSAC's suggested cash limit): only £166 million was paid out. Some managers went further and used monthly expenditure profiles (which were supposed to be guidance only) as fixed monthly allocations, which were also not to be exceeded. In the second year, as the volume of demand has grown from a slow start, managing the local cash limits has become considerably more difficult. Local managers are increasingly inventing bizarre techniques – including ever-more refined distinctions between 'deserving' and 'non-deserving' claimants – as well as increasing the refusal rate for both grants and loans in order to hold the line (*see The Sunday Correspondent*, November 19 1989, p3). It remains to be seen whether this pressure results in adjustments to the cash limits or whether frontline staff within the DSS offices are left to bear the entire burden of operationalizing this particular economic objective. At the time of writing, the budget for 1990/91 has been effectively frozen for the second year running.

In the creation of the social fund, then, we can see the bringing together by the government of a number of important elements in its social policy – a diminution of the role of the state, the 'strengthening of the family', a reduction in public expenditure, the drawing of deeply ideological and divisive distinctions between sections of the (potential) workforce, the stress on individual and private as opposed to collective and public solutions to social problems – which have been continuing threads in the programmes of recent Tory governments. Taken together, within the confines of a small, and declining, expenditure they represent one of the sharpest indications of the continuing attack on democratic notions of collective responsibility for care of those least able to maintain a reasonable standard of living. It is the bringing together of these political strands which may have generated so great a concern with the social fund. The fund, then, has an ideological significance out of all proportion to its financial status. It contains so many threads of current social policy that it is crucial to the government for it to succeed on their terms. If it fails, the implications for social policy go far beyond the social fund itself.

Arms-length or hands-off?

For those who were to experience working alongside the social fund on a day-to-day basis (particularly local authority social workers, many of them concerned with declining Section 1/Section 12 budgets, welfare rights advisers and advice centre workers), there had emerged a clear consensus as to what was wrong with the fund. What proved to be more difficult in the period immediately before and after the commencement of the fund was to construct a policy to guide their relationship with the fund, and with Social Fund Officers (SFOs). Hardly anyone, as the precise shape of the fund emerged (virtually unscathed despite the wide-ranging critique of it), was prepared to argue for committed cooperation. The choice posed for advisers, in the debates (which ran from 1986 until at least the middle of 1989) polarized into two positions: non-cooperation ('hands-off') and determined advocacy ('arms-length'). (The determined advocacy position was known by a number of other names during the struggle to define it, including the 'rights approach', 'impartial advocacy' and 'aggressive advocacy', but I shall refer to it by the name by which it was finally, and most widely known.)

Arms-length?

The determined advocacy position was one around which most local authority social workers, welfare rights advisers and major national voluntary organizations finally grouped. Many separate attempts at defining guide-lines were made from 1986 onwards. Individual national voluntary organizations developed their own policy, as did various local authorities, and there were differences in emphasis which reflected the nature of a particular organization's relationship with the social fund. For example, voluntary organiza-tions were concerned about the knock-on effect of local authorities' refusal to accept the role suggested for them by the Social Fund Manual. 'Voluntary organisations and charities must recognise that they may be seen as a soft option by the SFOs. . . . Voluntary organisations may therefore be seen as an easier target by SFOs for gaining information, assistance in assessment etc. . . . other agencies may also see them as an alternative source of help' (Social Security Consortium, 1988, p2). However, there did emerge a common core of principles which were reflected in most 'determined advocacy' guidelines.

There is insufficient space to detail the individual guidelines here, and the reader can refer to particular organizations for details of their policies as well as to an article by Lister which reviews the process by which several of the more influential ones were drawn up (Lister, 1989a). Probably the key documents were those produced by the local authority associations in England and Wales, and Scotland (the Association of Metropolitan Authorities–AMA, Association of County Councils—ACC, and Convention of Scottish Local Authorities—COSLA, which produced a common guide), the professional social work association, BASW (British Association of Social Workers), and, within the voluntary sector, those of NACAB (the National Association of Citizens' Advice Bureaux) and the Social Security Consortium (SSC), acting as the national coordinating body for the views of voluntary groups.

The position of the local authority associations was eventually summarized in a practice guide and position statement (AMA/ACC, 1988). In it the associations repeated their view that the social fund '. . . should have no place in a social security system . . . (and that) particular objection is taken to the fund's emphasis on the prioritization of need' (*ibid*, p1). Responsibility for income maintenance should remain with the DHSS, clients were to decide themselves what their needs were (rather than social workers who were to resist being drawn into joint assessments of need with SFOs) and 'the appropriate response for local authority fieldworkers is to provide advocacy as the representative of clients wishing to apply to the social fund' (*Ibid*, p2).

The main elements of determined advocacy were:

1 Claimant sovereignty in deciding what his/her needs were with social workers acting as representative *for* a claimant but not co-manager of a claim *with* an SFO.
2 Local SFO priorities should be disregarded so that each claim could be supported on its merits.
3 Grants rather than loans should be pursued.
4 Any refusal to make an award should be followed by a request for a review.

The approach 'recognises that whilst it would be preferable not to have to deal with the social fund, claimants may not have that luxury and will need impartial help to get the best that they can from the fund' (SSC, 1988, p15). Similarly although BASW, like the local authority associations, had initially taken a stance of non-cooperation, it too concluded that determined advocacy was the appropriate stance to adopt. (This was not without some dissension, some social workers continuing to argue that advocating for some clients was still, within the confines of a cash limit, an implicit form of prioritization of clients' needs.)

In relation to monitoring, the local authority associations (and other determined advocates) were clear about its importance.

25. Local authorities may wish to institute systematic monitoring of the social fund's impact on clients and local authority services. Authorities concerned that the fund remain in the public eye will be clear about the crucial importance of monitoring.

26.   Monitoring would aim to ensure that the impact of the social fund
       is systematically and objectively recorded and exposed to public
       view and to ensure that the local authority's policies in response to
       the social fund are operating as effectively as possible. Monitoring
       should attempt to establish the effects of the fund on particular
       vulnerable groups such as people with disabilities, single parents,
       and people in ethnic minority groups.

                                                   (AMA/ACC, *op.cit*, p9)

The action plan for social workers given as an appendix to the
practice guide also encouraged them to participate in monitoring
exercises.

The scope of these exercises was not defined in the practice guide
and it was left to the SSC later in the year, addressing an audience
of voluntary organizations, to spell out the kinds of data which
needed to be collected (SSC, 1988, p16). These included details
of those seeking help from the social fund (outcome of applications,
repayment rates, effects on those refused etc.), details of the effects
on organizations (requests for information from SFOs, referrals from
SFOs, increasing demand on charities etc.) and information on the
extent to which the social fund discriminated in terms of age, sex or
race. The SSC also re-emphasized the wider political significance
of monitoring. 'Campaign work, using the results of monitoring,
would obviously include pressure on MPs and using the local
media' (*ibid*).

This guidance was elaborated on by the London Advice Services
Alliance (LASA) which shortly afterwards published a pack of
information for organizations wishing to monitor the fund (LASA,
1988). This offered organizations three specimen monitoring forms,
two for use in advice centres and one by grant-giving charities, and
advice on how to conduct campaigns using data derived from
monitoring. LASA's argument for monitoring was that it 'will
provide the evidence needed to press for its abolition or radical
reform beneficial to claimants. The government has shown itself
vulnerable to criticism on social security policy when public and
media pressure is strong' (*ibid.*).

Hands-off?

The policy of non-cooperation with the fund was, according to
one commentator, originally widely advocated by advice agencies
(Arnott, 1988, p23) as well as being the original stance taken by
many organizations (including BASW and local authority associations) which later shifted their ground. However, despite the fact that
it was offered in the SSC's guide for voluntary organizations (SSC,
1988) as an equal option to that of determined advocacy, only those

organizations in membership of the Federation of Independent Advice Centres (FIAC) or the National Campaign Against Social Security Cuts and a few other organizations, including a number of trade union branches and the city of Liverpool, were to attempt to carry out the principles of non-cooperation. The SSC defined non-cooperation as follows.

Advisers would
- insist that all claims be considered for grants not loans
- insist that all needs are of equal priority
- encourage all clients to claim as many payments as they need, as often as they need
- encourage all claimants to seek reviews if refused a payment
- encourage all claimants who lost on review to complain to their MP
- refuse to deal with the DHSS for any reason. (SSC, 1988, p14)

The SSC commentary on this position suggested the inherent political dangers in it as well as the practical difficulties. 'Non-cooperation with the social fund would require a commitment to opposition to the fund which many advice agencies may not be in a position to make. A joint commitment . . . might well prove the social fund unworkable. However, such coordination would not be easy to obtain and it is likely that advisers will see this approach as having such an adverse effect on claimants that claimants themselves must have the right to make the decision not to cooperate with the fund' (*ibid*). At its national conference in 1987, FIAC was able to obtain a virtually unanimous vote in favour of the position of non-cooperation. By mid-1988 there had been a significant—though not decisive—shift of opinion within FIAC towards the position of determined advocacy, in the light of some months' experience of working with the fund.

The SSC's definition of non-cooperation was not explicit on the issue of monitoring although the 'refusal to deal with the DHSS for any reason' appears to imply that even monitoring of the fund to confirm its presumed unhelpful effect on claimants is ruled off-limits. Certainly this was the interpretation of some social workers invited to become involved in the SSRC monitoring exercises (*see below*) who claimed that the position of non-cooperation which they had taken, in isolation from most of their colleagues, required that they also 'non-cooperate' with any research into the impact of the fund.

FIAC itself, however, in its policy statement for member organizations, does refer directly to the value of monitoring. 'All member centres should campaign actively against the social fund, in particular by lobbying MPs, referring to these cases and by using the local and national media to expose the misery of the social fund'

(FIAC, 1989), and '. . . advisers and agencies should systematically monitor claimants with needs which would have been able to attract single payments. This monitoring is not only aimed at long-term statistical research but it is intended to provide hard information of use in campaigning around the issue, highlighting hardship in the media and putting pressure on the government . . .' (*ibid*).

In the event, and as advisers have struggled with the interpretations of their particular guidance in practice, it has seemed that 'there was less that divided the two positions than they had in common' (Craig, 1989, pvi). Indeed, as the secretary of FIAC observed at an early stage, the two policies differed only in the area of individual advocacy. FIAC was opposed to this on the grounds that '(i) it runs counter to FIAC's constitutional aims and (ii) that individual advocacy means cooperating with the social fund' (Holloway, 1989). The first of these arguments was based on the view that most FIAC agencies were 'bound to serve the interests of the community as a whole' (a statement which, in all probability, the majority of agencies pursuing the determined advocacy position would also claim for their own). The second seems tautologous.

The difference between the two positions may be becoming barely perceptible (and Holloway later reports on particular non-cooperating advice centres which have 'softened' their line in the direction of determined advocacy). Nevertheless, the differences were asserted at the height of the debate to be real enough. The nuances in the debate and differing interpretations led to considerable confusion which the government was able, mischievously, to exploit by accusing 'non-cooperating' local authorities, of which there were in reality not even a handful, of being responsible for only limited take-up of the fund in the first year. This confusion was still apparent in the results of a BASW monitoring survey of its membership in early 1989 which revealed that 14 per cent of local authorities covered by the survey were formally 'non-cooperating' but nevertheless permitting their social workers to assist clients in making a claim to the social fund.

The twists and turns of this debate are perhaps most fully demonstrated by the experience of NALGO, the local government union covering most social work grades,[1] which moved from a stance of non-cooperation through one of determined advocacy to a somewhat *laissez faire* position permitting individual branches to form their own policies in the light both of the AMA/ACC guidance and of local conditions. What did perhaps emerge most clearly from the arguments was a clear consensus on the need to monitor the fund, independently of the DSS, and on the political uses to which monitoring could be put. We can now turn to examine some of the more significant monitoring initiatives which emerged.

Watching it

Of the range of monitoring initiatives established from the end of 1987, I propose to examine only three in detail, for reasons of space. These are the work of the Nottingham University Benefits Research Unit (NBRU), the Social Security Research Consortium (SSRC), and the Social Security Consortium (no relation). All of these initiatives are continuing at the time of writing but some of their early findings can be referred to in passing. Before discussing each of these, I should also mention briefly four other key sets of monitoring arrangements.

The DSS is, of course, conducting its own internal monitoring, details of which are available in the first annual report of the social fund of the Secretary of State (DSS, 1989a)[2]. Despite the unprecedented scope of statistical material provided as annexes to the report, it is difficult to see it as other than a political justification for the fund's existence. In the light of reported experience of the fund during the first year, the Secretary of State at times stretched the credulity of even the most generous of observers. In addition, and somewhat at a distance from the DSS, the Social Fund Commissioner is monitoring the quality of reviews carried out at the second tier review stage by Social Fund Inspectors (DSS, 1989b). The Commissioner is not responsible for assessing the quality of decision-making by SFOs.

Third, the DSS has funded the Social Policy Research Unit at York University (SPRU) to undertake what is coming to be known as the official independent evaluation of the social fund. It will have as its centrepiece '. . . a survey of successful and unsuccessful social fund applicants as well as people who have not applied for help from the fund' (SPRU, Press Release, 3.4.89). This research will be conducted over a two-year period making use of existing DSS local office statistics from approximately 10 per cent of offices and with, it is hoped, the cooperation of SFOs and social fund managers. Needs unmet by the social fund are expected to be defined in terms of the perceptions of SFOs and through discussion with local advisers. This research will thus, to some extent, begin to explore the problematic area of unmet need although the role of SFOs in this process has been questioned.

Finally, the Policy Studies Institute has secured a grant from the Economic and Social Research Council (ESRC) to undertake an assessment of the review procedure, as part of the ESRC larger research initiative on 'Citizen Grievances and Administrative Action'. This research, which commenced in late 1989, is based on an examination of a sample of case studies of review applications in eight local offices, with a view to assessing 'the secondary decision-making procedure in the light of alternative sets of objectives which might be set by social fund applicants' (PSI, job details, August 1989). Again, the DSS local office records are to be made available to the research team. For each case study, all participants—claimant, adviser, local DSS office staff and SFO—would be interviewed. The latter two research projects will not have data available until 1990/91.

Nottingham Benefits Research Unit

The NBRU Social Fund Project was established with the support of the Social Services Research Group (SSRG) in 1987. The SSRG is a 'forum for the exchange of ideas on research into the social services' and has a membership including people working in research, planning and development in local authorities, voluntary organizations and academic bodies. NBRU itself has been in existence since 1981, undertaking research into welfare rights and social security; the Social Fund Project, which commenced work in April 1988, is currently the unit's largest research programme.

The core of the project is joint monitoring of social fund referrals carried out by a sample of 87 local offices in social services/work departments in 27 local authorities in England, Wales (one authority) and Scotland (two authorities). This monitoring is carried out at three-month intervals through an examination of new referrals and existing cases, using standardized recording forms. Known as *Referral Snapshots* and *Case Review Exercises*, each lasts for five working days. Local authorities opted in on a fee-paying basis (£3500 flat-rate) and were offered some flexibility as to the extent of their involvement, subject to a common recording approach. Thus local social services research officers were able to determine how many local offices participated and which offices they were—generally between two and four offices took part from each authority.

The NBRU stressed both the national dimension of the project—whereby authorities would be enabled to contrast experience with that of other authorities—and the aspect of frequent feedback to individual local authorities to enable them to monitor those of their own policies likely to be most affected by the social fund (Section 1, welfare rights, referrals to other agencies etc.). The initial aims of the project included '1) to monitor the policies and procedures that Departments adopt in relation to the Social Fund, 2) to examine the consistency of policy operation within Social Services Departments and 3) to monitor Section One expenditure before and after the introduction of the Social Fund' (NBRU, 1987). Other aims included an examination of the use made by SFOs of the resources held by voluntary organizations and charitable trusts.

The NBRU's initial findings have been reported largely through three channels. In September 1988 the Unit established its own

Bulletin, *Benefits Research*. Initially, the Bulletin reported mainly on the findings of the in-house research, but by mid-1989 its scope had been widened to include research reports from non-NBRU sources as well as political comment and case material submitted by other researchers.

Second, the Unit published a series of occasional papers related to specific aspects of its social fund research, such as summaries of the snapshots. In *Boundary Wars* (Svenson, 1988), the Unit contrasted local authority policy responses to the social fund, within the context of the BASW and AMA/ACC position statements. A later report, *Vulnerable Clients* (Becker, 1989), presented the findings of the first Case Review Exercise. This involved 347 social work clients, one third of whom had specific social fund or financial problems, particularly with community care grants (CCGs). It also reflected the dual focus which had begun to emerge in many monitoring reports, one concerned with the impact on clients or users of a service and the other the impact on the organization itself. This report concluded not only that social work clients were increasingly experiencing financial difficulties as a result of the social fund (and the wider social security changes), but that these difficulties were increasingly being brought to the doors of social services departments.

Third, the Unit negotiated with *Community Care* magazine a regular feature 'Fundamentals' which appears bi-monthly in the magazine. These features summarize the work of the Project for a wider readership but again include other material. For example, articles by Lynes (Lynes, 1988) and Craig (Craig, 1988) examined trends in local office spending patterns based on separate analyses of the local office data provided centrally by the DSS. An analysis of this data had also been the subject of an earlier, and controversial paper from the NBRU. The DSS had commenced providing this data—numbers of grants and loans awarded and refused, monthly spending totals, state of the budget—to a few researchers during the summer of 1988. Prior to this, it was only available to those with access to the House of Commons Library. A comparison of data supplied direct from local offices to the NBRU with that in the House of Commons revealed serious numerical discrepancies and alerted outside researchers to some disturbing shortcomings of the social fund microcomputer, a theme to which other researchers were to return later (Baker, Becker and Svenson, 1988).

Although the NBRU made no claim as to the representativeness of its sample of authorities, the population covered by them comprised 14.5 million people, more than 25 per cent of the UK population. Within them, almost two million people were dependent on Income Support. By July 1989, with five snapshots or case review exercises completed, more than 1700 people with financial and social fund problems had been monitored. Reporting on the cumulative impression created from these snapshots (one of

'Small Change'), Becker pointed to the strengths and weaknesses inherent in this kind of monitoring. 'Each individual snapshot tells us something about the type of people seeking help from personal social services in that particular week—and also something about their problems and what happens to them. But taken as a series, the snapshots create a unique picture of how these demands on social services—and responses—change over time' (Becker, 1989b). The strength of this monitoring is the picture developed from a growing volume of cases recorded which can show trends and make comparisons possible between authorities and areas and over time. The weaknesses, which NBRU's research shares with other monitoring projects, are that it offers only a fleeting and partial glimpse of any one individual client's position, and that it only reflects the position of those in contact with the agency.

Social Security Research Consortium

The SSRC is a grouping of researchers based throughout the UK, with an interest in social security. The Consortium emerged from discussions between a group of these researchers in 1987. Some had already undertaken research into the issues surrounding social services/social security boundary problems and had been party to the discussions within local authorities leading to the AMA/ACC position statement. A further factor which shaped the SSRC approach was that it was then felt that 'the government will neither conduct nor sponsor social fund monitoring and that major funding from alternative sources is not forthcoming' (SSRC, 1987). Parliamentary answers indicated that the government had no plans originally to conduct its own monitoring. However, it is, as we have seen, now both carrying out internal monitoring and sponsoring the SPRU research (perhaps prompted by the development of external research programmes) and the SSRC has been able to attract funding from charitable foundations for its own research.

The initial focus of the SSRC was, like the NBRU, to examine the impact of the social fund on the clients and work of social services departments. There is no commonly agreed explanation as to why those active in the early stages of the NBRU and the SSRC were unable to develop a single or joint approach. The two groupings did, however, despite some initial tensions, agree to a protocol which allowed each to approach separate local authorities offering different kinds of research package. These, to some extent, reflect their separate stances towards funding.

The SSRC, unlike the NBRU, attempted to achieve a statistically valid 10 per cent sample of local authorities based on 'a stratified frame of British authorities, reflecting different geographical regions, tiers of government and variations in political control' (*ibid*). Researchers were to be recruited in each of the sample areas to coordinate the research and the data analysed centrally (at Lancaster University). The local authority associations endorsed the research and provided a steering group to discuss progress but were unable to provide more than token funding for it.

The centrepiece of the SSRC research initially was to be based on detailed questionnaires administered by social workers to clients referred to them with financial or social fund problems during a specified four-week period. The questionnaires were to be followed up by researchers with semi-structured qualitative interviews and group discussions with social workers. Again a dual focus is evident: the research was expected to throw some light both on the effects on client-claimants, e.g. the difficulties they experienced with loans, and on the social services departments themselves, e.g. the boundaries between cash and care, particularly in relation to CCGs.

The pilot study was carried out in eight local authorities in the summer of 1988. Findings were reported in a series of documents during 1989 (Stewart and Stewart, 1989; Walker 1989; Stewart, Stewart and Walker, 1989). By the time the pilot had been analysed, it was clear that the original methodological strength of the SSRC's work would have to be diluted for a number of reasons. Several local authorities had withdrawn from the research for reasons unconnected with it and others had changed political control; the commitment of energy and resources of local authorities and the volume of cases recorded varied markedly (as with the NBRU); as a result of local factors, despite standard recording sheets, the ways in which potential 'social fund applicants' were processed led to an uneven quality of recording. Nevertheless, the situations of over 300 clients were recorded in the pilot survey and 50 social workers were interviewed; in the main study, covering more than 20 local authorities, four times as many questionnaires were completed with approximately 100 social worker and other interviews.

The conclusions of the pilot survey were summarized by Lister. As well as challenging the '. . . somewhat complacent statement by the Social Services Secretary that the "social fund is now working well". . .' (Lister, 1989b, p16) for claimants, the pilot research revealed the considerable difficulties local authorities and their social workers were having in interpreting and operating such guidance as they had with regard to the fund. The findings underlined '. . . the need for local authorities and other agencies to clarify for their workers the meaning of whatever policy is adopted towards the social fund and to ensure that they are trained in how to implement that policy. They also highlight, once more, social workers' general lack of knowledge about and training in social security matters. . .' (*ibid*, p18). The findings of the main survey, undertaken in the spring of 1989, will be published shortly. Similar parallel studies were conducted within NACAB and the Probation Service and are the subject of separate reports.

Although the primary focus of the SSRC's work was with local authorities, it was recognised that this would provide only a partial picture of the impact of the fund. Consequently, a number of researchers developed parallel work with local voluntary advice centres using similar research instruments. This resulted in week or two-week long exercises involving between four and eight advice centres in five areas. Their findings have been reported in *Community Care* (Alcock, Craig, Hill and Vamplew, 1989). As well as providing further 'distressing evidence of the shift from public to private welfare in the late 1980s' as claimants were referred on to charities and trusts, this monitoring, alongside that of the statutory sector, was able to throw some light on the differing uses made of the various advice sources in particular areas. However, and again in common with the NBRU work, it provided but a fleeting sight of a claimant's story. Those, for example, who were advised to apply for a grant or ask for a refusal to be reviewed rarely returned to tell the rest of their tale. Like NBRU's work, the value of this SSRC work may be more in the overall patterns and trends that it reveals, even acknowledging the limited range of claimants it is able to reach.

It was partly to address this problem (and partly also to explore the dimension of race as a significant element in the operation of a discretionary system) that a third strand of monitoring has been developed within the SSRC framework. This involves interviewing a sample of income support claimants in Bradford recruited on a random basis and not through agencies. This has been made possible through charitable funding and has involved considerable problems in the construction of a sample, given the unwillingness of the DSS and the local authority to make a suitable sampling frame available. The approach may be extended to other areas. This kind of monitoring, based on in-depth semi-structured schedules, will provide a more rounded view of claimants' experience of the social fund in relation to broader questions such as the management of debt and house-hold budgeting in low income families.[3] It will also permit exploration of the problem of defining unmet need from the perspective of the claimant.

All other major monitoring initiatives have reached a common conclusion regarding the limitations of monitoring the social fund through agencies. It is not only that agencies often quickly lose touch with those who apply to the social fund, once a decision is made, or with those who decide not to apply; there is, as Davies puts it, '. . . insufficient information available as to what is actually happening to people who are *not* applying to the social fund . . . (and a) need for ongoing research aimed at monitoring the *longer-term* effects of the social fund . . . on claimants . . .' (Davies, 1989—my emphases).[4]

The type of research being conducted in Bradford exchanges width for depth, and brings its own political problems. A similar piece of research, only marginally concerned with the social fund, was conducted by SPRU for the Tyneside Child Poverty Action Group shortly before the April 1988 changes were introduced. The response of the Social Security Secretary indicated the likely approach the government might take towards small-scale in-depth research: it was, he indicated in effect, to be disregarded because it involved too small a sample to be of significance (60 families were interviewed). This dismissive remark was an echo of one made at the January 1989 conference organised by *Community Care* and the SSRC to discuss the initial research findings from the SSRC. Here the DSS spokesman indicated that he would only be interested in looking at 'hard data' from research.

Social Security Consortium

The last of the monitoring initiatives to be reviewed briefly here is that of the SSC. It is, in reality, not one initiative but a number which have been coordinated through the SSC. There has been no attempt to use common research instruments (although some use has been made of the standard pro-formas issued in the LASA pack—see above). In a few cases, the monitoring has been little more than a trawl from the central office of voluntary organizations to their branches seeking information on their experience of the social fund. Many have, however, attempted a more rigorous approach.

The SSC was established in 1986 '. . . to act as a focus for the many voluntary and community organizations campaigning against the provisions of the 1986 Social Security Bill' (Craig, 1989, pvi). Once the Bill had been enacted, the SSC took on the role of coordinating voluntary sector monitoring of the fund, generally within the context of the AMA/ACC guidelines. A subgroup oversaw this work and began to canvas evidence from organizations throughout the early part of 1989. This evidence was the basis for a booklet later in the year (Craig, ed, 1989). Although, as the introduction to the booklet points out, the quality of the evidence acquired was uneven and the range of issues addressed by it widely varying in scope, what struck the compilers of the booklet was '. . . the frequency with which the same clear themes emerged' (Craig, 1989, pviii). Was the social fund effective and efficient in the terms laid down by the Secretary of State? Was the process of 'considered decision-making' an advance on that obtained during the single payments regime? Were claimants' needs being indentified clearly and met in full? On all these grounds, the Consortium's evidence found the fund to be lacking. In the conclusion to the booklet, Lister summarized the evidence thus: '. . . the prognosis must be a gloomy one. It is important that both the voluntary and statutory sectors . . . continue to monitor the effects of the social fund both on claimants and their agencies. . . . every agency working with social security claimants has a responsibility to ensure that . . . the "privatization" of need is made a public issue' (Lister, 1989b, p70).

Keep on monitoring?

Lister's call goes to the heart of the monitoring issue. Through the social fund, as through many other recent pieces of social policy (some of which are discussed elsewhere in this volume), the government has shifted the responsibility for meeting social needs steadily out of the public, collective arena into the private individualized sector. In the case of the social fund, this means not only moving the burden onto voluntary agencies, charities and grant-giving trusts but towards credit companies, loan sharks and second-hand furniture and electrical goods stores. And at the back of this line stands the family. Regardless of its objective economic circumstances or the extent to which, in reality, it fits with the ideal type the government constructs for it[5], the family is enjoined to support its members who have fallen on hard times.

This process, because of the way the social fund has been structured, was liable to happen in thousands of isolated, obscure and private ways. Indeed, it is precisely this tendency to privatize poverty which enables the government to resist attempts to define it as a growing problem and to deflect demands for further action. The value of monitoring—as the initiatives described above demonstrate—is to keep the issues of poverty and political responsibility for dealing with it on the public agenda. It was never enough to rely on the government's own monitoring, as the bland annual report of the Secretary of State for Social Security and the unyielding responses to persistent questioning in Parliament have confirmed. Whether the cumulative effect of the various monitoring exercises can produce any changes in the scheme remains to be seen. We have already observed that critical comment based on small-scale research into aspects of the fund is dismissed as being unrepresentative (e.g. the SPRU/Tyneside CPAG report mentioned earlier or the DSS response to one researcher's interviews with some Social Fund Officers: *see* Craig, 1988a; Lloyd, 1989) even where such comment confirms findings reported from other quarters. The remarkable features of social fund monitoring are its extensiveness and the degree to which there is unanimity (at least outside the DSS) as to the fund's shortcomings in practice.

The DSS – and the government as a whole – remains resistant to making any but the most superficial changes despite this fundamental critique. But that is a problem of the politics of social policy which goes far wider than the social fund: the ideological basis of the social fund merely reveals it more sharply. The government increasingly has a reputation for cancelling, suppressing or distorting social policy research of which it disapproves. Faced with this, researchers can only defend the integrity of their research and seek new ways of reaching wider audiences with their findings.

Notes

1   *See* for example press coverage on NALGO debates on the social fund e.g. *Social Services Insight*, 5.2.88, p3; *Social Work Today*, 21.7.88, p2; *Community Care*, 24.11.88, p1 and 22.6.89, p1.

2   During the first year of the social fund, the DHSS was split into two parts. The Department of Social Security (DSS) then took responsibility for the social fund.

3   The Policy Studies Institute is conducting research into consumer credit and debt which, although much more wide-ranging, is planned to have some emphasis on the circumstances of low income families.

4   Some anecdotal information is beginning to emerge. For example, an exercise in one local office involving home visiting revealed 67 cases where a successful CCG award was likely, in a three-month period. Replicated across all local offices, this would almost double the demand nationally for CCGs in a year.

5   Many young people wishing to live independently of their parents are obliged by social security legislation to invent or embellish stories of family breakdown in order to claim benefit independently. Others are obliged to remain at home despite the threat of physical or sexual abuse rather than reveal their stories over a DSS counter.

References

Alcock, P, Craig, G, Hill, M, Vamplew, C (1989) Reduced Expectations. *Community Care*, 24 August, pp16–17.

AMA/ACC (1988) *Social Fund-Position Statement and Practice Guide*. London, January.

Arnott, H (1988) What Price the Social Fund? *Legal Action*, April, p5 and p23.

Baker, B, Becker, S, Svenson, M (1988) *Ten Days in June*. Nottingham Benefits Research Unit, July.

Becker, S (1989a) *Vulnerable Clients*. Nottingham Benefits Research Unit, February.

Becker, S (1989b) Small Change. *Benefits Research*, Issue 3, Nottingham Benefits Research Unit, July, p9.

Bennett, F (1989) The Social Fund in Context. In G Craig (ed) *Your Flexible Friend?* London, Social Security Consortium.

Berthoud, R (1987) The Social Fund – Will It Work? *Policy Studies*, 8, part 1.

Berthoud, R (1985) *The Examination of Social Security*. London, Policy Studies Institute.

Bradshaw, J (1987) The Social Fund. In M. Brenton and C. Ungerson (eds) *Yearbook of Social Policy, 1986/7*. Harlow, Longman.

Craig, G (1988a) The Nightmare Lottery of the Social Fund. *Social Work Today*, 24 November, pp15–17.

Craig, G (1988b) And the Wheel of Fortune. *Community Care*, 8 December, ppiii–iv.

Craig, G (1989) Introduction. In G. Craig (ed) *Your Flexible Friend?* London, Social Security Consortium.

Craig, G (ed) (1989) *Your Flexible Friend?* London, Social Security Consortium.

Craig, G and Coxall, J (eds) (1989) *Monitoring the Social Fund – A Bibliography, 1985–89*. Bradford University Applied Social Studies Department.

Davies, C (1989) Issues for the Claimant. In G Graig (ed) *Your Flexible Friend?* London, Social Security Consortium.

DSS (1989a) Annual Report by the Secretary of State for Social Security on the Social Fund, 1988–89. London, HMSO, Cm. 748.

DSS (1989b) Annual Report of the Social Fund Commissioner for 1988–89 on the standards of reviews by Social Fund Inspectors. London, HMSO.

Federation of Independent Advice Centres (1987) *Social Fund: Policy Guidelines*.

Holloway, A (1989) *The Social Fund – How Have Advice Agencies Responded?* Ll.B. Dissertation, Unpublished, Brunel University.

LASA (1988) *Monitoring the Social Fund – Information and Guidance on the Monitoring Process*. London Advice Services Alliance.

Lister, R and Lakhani, B (1987) *A Great Retreat in Fairness*. London, CPAG.

Lister, R (1989a) Defending the Cash/Care Frontier – Social work and the social fund. In P Carter, T Jeffs and M Smith (eds) *Social Work and Social Welfare Yearbook* 1. Milton Keynes, Open University Press.

Lister, R (1989b) The Social Security Research Consortium. *Benefits Research*, Issue 3, Nottingham Benefits Research Unit, July, pp 16–18.

Lister, R (1989c) Privatising Need. In G. Craig (ed.), *Your Flexible Friend?* London, Social Security Consortium.

Lloyd, P (1989) In Defence of the Social Fund. *Social Work Today*, 19 January, p12.

Lynes, T (1988) The Numbers Game. *Community Care*, 12 December, p22.

Mullen, T (1989) The Social Fund – cash-limiting Social Security. *Modern Law Review*, January, pp64–92.

NBRU (1987) *The Social Fund Project – A Proposal for a Collaborative Project*. Nottingham Benefits Research Unit.

SSAC (1987) *The Draft Social Fund Manual: Report by the Social Security Advisory Committee*. London, HMSO.

Social Security Consortium (1988) *The Social Fund and Voluntary Organisations – How Do You Respond?* London, SSC.

Stewart, G and Stewart, J (1989) Fund of Bad Will. *Community Care*, 26 January, pp20–21.

Stewart, G, Stewart, J, and Walker, C (1989) *The Social Fund*. ACC, London.

Svenson, M (1989) *Boundary Wars*. Nottingham Benefits Research Unit.

Ward, S (ed) (1987) *Of Little Benefit: An Update*. London, Social Security Consortium.

Walker, C (1989) A Heavy Burden. *Community Care*, 29 June, pp16–18.

8 The Prime Minister's Review of the National Health Service and the 1989 White Paper *Working For Patients*

Calum Paton

Introduction

This chapter discusses the Prime Minister's Review of the National Health Service and the resultant White Paper, *Working for Patients*. Legislation embodying both this White Paper and the White Paper on Community Care (following the second Griffiths Report, *Community Care: Agenda for Action*) was introduced to Parliament in November 1989, covering England, Wales and Scotland. The article reviews the policy debates prior to the NHS Review, the main aspects of the White Paper, *Working for Patients*, and how they relate to previous NHS policy initiatives. The second part of the chapter discusses the intellectual and analytical foundations of the linchpin of the White Paper – namely, the concept of the 'internal market' in health care. In particular, attention is drawn to parallels and distinctions between US health policy and trends and the ideas underpinning the British White Paper. The politics of the whole episode are then discussed, focusing on the medical profession in particular and also upon relations between government and management. Finally, by way of conclusion, some of the dangers inherent in the policies embraced by the White Paper are outlined.

Part I: The Review and White Paper

The 'Prime Minister's Review', announced in January 1988, was so called because the Prime Minister herself announced a fundamental review into the future of the NHS in response to questions on *Panorama* – unknown in advance by Ministers, civil servants or the Conservative Party. The Review process continued a trend in the Conservative administration of by-passing traditional policy-making bodies or investigatory mechanisms such as Royal Commissions. Instead of Departmental officials from the policy divisions of the Department of Health as well as the Permanent Secretary and others at the top of the office constituting the key personnel in the Review, informal deliberations constituted the key sessions of the process. These were dominated in the early stages by the Prime Minister herself and dominated throughout by more informal advisers such as those in the No 10 Policy Unit, former members of that unit (such as its former head John Redwood and former health and social policy member David Willetts) and members of 'think-tanks' – the Centre for Policy Studies in particular, but also the Adam Smith Institute (and in the early days, the Institute of Economic Affairs Health Unit, before its prescriptions for dismembering the NHS's public financing system ran aground on an eventual pragmatism).

The Review Committee was formally chaired by the Prime Minister and its other members were the Chancellor of the Exchequer, Nigel Lawson; the Chief Secretary to the Treasury, John Major; the Secretaries of State for Scotland and Wales, Malcolm Rifkind and Peter Walker; and the Social Services Secretary and Minister of Health, John Moore and Tony Newton, the former later replaced by the Health Secretary Kenneth Clarke when the Department was split at the end of July 1988. The Civil Servant leading the Secretariat was Strachan Heppel, Deputy Secretary in Social Security. Economic advisers (permanent and seconded) in the Department also contributed.

The Review was originally supposed to report by the summer of 1988 – again, no overtones of the Royal Commission taking minutes and lasting years! But dispute over policy and difficulty in devising practical reform proposals prolonged its deliberations until early 1989, with the White Paper representing its written conclusions without any intervening 'final papers'.

The Review Committee met weekly, with limited contributions from private health care executives, businessmen (including Sir Roy Griffiths, at this time Deputy Chairman of the NHS Management Board and the PM's personal adviser) and generalists from the policy community on the right-wing of politics. There was no consultation on a formal basis with the British Medical Association, the medical Royal Colleges, other health care professions' official bodies or the public. Invited 'contributions' on an *ad hoc* basis from academics and others were – inevitably selectively – considered. The Prime Minister took an interventionist, if intermittent, role, personally amending policy papers and setting the agenda by ruling out options, if not by deciding on policy details.

In the end, the Review, in an attempt to maintain public financing yet escape the allegedly 'bureaucratic' system of planned provision adopted the core ideas of 'provider' markets within the NHS. Politically, some of the more right-wing advisers saw the Review's conclusions as a half-way house to more thoroughgoing privatization in a fourth Conservative term. When John Moore was moved away from Health, much of this generalist futurology diminished. The Prime Minister herself had seen the NHS as a 'black hole' – she was not necessarily hostile to public spending on it *per se*, but was unhappy at 'more money' meaning 'more criticism' as to cuts. So measuring outputs and outcomes in health care was her (unstated) objective – including a concern for value for money. Naturally her opponents saw it differently. What the Review did enhance was Prime Ministerial as opposed to cabinet or consultative government.

The stages of the PM's Review

It is important to remember the historical background to the Prime Minister's Review of the National Health Service. Growing concern, expressed especially in 1985 and again towards the end of 1987, about under-funding of the National Health Service was occasioned by alleged crises in large teaching hospitals, in London and Birmingham especially. The government felt increasingly on the defensive about the politics and financing of the National Health Service. Eventually the Prime Minister decided to try to move on to the offensive and announced the fundamental review into the future of the National Health Service at the beginning of 1988. Her skill lay in transforming what had been a debate about whether funding was adequate or not into a debate about the nature of the delivery of health care. When the Review's conclusions were published on 1 February 1989 as the White Paper *Working for Patients*, the debate had been transformed from one about the 'demand' or financing side of health care into one about the efficient delivery of health care through provider markets.

How did this come about? Let us consider the evolution of the Review. Apart from a brief investigation in 1981–82 of alternative systems of financing for health care, this was the first time since the introduction of the National Health Service in 1948 that radical alternatives to a National Health Services model of funding health care were being seriously considered in Britain. John Moore the Secretary of State from 1987 to 1988 was keen on examining alternative systems of financing: principally, various health insurance models ranging from National Health Insurance (publicly funded in the main) through to various alternatives in the realm of private insurance; vouchers to individuals earmarked for health care; and significant tax relief for private insurance.

The first stage of the review led to much pamphleteering by radical right-wing think-tanks, such as the Institute of Economic Affairs Health Unit, the Centre for Policy Studies and the Adam Smith Institute (Green, 1988; Willetts and Goldsmith, 1988; Redwood, 1988; Redwood and Letwin, 1988; Butler and Pirie, 1988). Their proposals were very general and concerned with both the financing and provision of health care. In the end Moore personally chose the option of a 'financing' initiative – allowing individuals to 'contract out' of the NHS on the analogy of 'contracting out' of state pensions – a policy with which Strachan Heppel, the Deputy Secretary in the DHSS heading the administration of the Review, was identified. (Heppel was a social security, not health, specialist.) But such options were anathema to the treasury (as they meant 'unnecessary' tax relief to those already with private insurance and, more importantly, the loss of direct revenue on a large scale) and politically very risky. Even Mrs Thatcher felt she could not move against the NHS, and her personal advisers felt that the radical policy agenda for the third term of office was already taking its toll on government energy and taxing public patience.

Given the deep political unpopularity of radical moves away from a tax-funded NHS, there was difficulty in designing proposals compatible with a radical review of the NHS yet within the bounds of political pragmatism. The Prime Minister's dissatisfaction with Moore's 'radical' yet impractical proposals on the *financing* side yet absence of ideas concerning the *provision* of health care (on the supply-side) led to his dismissal in July 1988 from the Department of Health half of his job (and later complete dismissal in 1989). The Department was now split into two departments, Health and Social Security. Moore's poor performance in dealing with his critics, in particular in Parliament, had not helped his case.

Phase Two of the Review was marked by consolidation by the new Secretary of State for Health, Kenneth Clarke, formerly Minister of State in the Department from 1982–85. Clarke, a supporter of the National Health Service when set against many of his more sceptical conservative colleagues, was thought likely to abandon radical ideas altogether and to go further down the road of efficient 'public management' as represented by the Griffiths Inquiry in 1983 (Griffiths, 1983) with which he (rather than the Secretary of State at the time, Norman Fowler) had been particularly identified. Thus it was likely that existing initiatives for better management of public money, such as resource management, and measures such as clinical audit would be continued and 'beefed up'. It was further thought that, as well as forcing doctors to take responsibility for specialty and departmental budgets, Clarke might seek to put NHS clinicians on short-term contracts in return for higher salaries.

However, the Review entered Phase Three when the Prime Minister's dissatisfaction with the lack of a radical agenda led to the adoption of radical ideas on the 'supply-side' of health care. The concept of provider markets, a broader version of Professor Alain Enthoven's concept of the internal market (Enthoven, 1985), was the linchpin of the Review. Other less radical components of the Review included further moves to medical audit and the control of Family Practitioner services. Furthermore the move to a corporate management model for health care was enhanced, as the NHS Supervisory Board (now wholly defunct) and the NHS Management Board were replaced with (respectively) an NHS Policy Board composed primarily of Ministers and businessmen, and an NHS Executive, to be responsible for implementation of ministerial strategy (Department of Health, 1989a).

The background of the Griffiths Report, 1983

The Griffiths Report had set out a blueprint which would 'take politics out of the NHS' and provide a corporate management board as in nationalized industries. The aim was that 'management could be left to manage'. However, as the first Chief Executive and Chairman of the NHS Management Board, Victor Paige, pointed out on resigning in frustration, this was never politically realistic. The White Paper arrangements have now *centralized* political control and made NHS management, from the new Management Executive through to the more tightly managed Regional and District Health Authorities, more likely to act at the behest of political priorities. It is a likely consequence of the White Paper's implementation that political intervention in health care will become more direct rather than less obtrusive, albeit in the context of a corporate management structure. Already, by the end of 1989, the ambulance dispute has suggested that the NHS Management Executive is likely to act as a conduit for political directives rather than as an autonomous management board.

These developments are of course part of an attempt to clear up some inconsistencies in the pre-White Paper NHS. A problem with the 'half-way house' of the Griffiths Report had been that the new managerial line of control from the Secretary of State and the NHS Management Board through to Regional and District General Managers had cut across other lines of control. The Secretary of State also was at the top of a 'line' linking Regional Chairmen and Regional Health Authorities with District Chairmen and District Health Authorities. The Chief Medical Officer was the head of a medical 'line' of control through Regional down to District Medical

Officers. A major consequence of the 1989 White Paper is to diminish lines of control other than the key political/managerial one. Health authorities are no longer to be quasi-independent, drawing members from professional groups, public interest groups, trade unions and the public at large. Instead they are to be effectively Corporate Boards.

Thus health authorities will no longer be loosely representative bodies rooted in their communities, but mere adjuncts to their local management boards. Alternative sources of advice to the Department of Health, whether through lay authorities or through the medical professions, are to be subjugated to the new structures, entrenching general management, which establish firm lines of control 'from the top down'. The irony here is that political unpopularity deriving from rationalizing measures (eg hospital closures) may not be deflected to the 'locally responsible' managers, as Ministers hope, but channelled upwards to Ministers, no longer 'protected' from themselves by independent-minded health authorities.

Contents of the White Paper

The eight Working Papers which followed the White Paper after two weeks did not provide much more detail than the Paper itself. The key themes of the White Paper are reflected in the titles of the Working Papers, which are only marginally amended in the following list, of which the first three are discussed below in more detail.

1 Self-governing hospitals
2 Funding and contracts for hospital services
3 Practice budgets for GPs
4 Indicative prescribing budgets for GPs
5 Capital charges
6 Medical audit
7 NHS Consultants: appointments, contracts and awards
8 Implications for Family Practitioner Committees (Department of Health, 1989b).

Self-governing hospitals

The most plausible rationale for self-governing hospitals is to 'free up' providing institutions to compete as flexible actors in the market place. 'Hospitals' are for the purposes of this theory to include all forms of health care: Secretary of State Kenneth Clarke announced later, under some pressure, that community units, or parts of them, would also be allowed to opt out. As in education, the ideology argues that independent institutions are more able to set their own objectives and manage their resources and then make themselves

appealing to the client, whether the parent (in education) or the sick
person's advocate (in the NHS) – i.e. the health manager acting as
purchaser of health care.

Contracting for services

Funding and *provision* are now, in theory, separated. The District
is the purchaser, having been given funds by the Department
of Health via the Region. Contracts with providers (whether
self-governing hospitals and units or directly managed units) are
made by the District, which determines the mix of services to be
provided. This allows the District in theory to promote clarity of
thought in determining its care mix, and certainly does not involve
a priori any diminution of the claims of 'priority' groups such as
the elderly, chronically ill and mentally ill, and of, for example,
community care.

However, in practice, this measure may have robbed the NHS
of a considerable amount of flexibility. For the difficulties inherent
in predicting and costing need for health care, when quantified
by a system of contracts, may produce a more bureaucratic and
regulated NHS than existed prior to the White Paper. Districts are to
be the purchasers of health care for their residents. Thus patients and
GPs will have their preferences subjugated to those of managers.
Pre-White Paper, GP referral was not controlled, even if the money
did not always 'follow the patient' quickly because of the operation
of the resource allocation formula. Post-White Paper, although the
money will 'follow the patient', with units paid in proportion to their
workload, referrals will be rationed. This will be done 'rationally' in
the eyes of the White Paper's defenders, by managers. The age of
a rationed NHS, long existing informally, has formally dawned.

The main problem is that Districts will *in fact* be both purchasers
and providers. A real marketplace in provision cannot be established
for this reason, and also because Regions and Districts need to
have some certainty as to where patients will be treated in order
to provide resources accordingly. Furthermore, the new policy of
'charging for capital' (Department of Health, 1989c) means that
Regions will be the *banker* which provides hospitals and units with
capital or denies them. Capital charging is intended to ensure that
prices of services reflect capital costs (depreciation and rental of
capital, on accounting principles) – that is, that costs are global,
as in the private sector, where any purchase generally reflects the
total cost of production and not just the running costs. Making the
Region the disburser of capital, on the 'provision' side, was
thought necessary since the District was the purchaser on the
'demand' side. The roles of purchaser and provider were already
confused, or inadequately separated – this confusion could not but
be accentuated by making the District the disburser of capital to

providing units as well as purchaser from them, but making the Region the banker gave it a significant, if backdoor, planning role.

In practice, therefore, Regions and Districts will effectively be planning services in an even more 'top heavy' manner than before. The rhetoric is competition; the reality is bureaucratic planning with the language of contracts and managed competition to make it respectable in the eyes of a government to which 'planning' is a dirty word.

GP budgets for hospital care

The intention behind offering practice budgets to those GP practices with populations of more than 11,000, and with an ability to demonstrate the capacity to manage their own budgets (for certain defined aspects of hospital care), is to provide a rival purchaser to the District Health Authority and to make providers more conscious of the need to 'sell themselves' to purchasers. Since GP practices which 'opt out' are to be funded directly by the Region, any resulting shortfall in Regional monies for Districts will have to be spread over hospitals and units, which in turn will have to sell themselves to the general practices.

In practice it has proved a very difficult task to find an equitable and yet manageable formula by which GPs' populations' needs could be gauged. The government wanted to avoid the alleged rigidities of the Resource Allocation Working Party (RAWP) approach, used up to now for hospital and community services, but has become committed to even more minuscule calculations. Moreover, allocating to smaller catchment populations (in GP practices) further diminishes the broad advantages of the NHS system of resource allocation and planning which brought with it an ability to spread risk over large catchment areas, plan services accordingly and respond to unexpected need relatively flexibly.

Implementation

The problem is that the Department of Health is defining the success of the White Paper in terms of process – how many hospitals 'opt out'; how contracts are drawn up – rather than outcomes defined by the criterion of how far the health status of a target population is improved.

A major danger is that 'regulating competition' is a much more bureaucratic and cumbersome exercise than merely running a planned public health service. This may go against the prevailing political rhetoric, but is a lesson which we would do well to absorb from the United States. Protecting the needs of 'untrendy' local services and poorer local populations and groups is a major challenge following the Review and White Paper. The internal market was originally

E

suggested by Alain Enthoven, 1985 as a means of solving the problems faced by large teaching hospitals who were losing money under the RAWP formula. That is, gaining Districts (purchasers) outside London could buy services from losing Districts' hospitals – allowing, for example, London teaching hospitals to be rewarded for work done for other Districts. The essence of Enthoven's idea was to ensure that workload was adequately rewarded. The RAWP formula had in fact sought to provide funds to compensate Districts for work for other Districts, but it did so only indirectly and slowly. Ironically, the White Paper may now herald the closure of 'expensive' London services (other than those in self-governing hospitals) and a move of provision to the provinces which was never achieved by direct planning in the 1960s and 1970s. This is because Districts outside London may eschew London's services on the grounds of cost. Hence Enthoven's assumption that the 'quality' of services in London would save them may not be realized.

What is more, progressing by means of pilot projects was advocated by Alain Enthoven, and this advice has not been taken by the government. In defence of the government, it can be argued that the opting out of hospitals which occurs gradually, and the gradual evolution of practice budgets for some general practices, will in effect take the form of pilot projects. However, the political need to 'make things succeed' will probably prevent scientific assessment of developments, as extra money may well be pumped in to prevent the failure of 'showpiece' initiatives.

GPs (in some cases) and health authority management will have to make decisions as to priorities. Reconciling the decision of GPs with the decision of authorities is a major challenge facing the White Paper's implementation. 'Working *for* Patients' may be an appropriate title, then, for the White Paper since we are not talking of direct, individual 'consumer sovereignty' by the patient. Rather, definition of the needs of patients will have to be made through consensus between doctors, managers and health authorities – naturally dependent at the end of the day on the government in a centrally funded system.

Rationing of health care at the point of purchase, by a global purchaser, rather than allowing rationing to be done informally by providers of care, is the key theme of the White Paper. However, the status of the District Health Authority as a monopsonistic public purchaser was diluted by giving optional budgets to GPs for certain categories of non-immediate hospital care. This policy was opposed by many involved in the NHS Review. However, in the end, it 'slipped in', supported by those – and primarily the Prime Minister – who liked the sound of 'pluralism in financing' without necessarily thinking through the consequences.

It is worth noting that the White Paper on community care responding to the second Griffiths Report of 1988, which has been addressed along with the NHS White Paper in the Health Service Bill of November 1989, also has as its essential element the distinction between the purchaser and the provider with the assumption that rationing and choice are exercised by the purchaser (Griffiths, 1988).

The regulation of competition and the internal market

Regulation of competition has inevitably accompanied the 'pro-competitive' strategy of the White Paper. There is seemingly to be an uneasy reconciliation of planning and competition (which are not necessarily opposed, but which had been opposed in the government's rhetoric).

All in all, no other health system in the world combines substantially centralized public financing and a fragmented, competitive strategy on the supply-side. There is no obvious economic, social or political theory to predict the likely success of the policy. In that sense it was either an act of faith or an unfortunate political blunder forced by the momentum personally given to the Review by the Prime Minister.

The essence of the internal market is that health care will be purchased on behalf of patients from competing providers, not all of whom will be local. It is 'internal', because the providers are NHS units, selling services to District Health Authorities and (in some cases) general practitioners. An 'external' market would involve private sector providers also.

Some *caveats* can be considered:

1 Can hospitals or facilities expand and contract in line with demand; is the market model realistic? There is an analogy here with schools in the education debate. Furthermore, is it choice by patients or managers on the demand side or choice by suppliers which will determine the patient's lot? If good schools are a scarce commodity, the phenomenon most evident can be parents and children competing for schools not schools competing for children in a buyer's market. If the analogous situation applies in health care, the major danger will be that hospitals and providers have an incentive to discriminate against less 'profitable' patients (ie more expensive and 'difficult' patients) more than in the pre-White Paper system. Regulations to prevent this would be more bureaucratic than the much-maligned public planning which competition is allegedly to supersede. Unlike in the USA, demand exceeds supply in health care. In the USA, there is much spare capacity in hospitals.

2 The incentive to admit and receive patients on a market model, and boost one's income as a result (or the income

of one's institution) may necessitate a 'gatekeeper' after the GP referral to prevent US style 'excessive care'. This may increase the costs and diminish the efficiency of the reform. Furthermore, providers may collude to the consumer's disadvantage (Ranade, 1989). For example, prices may be set higher than efficiency in a competitive market would dictate. This can only be circumvented by translating 'competition' into Health Authority-dominated planning by the back door. The question then arises, why bother with the reforms?

3   How will hospitals compete
    – on grounds of cost, quality, or outcome?
    – Will there be a bias to a culture of quantity not quality?
    Again there may be an analogy with the education debate. Which performance indicators will be used? Will they be adequate? Just as in education, liberal arts may be neglected by parents as indicators of the success of schools in favour of 'marketable' and quantifiable skills, the more esoteric areas of health care – and in particular teaching, education and research – may be relatively under-funded. Safeguards will be necessary to prevent this. The only alternative would be a full private market model for medical education as in the US, with all its unpleasant knock-on effects (expensive care, inequity in access to education and so forth).

4   What are the implications for staff security? How far is the Government prepared to go in diminishing the notion of NHS staff as part of the organization rather than merely units of production?

5   If the internal market is to lead, for example, to the closures of particular specialities, how will universally necessary services such as accident and emergency (which may for example be dependent upon orthopaedic departments) be protected?

6   Will there be adequate competition either to have a competitive effect on prices or to allow competition by criteria of quality? Lessons from the US's 'pro-competitive' phase of the 1980s suggest that attaining the former requires a greater locational concentration of hospitals than is common in most areas of Britain. Allowing the latter requires adequate finance in the system. This is true as regards some of the US's purchasers (those who have generous insurance) but not all; it is certainly *not* true in the British NHS.

Part II Lessons and warnings from the United States

It would be misleading to state that the NHS White Paper was modelled overtly on US health care. The Prime Minister's Review, while considering a variety of radical options in its early stages, was increasingly forced to accommodate both British political realities and the structure of a public health care system. However, the adoption of the ideas of 'provider markets' and the 'internal market' draws on a misguided perception that US health care is moving towards efficient 'supply side' competition.

Provider markets refer generally to the possibility of competition in delivering health care, and the placing by purchasers of contracts for stipulated services. These constraints may be with public or private providers. The purchaser in a British context is the District Health Authority, but in a US context may of course be the individual or employer. The internal market was the phrase adopted by Enthoven (1985) to show that he was proposing a model compatible with public sector provision: 'internal' refers to the fact that suppliers are NHS institutions. Enthoven's model draws inspiration from the US in that the District Health Authority in Britain is seen as capable of adopting some of the characteristics, and reacting to some of the incentives, inherent in the US Health Maintenance Organization, to be described below.

The key trend in US health care has been the replacement of weak and politically subverted planning in the 1970s by an allegedly 'pro-competitive' strategy in the 1980s. This has sometimes been linked to the phenomenon of for-profit, 'corporate' health care (Starr, 1983) – although the advances made in the early 1980s by large-scale entrepreneurial health organizations, which were tending to 'swallow up' smaller non-profit organizations, have been halted in the late 1980s, due to the high price of allegedly competitive for-profit medicine.

The alleged advantages of competition are the provision of health care services which are more responsive to the consumer, at higher quality and lower prices. However, in practice these advantages have not necessarily been reaped in the United States. The overall cost of health care in the United States remains a major problem. In response to this, a number of new types of financing mechanism have been developed, although traditional fee-for-service medicine reimbursed by the traditional commercial insurer still plays a significant role within the system. Government programmes cover particular categories of the population. The traditional non-profit insurers, such as Blue Cross and Blue Shield, still exist – although amended in the direction of greater cost control.

The major development affecting health care is the further expansion of Health Maintenance Organizations (and their cousins, Preferred Provider Organizations). The aim of these organizations, defined and discussed below, is to contract for more cost-effective health care (and, in some cases, simply cheaper health care). The overall salience of such programmes in limiting increases in the cost of US health care ought not be exaggerated, however, as costs continue to rise in the late 1980s – indeed have been rising faster than in the mid-1980s. The existence of substantial tax credits for private health care – which cost the Federal Exchequer more than the whole of the Medicaid programme – hardly encourages cost control, although various mechanisms to limit tax expenditures have been proposed.

In certain areas of the United States, there is still more regulation than competition (especially in East Coast States, such as Massachusetts, New York, New Jersey and Maryland). However, even where competition has developed the lessons which can be drawn vary. In some areas of the country, the existence of a competitive climate has led to more providers, lower costs, yet lower quality of health care (by the criterion of avoidable deaths) and less access by the poor – in that cross-subsidy to provide charity care for the poor out of rich payers' surpluses is less possible due to cut-throat competition. (This is not in itself an argument against competition, but an argument against competition in the absence of adequate financing for all.)

Often the pluralism in financing of US health care has meant that only a part of the purchasing market has become competitive (i.e. that part where insurers and payers are cost-conscious) and costs have simply been passed on to less controlled sections of the market. In some areas of the country, for example, competition does not seem to have affected the cost of health care (and has maybe even pushed it up) or the high level of excess capacity in the system. Indeed, by encouraging more providers into the market, excess capacity may be increased. Occupancy rates in US hospitals are generally low in comparison with Europe (the national average is between 50–60 per cent). Even when doctors are supposedly in surplus, institutions compete expensively to attract prestigious doctors, in turn to attract consumers.

'Opted out' hospitals may do this in Britain, forcing up wages generally for health workers, which cannot be replicated in the rest of the NHS. Private purchasing of health care would allow them to do this to a greater extent, by injecting new cash. If more money is not forthcoming, of course, this US characteristic may not apply in Britain. But neither will high quality of care occur, if competition merely entails cost-cutting.

Competition has apparently led in the US to a reduction in hospitalization. However, even this is difficult to disentangle: it could be an effect of the general trend in this direction which has been occurring in any case; or it could be a specific consequence of regulatory policies operating through reimbursement mechanisms which attempt to contain prices, using methodologies which group illnesses and define expected costs for treating them. So-called 'Diagnosis Related Groups' are the best known example of such cost regulation; they are used to price the care of a patient in a particular disease category, and they therefore encourage the removal from hospital of that patient as early as possible. Thus price control may be attributed to powerful factors other than competition between suppliers.

Health Maintenance Organizations

In the United States, the Health Maintenance Organization (HMO) has been developed to reconcile the incentives confronting the provider and the insurer: by merging them into one organisation. The Health Maintenance Organization receives annual capitations or premiums for its enrolled patients and then is responsible for providing care to them, whether directly or through sub-contracting. The essence of the Health Maintenance Organization is that what economists call 'the problem of the third party payer' is removed by uniting the insurer and the provider. HMOs may be non-profit or for-profit. They may provide services directly through owned facilities and, for example, salaried doctors (in the comprehensive type of HMOs) or they may contract for all the services they provide. However the dangers of under-supply of care may exist – just as, in the traditional private fee-for-service system in the United States, the dangers of over-supply certainly exist. RAND Corporation studies show that well-funded HMOs do a good job, but that less well funded HMOs, such as patients reliant on public funding may have to use, can adversely affect the health status over time of the elderly, the chronically sick and the poor (Paton, 1988). Adopting the *rationale* of the Health Maintenance Organization in Britain, as the White Paper seeks to do, is certainly a strategy which requires strict safeguards.

Preferred Provider Organizations are essentially a form of contract, normally between employers on behalf of their employees for their health care, which, due to bulk buying, achieve lower rates of insurance and lower prices for care. The *quid pro quo* is of course that the patient is not free to be referred anywhere. Employers furthermore are increasingly providing health insurance directly themselves.

Interestingly enough, federal legislation to promote competition has not been particularly significant. Earlier legislation, in the late 1960s and early 1970s, to promote planning was half-hearted and eventually stillborn due both to the ideological opposition to planning in the US and to the effect of US political structure, which has tended to water down health planning and prevent the coherent reconciliation of its different components (Paton, 1990). Competition has been promoted as planning has declined, with its proponents (Enthoven, 1988) arguing that managed health care organizations can promote *managed* competition which suits the US culture better than planning. The pre-planning phase, it is argued, was marked not by competition but by a rigged market whereby provider 'guilds' colluded with patients at the expense of cost-control.

Nevertheless, it should be made clear that competition is a US response (and only a partial one) to a US problem. There is no intellectual case in itself for arguing that British planning has similarly failed, and that competitive markets are needed in Britain.

Different types of competition

One should distinguish competition amongst providers of health care and competition amongst financiers (insurers and other payers or reimbursers of health care). In the United States, it may be that often alleged advantage of competition – high quality health care, for those who have access to the system – stems from the overall level of financing rather than competition. In copying the US model there is a danger that Britain would escape the negative side of competition (waste, as a pluralism of payers and financiers is exploited by the providing market) yet would fail to reap the advantage suggested by proponents of competition (high quality health care responsive to the consumer).

This is because competition in Britain, post-White Paper, is to occur on the 'supply-side' – a monopsonistic purchaser (with the minor exception of budgets held by general practitioners) will exist in Britain in the form of the District purchaser. In the absence of significantly more resources for health care, the effect upon responsibilities to the consumer is likely to be minimal. It is not the consumer who is sovereign in the post-White Paper NHS, but the District Manager as purchaser of health care.

Managed health care: US and UK

The majority of managerial reforms in recent years in US health care have applied to publicly funded programmes and embraced attempts to limit cost increases and to restrict access, geared also to cost-containment. A central government policy has been the regulation of reimbursement to providers, for example through the system of Diagnosis Related Groups, which groups diseases and derives expected costs for treating them, to be used in a system of price regulation. Cost control has also been attempted by directing patients and consumers to stipulated providers. The Medicare and Medicaid programmes have seen a flurry of such regulations in recent years, and costs have been increasingly passed to the patient through deductibles and coinsurance (forms of cost-sharing under insurance).

In Britain the thrust of the White Paper is towards managed health care, with decentralized budget-holders (health authority managers and to a much lesser extent GPs also) taking the place of the government at the macro level and doctors at the micro level in rationing health care on behalf of patients. Money will now follow the patient, but the patient will not be free to decide where to go. Managed health care of this sort would be completely unacceptable politically in the United States for the mainstream citizen who currently enjoys access to mainstream US health care. It is only programmes for the poor where this type of restriction prevails. In Britain, we have been used to a lower level of funding of health – by no means a disadvantage, as medicalization of life in the United States has many costs – but if the trend continues through the type of initiative pursued in the White Paper, private health care as a means of escaping bureaucratic, managed health care aimed at limiting public expenditure will become more attractive. Thus while particular individuals may well be sincere in proclaiming that the White Paper is geared to improving the NHS, the long-term social effects must not be discounted.

Part III The politics of the White Paper

Politically, the White Paper can be seen as a clever exercise in diverting attention from the 'under-funding' of the National Health Service by international standards (British Medical Association, 1988; British Medical Association, 1989). Under-funding occurs despite the fact that, also by international standards, the NHS is extremely efficient and effective at producing health outcomes from limited amounts of money. It is of course a contentious debate as to how much the health status of a country's population is related to its health service. There are those who point to the fact that differences in health status between social classes are as wide now as they were at the foundation of the NHS. However, the complexity of such debates apart, a good case can be made that the NHS has ameliorated what would have been an even worse situation. This is not to belittle the challenges still confronting public health in Britain: indeed it is to point to the greater challenges which require greater expenditure.

Nevertheless, the essence of the White Paper has been to focus attention upon the provision management of health care. It is hoped that, by decentralizing responsibility for provision to hospitals and units, the 'buck can be passed' as regards adequacy and quality of service.

Consequences of under-funding can now be blamed more squarely on 'inefficient local managers' who have allegedly been set free to manage. Health authorities are no longer to be representative institutions (the part-representative, part-appointed hybrid of the past) but slimmed-down executive management bodies. This development has some potentially positive features (especially given the uninformed political gerrymandering of health care which can take place at the local level). Yet in the context of the government's centralization of objectives but devolution of responsibility, the danger is that, as in other areas of public life, opposition to an over-reaching central government will be diminished.

The response of doctors was predictable. It was unfortunate for both the Secretary of State and doctors that the debate about the White Paper in general became confused with the debate about the new contract for GPs. Doctors' fears as to professional autonomy, and levels of remuneration, have been accompanied by a genuine fear that the benefits of a publicly planned National Health Service (which they have come to accept enthusiastically, however slowly) are in danger of being lost as a result of the White Paper. Much argument against the White Paper by clinicians and general practitioners has often been rooted in an altruistic defence of the service, despite the fact that the BMA remains both an interest group and a trade union.

Hard-headed health service general managers, no longer the well-meaning but meddlesome 'lay administrators' of the medical profession's rhetoric, are now much more agents of central policy than they have been in the past. Health authorities have become politicized in line with central government's wishes, as appointment of Regional and District Chairmen by the Secretary of State has become much more dominated by party political considerations. General managers are now seen as spokesmen for the 'health service corporations' which they direct; and in terms of loyalty they are, somewhat implausibly, expected to combine the discretion of the civil servant with the evangelism of the private sector company director on behalf of ministerially-defined health service objectives. It is not surprising that, in this context, the medical profession is on certain occasions both sceptical and obstructive when it comes to the implementation by managers of often ill-thought out and politically motivated 'initiatives' in the National Health Service – not least when these initiatives are given neither time nor resources to succeed before the next 'flavour of the month' has taken over.

The NHS general manager is now a part 'political' appointment, expected to be 'one of us' in an increasingly politicized service, consistent with the government's, politicization of public service. While there are some promising aspects of the White Paper, the politicized and ideological environment in which it is being implemented holds many dangers for a publicly planned health service where resources are directed to those most in need. Ideologies and slogans are being adopted from the language of competitive health care in the United States which betray little knowledge of that country's mixed experience with competition. As in other areas of British public life, we have the irony that 'US inspired' competitive or privatization initiatives are being uncritically fostered.

The response of all other NHS professions – including nurses, paramedics and ancillaries – is hostile to the White Paper. However the fundamental political reality is that the Secretary of State for Health is reliant for career advancement upon 'making something of' the implementation of the White Paper; and by the time further health policy is constructed, he may well be at another Ministry. There are those in the Conservative party, inspired by the Prime Minister herself, who are distrustful of the idea of a publicly financed health service which is more than merely a welfare wedge for the poor. The prospect is that such advisers could have their way in a fourth Conservative administration after the next general election. It is the conflict between the pragmatists and such zealots which in many cases surfaced during the Prime Minister's Review. The right wing think-tanks put forward radical ideas very much geared towards amending if not replacing the National Health Service in the direction of both private financing and private provision. In the end, the public's strong belief in the NHS – and a number of severe difficulties in other policy areas – persuaded the Prime Minister that these think-tanks could not presently be risked with the comprehensive design of British health policy. The danger is that, if the half-way house of partial competition which the White Paper embraces is seen to create severe problems for the National Health Service, it will be open to the more radical wing of the Conservative party to argue that 'full competition' and greater privatization more generally are necessary to salvage things. That of course is a political debate which must await the future.

The politics of the British Medical Association

During the debate in 1989 about the White Paper on the National Health Service, the Secretary of State, Kenneth Clarke, accused the British Medical Association of always opposing radical change – whether the creation of the NHS and the debate leading up to that in the 1940s, or what Clarke sees as improvement to the NHS for the 1990s. The charge is highly misleading. There is, of course, no doubt that in the 1940s the British Medical Association represented much hostility by doctors to the proposed National Health Service. In this they were largely supported by significant elements of the Conservative party. So what has changed? Has the Conservative party suddenly become the defender of the National Health Service? Has the British Medical Association, in the guise of defending the National Health Service, simply continued its tradition of opposing meaningful and worthwhile reform?

The Conservative party was always prepared to support private doctors in their fight to be free of government regulation, monitoring of contracts and monitoring of costs as long as they were dealing with private patients not paid for substantially by the public purse. Once the National Health Service had been established and become both institutionalized and popular, Conservative governments, like Labour governments, found themselves paymasters of a publicly funded health care system. They are therefore interested in receiving value for money in this system. The medical profession in turn has gone from the position of opposition to the National Health Service to one of support for its social ideals (with, of course, some exceptions, especially those who practise largely in the private sector), while showing some natural caution and reluctance to be 'over-monitored' and 'over-regulated' as to cost quality of services provided by doctors.

The irony is that, were we talking about the private sector (including private consumption of medical care), the Conservatives would in all likelihood be firmly supporting the doctors in their desire not to be 'over-regulated' by schemes such as resource management and price controls. In other words the Conservative government wants to limit public spending on health care and regulate the medical profession accordingly, while encouraging private care which can set its own terms of existence. While Mr Clarke may not personally have designed or approved such a strategy, it is his fortune or misfortune to be the Minister in charge of presiding over exactly such a policy. There is a similar situation in the United States, where government regulators on the right-wing of politics seek to cut costs and regulate to a great degree in the public sector, while leaving the private sector relatively free from regulation. By and large, in the US restrictions on prices in health care as represented by Diagnosis Related Groups (DRGs) apply to Medicare but not to the private sector. Regulation is geared to saving public money, not linked to a universal strategy for equitably provided health care. The danger is that the same is now happening in the United Kingdom, albeit in a very different context.

So, has the BMA been historically inconsistent? The BMA has gradually changed its attitude, as has the medical profession as a whole. This is not to deny that there are some self-interested and over cautious reactions to both the White Paper and other health care initiatives. Doctors will always 'over-oppose' regulatory schemes which affect them – as will all professions. However, to portray the BMA as opposing everything, Mr Clarke makes selective use of the reality that the BMA's original opposition was to the NHS and that its opposition is currently geared to protecting the NHS. The Conservative party has of course undergone a more significant sea change. It is now leading the fight to regulate the medical profession – allegedly on behalf of the public interest but in fact acting upon a desire to divert the terms of debate about the National Health Service away from funding levels by comparison with the rest of Europe.

Part IV Conclusion

The advantage of the NHS, by international standards, has been its cost-effective public provision through planning. This is in danger of being substantially lost. Even where intervention occurs, it will be through cumbersome regulation rather than systematic planning.

For example, self-governing hospitals will not be allowed to 'cross-subsidise . . . to allow keener pricing of those services subject to competition' (Working Paper 1, p 11). This will require detailed 'public interest' regulation. Protecting local services will also require cumbersome regulation, giving the lie to the idea that markets are more efficient. GP budgets, if subject to unforeseen pressure, are to be bailed out by District Health Authority 'contingency funds', as discussed in Working Paper 3 (Department of Health, 1989c). These will require specially demarcated budgets, reducing flexibility. Furthermore, giving (some) GPs' budgets for (some) hospital care will diminish the money available for Districts' contracts with hospitals, increasing financial shortfalls for hospitals which can only be made up by their selling services to GP practices. In practice this will reduce the capacity for planning services based on awareness of long-term, stable demand.

Overall, the creation of a number of *distinct, cash-limited budgets* will lead to '*cost shifting*' – attempts to reduce expenditure by 'shifting' costs onto another budget. If Districts or GPs have contracts, for example, for limited numbers of outpatient consultations, there will be a temptation to shift some referrals to Accident and Emergency. This is allegedly to be 'monitored', as stated in Working Paper 3, but the task is highly complex. GP referrals which later lead to intra- or inter-hospital (or tertiary) referral may have to be paid out of GP budgets without the GP having knowledge in advance of the likely cost. Working Paper 3 expects the GP to foresee all. All in all, regulatory labyrinths will be necessary to police the market.

The clause about self-governing hospitals and community units is the most damaging and irrelevant clause within the White Paper. Competitive principles, provider markets and in particular the operation of the internal market could have gone ahead without institutions opting out. In practice, suspicion of future full privatization is being fuelled.

There is no statement as to outcomes or improvements expected from this policy – the government is falling into the trap of judging success by achievement of mechanistic management targets rather than health service (health status) outcomes. The policy, moreover, is likely to be subverted. In the arena of education policy, schools may seek to 'opt out' to subvert rational planning and avoid closure. While admittedly vigilance by the Department of Health may stop this happening in the health arena, a lot of managerial effort has already gone into negotiations to seek to obtain local and short-term financial advantage from the policy.

In the long term, if hospitals which 'opt out' of District Health Authority control and become self-governing succeed in selling their services to private purchasers (whether individuals, firms on behalf of their employees or insurance groups acting as Health Maintenance Organizations) then they will seek less and less of their core business from District Health Authorities or NHS GP practices. In consequence, unless a system of tight and intricate regulation (which would make a nonsense of pro-competitive strategy) is brought into operation or much more money is procured for the NHS, public services will have to be purchased substantially from a diminishing supply of directly managed NHS hospitals and units.

Medical (and perhaps other) staff at self-governing hospitals may be attracted by higher income and better conditions, forcing up prices and forcing the NHS's purchasing Districts to 'shop' elsewhere wherever possible – *or* to have less budget left for other, directly managed units. This is likely to happen in London, if anywhere.

There is little evidence from the United States that, even when there are pressures to reduce costs, hospitals acting competitively are able to do so. This has applied even in recent years when there has been an alleged glut of doctors in the United States. There is anything but a glut in Britain: in fact, a main problem envisaged for the growth of the private sector is where the medical manpower and nursing manpower would come from. It could only come about through diminished supply of such manpower to the NHS, *unless private medical education both takes off and expands quickly*. That is why private hospitals or 'profitable' NHS self-governing hospitals may bid up the salaries of doctors and the price of care, disadvantaging residual NHS institutions.

In this scenario there is likely to be a flight of provision from poor areas, with residual populations suffering as their institutions or GP practices become more run-down, with less subscriptions and less financing. Thus the question is, competition to benefit whom?

The danger of growing inegalitarianism will be increased if private money is increasingly allowed into the system, whether through the purchasing of private health care in the hospital sector or through the admission, by future Conservative legislation, of private money into the arena of primary care: for example, by allowing patients to 'top-up' their publicly-provided capitation payments with private resources. The verbal stress in the White Paper on capitation rather than on the tacitly retained, population-based, systematic system of

RAWP (NHS Management Board, 1988) may be considered to be a prelude to greater stress upon the individual's needs, with the individual's right to pay being adopted in the future. Currently this policy is advocated by right-wingers, as they have also done in the education debate in advocating that vouchers for schooling both be provided to parents and 'topped-up' with private money where parents wish.

It is ironical to return the hospital sector – indeed, the whole system – to the uncoordinated state of pre-1948. Indeed, there is a good whiff of nostalgia – as with much of the 'new' right – in the reforms, despite their brave new world imagery of markets enhanced by 'high tech' corporate management.

References

British Medical Association (1988) Evidence to the government internal review of the National Health Service. *British Medical Journal*, 296, pp 1411–8.

British Medical Association (1989) *Special report on the Government's White Paper, Working for Patients*. London, British Medical Association.

Butler, E and Pirie, M (1988) *The health of nations*. London, Adam Smith Institute.

Department of Health and Social Security (1976) *Sharing resources for health in England* (The RAWP Report). London, HMSO.

Department of Health (1989a) *Working for Patients* (The NHS White Paper). Cmnd. 555, London, HMSO.

Department of Health (1989b) *Working Papers 1–8* (The NHS White Paper). London, HMSO.

Department of Health (1989c) *Working Paper 3* (The NHS White Paper). London, HMSO.

Enthoven, A (1985) *Reflections on the management of the National Health Service*. London, Nuffield Provincial Hospitals Trust.

Enthoven, A (1988) *The theory and practice of managed competition*. Amsterdam, Elsevier.

Green, D (1988) *Everyone a private patient*. London, Institute of Economic Affairs Health Unit.

Griffiths, R (1983) *Letter to the Secretary of State* (The Griffiths Inquiry Report). London, HMSO.

Griffiths, R (1988) *Community care: agenda for action*. London, HMSO.

NHS Management Board (1988) *Review of the Resource Allocation Working Party Formula. Final report*. London, HMSO.

Paton, C (1988) Trouble with the health maintenance organization. *British Medical Journal*, vol 297, pp 934–5.

Paton, C (1990) *US health politics: public policy and political theory*. Aldershot, Gower.

Ranade, W (1989) *To market, to market*. Birmingham, National Association of Health Authorities.

Redwood, J (1988) *In sickness and in health: managing change in the NHS*. London, Centre for Policy Studies.

Redwood, J and Letwin, O (1988) *Britain's biggest enterprise: ideas for radical reform of the NHS*. London, Centre for Policy Studies.

Starr, P (1983) *The Social Transformation of American Medicine*. Cambridge, MA, Harvard University Press.

Willetts, D and Goldsmith, M (1988) *Managed health care: a new system for a better health service*. London, Centre for Policy Studies.

9   National health services, resource constraints and shortages: a comparison of Soviet and British experiences

Christopher M. Davis

Introduction

The Soviet Union and Great Britain provide most medical services to their populations without direct charge through networks of publicly-owned, state-financed institutions. The national health services in these two countries have numerous similar characteristics as a result of their common organizational forms, the impacts of universal influences, and the shared needs to confront many of the same challenges (such as how to cope with a virtually insatiable demand for medical care with limited resources). However, each health service also has unique features that have been determined by the nations' differing histories, political systems, economic organization, and cultural traits.[1]

This study attempts to make a contribution to the international comparison of medical systems by assessing the relative strengths of universal and specific forces on medical institution behaviour in the USSR and UK during the period 1965–85. The initial section briefly reviews the political, economic and social environments of the two countries in order to provide a foundation for the subsequent evaluation of several questions concerning their influence on health services. How important are political variables in determining medical system characteristics? Does it matter that the USSR had, at least until the Gorbachev era reforms, an authoritarian political system under the monopoly control of the Communist Party whereas

Britain has had a multi-party democracy? Is the performance of a national health service affected by the type of economic system within which it functions (centrally planned economy in the USSR versus capitalist market economy in the UK)? Do the social, cultural and psychological features of the populations in the Soviet Union and Britain have differing effects on the behaviour of their members with respect to personal health habits, utilization of medical services, and relationships between patients and medical staff?

In any comparison of health services there are numerous interesting issues that could be analysed. Due to space constraints the second section examines only five: (1) Is demand for medical care growing rapidly?, (2) How effective are health cost containment programmes?, (3) How pervasive are shortages in the health systems?, (4) Are medical services distributed through rationing schemes?, and (5) Has technological progress been similar in the two systems and has it promoted a convergence of the characteristics of the national health services?[2]

The topics covered and methodological approach utilized in this chapter are similar to those in the book *The Painful Prescription* by Aaron and Schwartz (1984), which examines rationing of hospital care in two different types of medical systems, the mixed private-public one of the US and the national health service of the UK. Their main concern, and one of those of this study, is to improve understanding:

> of what kinds of choices budget limits have forced on British health planners, doctors and patients and of what stresses such budget limits have generated within the political system that imposed them (Aaron and Schwartz, 1984, p 11).

Due to space constraints the presentation of the analysis of the Soviet case is abbreviated in places. Fuller discussion of issues and documentation of arguments can be found in previous works of this author (Davis, 1983a, 1987, 1988, 1989ab). One further introductory qualification is that although the Gorbachev-era health service is afflicted by many of the problems identified below, significant reforms were introduced during 1985–90 that already have changed its personnel, organization, and policies, and could improve its circumstances and performance in the 1990s (Davis, 1987).

Health service environments and organizations

Political, economic and social environments
The behaviour of medical establishments and the people associated with them (e.g. patients, medical staff, government decision

makers) in the UK and USSR is affected not only by universal forces, but also by the specific political, economic and social environments of the two countries. For general information on the Soviet political, economic and social systems *see* Ellman, 1973; Matthews, 1978; Lane, 1978; Hough and Fainsod, 1979; Kornai, 1980; and Gregory and Stuart, 1981. Assessments of the environment of the British NHS can be found in numerous sources (Culyer, 1976; Aaron and Schwartz, 1984; Butler and Vaile, 1984; Mooney, 1986) and of the Soviet one in Field, 1967; Kaser, 1976; Ryan, 1978; George and Manning, 1980; and Davis, 1983b, 1988, 1989ab. For the purposes of this chapter the assertions about system characteristics made in Table 9.1 should suffice. In subsequent sections the various features of the environments are discussed within the context of the analysis of the five issues mentioned above.

Health production processes

Changes in the population's health in both the UK and USSR are generated by a complex health production process that involves the activities and interactions of seven main institutions: consumers, medical system, medical supply network (e.g. pharmacies), medical industry, biomedical research and development (R&D), medical foreign trade, and the central health bureaucracy (Davis, 1987, 1988). Each of these institutions generates measurable outputs, uses inputs of labour, capital and intermediate goods, obtains finance from various sources, and has linkages with the others.

It should be obvious that there are many different features of Soviet and British health sector institutions. For example, in the UK pharmacies and pharmaceutical factories are privately owned whereas in the USSR they are state enterprises. Nevertheless, it can be argued that the two national health services have similar functions within the health production process. First, the health systems attempt to prevent or cure the population's illness, which changes in pattern and magnitude in response to developments in demographic, consumption, and environmental forces.[3] Second, medical services are intermediate outputs in the health production process, which has as its final goal the improvement in the population's health, and therefore have only limited influence on health outcomes. Third, the quantity and quality of medical service outputs are determined by the efficiency of production of medical establishments and the scale and quality of their inputs of labour, capital (buildings and equipment) and intermediate goods (medicines, medical supplies, food). Fourth, the technological state of the medical system is a function of both its demands and the supply from domestic medical industry or foreign trade organizations.

Table 9.1 A comparison of the features of the environments of the
UK and USSR health services, 1965–1985

Political system

UK	USSR
Emphasis on individual rights	Emphasis on the collective and the state
Multiple political parties	Single Communist Party
Contested elections	Uncontested elections
Free press	Censored press
Firm party discipline	Rigid party discipline
Strong popular support for the NHS	Strong popular support for the NHS
Popular dissatisfaction with performance of NHS an important political issue	Popular dissatisfaction with performance of NHS an insignificant political issue

Economic system

UK	USSR
Most property in private sector	Most property in state sector
Market regulation of the economy	Central plan regulation of the economy
Consumers have strong market power relative to suppliers (buyers' market)	Consumers have weak market power relative to suppliers (sellers' market)
Weak government control of income and consumption	Strong government control of income and consumption
Economy open to world competition (private control of foreign trade)	Economy closed to world competition (state monopoly of foreign trade)
High consumption share of national income	Low consumption share of national income
Chronic excess supply in consumption markets	Chronic excess demand in consumption markets
Unequal distribution of income and wealth	Unequal distribution of income and privileges
State-owned NHS an anomaly in market economy	State-owned NHS typical component of centrally planned economy

Table 9.1 (contd)

Social system	
UK	*USSR*
Significant ethnic diversity in population	Great ethnic diversity in population
Highly educated population	Highly educated population
Moderate popular resistance to attempts by state to constrain individual's right to obtain maximum satisfaction of needs	Popular acceptance of right of state to constrain individual's attempt to obtain adequate satisfaction of needs
Citizens moderately destructive of own health (alcoholism, smoking, drugs, poor driving)	Citizens unusually destructive of own health (alcoholism, smoking, poor diet)
Popular sympathy for NHS and its staff	Popular sympathy for NHS and its staff
Popular assumption that free medical care is a right	Popular assumption that free medical care is a right
Popular willingness to accept doctors' authority	Popular willingness to accept doctors' authorority
Popular acceptance of reasonable constraints on availability of medical services	Popular expectation of severe constraints on availability of medical services
Population measures NHS performance relative to best standards in world	Population measures NHS performance relative to past standards in USSR

National health service organization

UK

The features of the British NHS are well known and evaluated in numerous other sources (Culyer, 1976; Butler and Vaile, 1984; Mooney, 1986). Suffice it to say that it is owned and managed by the state and provides medical care of all types to the population free of direct charge. The NHS is comprised of the following three main services (with shares of the 1985 budget in brackets): hospitals (58.1 per cent); family practitioners (22.6 per cent); and community health (6.5 per cent) (Office, 1987, Table 2.7). Part of the remaining 12.8 per cent of the budget finances the administration of the NHS by the Department of Health and Social Security and the regional and district health authorities.

In the period under study the medical system expanded in size, increased its output, and improved its efficiency. From 1970 to 1985 employment in the NHS grew from 741,000 to 1,223,000 and the provision of various services increased: total hospital discharges (including deaths) rose from 6,246,000 to 7,876,000 and the number of GP consultations grew from 229 million in 1975 to 251 million in 1985 (Office, 1987, Tables 2.5, 3.25, and 4.11). During the 1970–85 period there were declines in the numbers of hospitals from 2,931 to 2,423 and of hospital beds from 530,511 to 426,448 (Office, 1987, Tables 3.8 and 3.8 (a)). But the latter trends reflected a policy of closing down small or redundant hospitals and a practice of improving efficiency: the average length of stay per acute bed dropped from 11.6 days to 7.7 days and the throughput indicators of annual discharges (including deaths) per acute bed rose from 23.3 to 35.1 (Office, 1987, Table 3.26).

Since the purpose of this chapter is to evaluate NHS responses to resource constraints, attention can be focused on several of its characteristics. First, there was no direct access to specialists as in the US. Patients obtained their first contact medical care from a general practitioner. Second, a sequential referral process existed in the NHS. GPs screened patients according to various criteria to determine which should be sent for diagnosis and treatment at district hospitals. Further screening then was carried out before patients were sent on to consultants at teaching hospitals. Third, hospital doctors were salaried employees, received no benefits from provision of extra treatment, were aware of resource constraints, and tried to maintain good relations with their colleagues who were involved with them in a zero-sum resource allocation game (Aaron and Schwartz, 1984).

USSR

The organization of the pre-reform medical system in the USSR developed over the past several decades in response to universal influences and specific political and economic forces within Soviet society.[4] As in the British case, its facilities were state-owned, finance came primarily from the government budget, and medical services were provided free of direct charge to the population. In 1985 the Soviet NHS: employed 7,235,000 people (including 1,170,000 doctors); possessed 233,000 hospitals and 391,000 outpatients clinics; and provided 3168 million outpatient doctor visits and 69.6 million hospitalizations (Davis, 1987, pp 316–17).

Although it was officially claimed that the health service was organized on principles derived from Marxist-Leninist ideology, empirical evidence suggests that several of these were more aspirations than descriptions of reality (Field, 1967; Ryan, 1978; George and Manning, 1980).[5] For example, the Soviet health system did not have a unified organization (Davis, 1988). First of all, several different authorities besides the Ministry of Health controlled medical facilities in departmental subsystems. Second, within the Ministry of Health there were two different types of closed subsystems (elite and industrial) and three open ones (capital city, provincial city, and rural). Each of these had somewhat different characteristics and provided medical care of varying quality to the population group it served. Third, a 'shadow' (or second economy) network of medical care existed that illegally made use of state facilities to provide medical assistance to many patients on a fee-for-service basis.

The medical profession in the USSR was quite different from its counterpart in Britain due to historical and political developments. In the case of Soviet doctors the salient features were as follows: the political power of doctors as an interest group was destroyed soon after the revolution; all doctors were salaried state employees; the practice of medicine was a low-wage profession; most doctors (70 per cent) were women; staff were used to working in accordance with state plans and subject to centrally determined budget constraints; and Soviet doctors were not concerned about complaints of patients, given the characteristics of the political system and society discussed above.

The organization of the delivery of medical care exhibited considerable diversity, reflecting differences between subsystems and client groups. First contact care of patients in large city, medium city, and rural district subsystems was organized on a territorial basis, according to place of residence, whereas access to services in elite, departmental and industrial subsystems depended upon place of work (Davis, 1988). Despite this complexity, there were some common features of first-contact care and patient referral in the USSR. In most cases the initial consultation between a patient and a general doctor occurred in an outpatient facility called a polyclinic. If the complaint could not be easily dealt with, a referral was made to either the polyclinic diagnostic department or a specialist doctor within the polyclinic. If the patient required hospitalization, the polyclinic referred the patient to a linked general hospital. This facility dealt with most cases, but a small percentage of patients required more sophisticated treatment. These were referred to specialized hospitals with large catchment areas.

Demands, constraints, shortages and rationing

During 1965–85 the Soviet and British health services were confronted by many similar phenomena and challenges: growing demand for medical services; tight budget constraints; technological advances that pushed back the frontier of feasible medical treatment; scarcity of specialized services; and the need for rationing. But the particular features of the environments described above meant that there were varying intensities of problems (such as inequality in distribution, shortages, and quality of care) and policy responses.

Demand for medical care

Health systems provide medical services to the population in response to demands that are initiated either by patients on an independent basis or by medical staff acting as agents of consumers (Culyer, 1976; Cullis and West, 1979; Mooney, 1986). In order to understand the degree of pressure on a health service to increase its output it is necessary to evaluate developments in demand. These are generated by a variety of factors. In the first instance demand is affected by conditions in the market for medical services (e.g. money and time prices for services) and the quantity and quality of medical services available. As general rules, demand decreases in response to price rises and grows with increases in medical service supply. Demand is influenced upward by growth in population disposable income, educational levels, the sophistication of medical technology and need for medical care. The latter is a function of prevalence of illness, which can be intensified by adverse developments in demography (e.g. ageing of the population), consumption (e.g. increased consumption of alcohol and cigarettes), and the environment (e.g. worsening industrial pollution).

Two demand-related aspects of illness patterns should be mentioned here. First, most health services treat only a portion of the illness in the society. The situation can be described by the concept of the morbidity iceberg, with the tip representing expressed demand and the base below the waterline as hidden illness (Butler and Vaile, 1984; Davis, 1988). Second, international experience indicates that as a nation becomes more urban and industrialized, living standards improve and there is a shift in its illness pattern that involves a decrease in nutritional and infectious diseases and an increase in degenerative illness (Butler and Vaile, 1984, pp 4–5).

UK

It is generally agreed that, due to the absence of a price barrier to medical treatment and various demand-inducing developments, the British NHS has consistently operated in an excess demand environment. According to Yates (1987, p 22):

> The demand for medical care, and in particular for surgical intervention, is absolutely enormous and has, throughout the history of the NHS, been much greater than the capacity of the health care services .... Over the last 30 years the situation has deteriorated because of tremendous scientific, technical, and medical advances that keep breaking new ground and make it possible to undertake types of surgery never previously dreamt of.

The developments in diagnostic and curative medical techniques and technologies that he refers to (and that are evaluated in the medical technology section below) have resulted in doctors uncovering more of the existing illness 'below the waterline' of the morbidity iceberg or calling in for treatment patients with known but hitherto incurable illness.

Several other factors have contributed as well to the growth of demand for medical services in the UK: the size of the total population increased from 54.5 million in 1965 to 56.5 million in 1985; the share of the elderly (those 65 years and older) in the population increased from 12 to 15 per cent during 1965–85; consumer knowledge of medical matters improved due to the rise in educational standards and greater dissemination of information through the media and formal health education programmes; real disposable personal income rose significantly; and, as indicated in the previous section, the supply of NHS medical services expanded in quantitative terms. In sum, throughout the period under study the NHS was under pressure to increase its output in order to cope with growing current period demand and the backlog of past demand of patients on waiting lists.

USSR
Over the two decades under study, the need for medical care in the Soviet Union also grew substantially due to developments in demography (population growth of about 50 million people, ageing, higher share of males), consumption (growth in alcoholism, smoking, and cholesterol intake), and the environment (increased pollution, worsening of sanitary conditions). Negative influences on citizens' health were not adequately offset by effective preventive medical programmes (Davis, 1983a, 1988).

In the period 1965–85 the USSR did not experience the expected transition in its illness pattern from one with a high percentage of infectious disease to one with predominantly degenerative illness, primarily due to its unbalanced development policy, especially its neglect of personal and public consumption. Instead, the Soviet illness pattern had some of the features of both industrialized and underdeveloped countries. The incidence of infectious diseases was higher in the USSR than in Britain or other industrialized nations, and there were unfavourable upward trends in the prevalence of typhoid and paratyphoid, diphtheria, whooping cough, measles, mumps, hepatitis and salmonellosis (Feshbach, 1983, 1986). Accidents and poisonings also rose, due to the rapid mechanization of Soviet society and growing consumption of alcohol (Dutton, 1979). In this period the Soviet population still suffered from a high incidence of nutritional disease, such as rickets and obesity, and respiratory illness, such as influenza and pneumonia (Davis and Feshbach, 1980). The most significant development was the increase in degenerative diseases caused by the ageing of the population, urbanization, stress, smoking, alcoholism, poor diet and pollution. The Soviet Union experienced coronary illness and cancer epidemics of growing severity that were reflected in the rise of the death rate from all cardiovascular disease from 247 deaths per 100,000 in 1960 to 459 in 1975 to 535 in 1983, and equivalent increases in cancer mortality (Dutton, 1979; Cooper and Schatzkin, 1982; Feshbach, 1986).

As mentioned above, the demand for medical services is a function of not only the population's needs but also developments in income, education, prices and supplies. In recent decades trends in virtually all of these variables in the USSR contributed to, or at least did not impede (e.g. the maintenance of a zero money price for medical care), the increase in demand.[6] This was reflected in the growth in the quantity of medical services consumed. From 1970 to 1985 the number of annual hospitalizations per 100 people increased from 21.5 to 25.1 and the number of outpatient visits to doctors (including home visits) per capita went up from 8.0 to 11.4 (Davis, 1987, 1988).

Health cost containment

In virtually all industrialized societies, expenditures on health have risen faster than national income over the past several decades. By 1985 the shares of health expenditure in GNP were in the 8–11 per cent range for France, West Germany, Netherlands, Sweden and the USA (Office, 1987, Table 2.2). The rising 'health burdens' elicited growing concern in these societies because of the high opportunity costs of the resources allocated to health, their inconsistency with government policies to reduce public expenditure, and evidence of inefficiency in the health production process. In consequence, most nations introduced health cost containment programmes (Culyer, 1989). In cases where cost containment was effective, however, it contributed to shortages in health systems and forced administrators and medical staff to make difficult choices concerning trade-offs between alternative claims on resources and rationing schemes.

UK

The book *The Painful Prescription* compares the US and UK health cost containment records. Aaron and Schwartz (1984, p 7) argue that spending controls in the US have been ineffective and that the level of medical care provided there is 'usually close to what would be provided if cost were no object and benefit to patients were the sole concern'. As a result, the health share of US GNP rose from 6.1 per cent in 1965 to 10.5 per cent in 1985 (US Bureau, 1984). In contrast, Britain was able to hold down the real growth of health expenditures due to seven features of its political system, society, and health service.[7]

Although these arguments are generally valid, available evidence indicates that Britain was successful in containing costs only relative to other OECD countries (Culyer, 1989). First, the index of NHS expenditure in constant prices rose from 100 in 1973 to 127 in 1985 (Office, 1987, Figure 2.4). Second, the NHS share of UK public expenditure increased from 10.1 per cent in 1965 to 13.0 per cent in 1985 (Office, 1987, Table 2.10). Third, the GNP share of NHS spending went up from 4.1 per cent in 1965 to 6.0 per cent in 1985 (Office, 1987, Table 2.3). As the previous section indicated, however, the population's demand for medical care grew rapidly during 1965–85. So the limits that were imposed on the health service were sufficiently stringent to ensure that excess demand remained throughout the period.

USSR
Features of the Soviet Union's political, economic, social and health systems created conditions of medical cost containment that were more favourable than those in Britain. In the Soviet Union the CPSU was the permanently ruling and only party. Its strong internal discipline ensured a high degree of support by the party and state bureacracies and by parliamentary bodies (e.g. the Supreme Soviet) for most policies. State ownership and control of the components of the health production process (medical facilities, pharmacies, medical industry, biomedical research institutes and foreign trade organizations) was more complete than in Britain. Within the medical system a similar sequential referral process existed. Since all medical staff in the USSR were salaried state employees and accustomed to working within plan-imposed constraints, it was even easier to screen patients and enforce centrally imposed budget limits. Finally, the average population member tended to accept decisions of authorities, had a modest individualistic drive, and had a relatively passive acceptance of illness-related suffering.

One component of an effective cost containment policy not discussed explicitly by Aaron and Schwartz (1984) is the government's setting of a relatively low priority for health in the resource allocation process. Without this feature, other conditions listed above would be insufficient to restrain expenditure. In the USSR the unimportance of the health sector was evidenced by the low wages of medical personnel, 'stingy' financial norms governing the calculation of medical institutions' budgets, unresponsiveness of health spending to growth in consumer demand for medical services, and chronic underfulfilment of health system expenditure plans for the purchase of medical commodities and capital investment (Davis, 1983a, 1989).

The combination of factors outlined above enabled the Soviet government to constrain severely the growth of national health spending (Davis, 1983a, 1987). Medically-related wage and price increases in real terms were held down to about 1–2 per cent a year. The growth rate of Ministry of Health expenditure was lower than that of the total state budget, a circumstance which reduced the health share of the budget from 6.5 per cent in 1965 to 4.6 per cent in 1985. As shown above, the health share of the UK budget rose. Expenditures on health from other sources did increase, so from 1970 to 1985 total health spending roughly doubled from 11.7 to 22.5 billion roubles. But this growth was from a low base and its rate declined from 6 per cent per annum in the period 1975–80 to 4 per cent in 1980–85. Success in the cost containment effort was reflected by the fact that the health shares of national income (using the Soviet measure of 'net material product utilized') remained stable at around 4 per cent while that of GNP, in contrast to UK experience, declined from 2.7 per cent in 1965 to 2.4 per cent in 1980 (US Congress, 1982; Davis, 1987).

Shortages in the health services

Shortages in a health system arise when the demand for medical services or commodities exceed available supplies (Cooper, 1975; Culyer, 1976). They can be observed in any country, at least on a temporary basis. In normal circumstances equilibrium can be returned to an excess demand market either by increasing the supply of the deficit good or by raising prices to market clearing levels. However, if no price barrier exists to restrain access to medical care shortages can only be minimized through restraining supplier-induced demand (e.g. as a matter of policy doctors do not detect as many cases of illness for treatment) or expanding the supply of medical services.

UK
The combination of rising demand for medical care and relatively tight budget constraints in Britain during 1965–85 generated many deficits and shortage-related phenomena in the NHS with respect to labour, buildings, technology, supplies, and provision of services. Some of these shortages can be detected using domestic British criteria (e.g. unfilled staff positions), whereas others can be identified on the basis of international comparisons.

In the case of labour, the central authorities in the NHS maintained tight controls over the creation of new staff positions and wage levels. By international standards there appeared to be fewer hospital doctors than necessary in some categories. Aaron and Schwartz (1984, pp 43, 50, 73) provide several examples of this: the norm for radiotherapists in the early 1980s was 1 per 200–250 new patients, the US had 1 per 177 patients whereas the UK had 1 per 288 patients; on a per capita basis the UK had one-tenth the number of oncologists and one-half the number of radiologists as the US. One policy adopted by UK administrators to cope with these shortages was to overwork junior doctors to the extent that it might have endangered patients' health. The low wages on offer in the NHS for other staff contributed to recruitment and retention difficulties. Aaron and Schwartz (1984, pp 33, 43) mention shortages of nurses for kidney dialysis centres and a 40 per cent deficit (in relation to an optimal level) of physicists at cancer radiotherapy centres.

Sustained tight budget limits had an adverse impact on the building component of the NHS capital investment programme. According to Aaron and Schwartz (1984, p 100) the UK annually spent $12 per capita on construction of medical facilities whereas the US figure was $25. As a consequence, in NHS facilities there were shortages of office and ward space, operating theatres, and intensive care units. Furthermore, prolonged scrimping on capital repairs meant that many existing hospitals were in a dilapidated condition.

In the environment of financial stringency that existed in Britain it was easier, for administrative and political reasons, to restrain the health system's acquisition of new technology than its wage bill. The UK had far fewer pieces of medical equipment on a population-adjusted basis than most other industrialized nations. Aaron and Schwartz (1984, pp 28, 41, 73) found that after adjusting for population differences Britain had relative to the US: one-sixth the CT (computed tomography) scanning capacity; one-fifth the number of intensive care hospital beds; far fewer X-ray machines in the offices of first contact doctors; and 44 per cent of the number of megavolt machines for radiation treatment of cancer. The statistical material in *Expensive Health Technologies* (Stocking, 1988) demonstrates that Britain was underprovided even relative to other EC countries (*see also* Table 9.2 below in the section on medical technology).

The deficits of labour and capital in the NHS constrained the provision of many important medical services to levels below those of other developed nations. Relative to the US on a population-adjusted basis the UK supplied its patients with: one-half as many diagnostic X-rays (and used only one-quarter as much film); one-third as much kidney dialysis (69 versus 230 people per million on dialysis); one-quarter as much parenteral nutrition treatment; one-tenth the number of coronary artery surgical operations (55 versus 490 bypass operations per million population); three-quarters as many hip replacement operations; one-sixth as much chemotherapy treatment for solid tumours; and one-fifth as many CT scans (Aaron and Schwartz, 1984, pp 33, 48, 55, 59, 64, 71, 73). Similar diagnostic and treatment discrepancies relative to other EC countries in 1986 are noted in Stocking (1988).

Although the analysis in this section demonstrates that shortages were prevalent in the NHS and had adverse effects on its performance, several other factors should be taken into account in a comparison with the situation in the USSR. First, the output of the NHS increased in Britain so the medical service shortages were relative to the growing demand. Second, the quantity of sophisticated technology in the NHS rose significantly in the period under study. For example, just from 1982 to 1986 there was a four-fold increase in the indicator of CT scanners per million population from 0.6 to 2.7 (Stocking, 1988, p 12). Third, British medical staff and patients were aware of international developments in medical techniques and technology and maintained pressure on spending authorities to improve supplies. Fourth, within the constraints of their budgets medical establishments in the UK were able to purchase any desired commodities, such as medicines and medical equipment, in input markets. That is, shortages existed within the NHS because of high demand and budget limits but not in other institutions of the health production process or in the country's capitalist economy. Fifth, the average quality of buildings and level of medical technology may have been lower in the NHS than in leading industrialized nations but it was far higher than in the Soviet Union.

USSR

Since the Soviet health system functioned in a chronic excess demand environment throughout the period 1965–85, it was afflicted by pervasive shortages. Detailed evidence supporting this general conclusion and the specific points made below is provided in other works by this author (Davis, 1983a, 1987, 1989ab). Due to space constraints only summaries are provided below.

In the USSR medical establishments open to the public frequently were unable to provide patients with adequate quantities of diagnostic and treatment services, especially those of a sophisticated nature. These short-falls reflected deficiencies in health service capital stock, labour and supplies. In many medical facilities there were crowded waiting rooms, cramped work spaces for staff, and location of diagnostic or treatment units in inappropriate areas. The amount of floor space per hospital bed was often below minimum sanitary levels because beds were crammed into insufficient ward areas or, not infrequently, placed in corridors. There were deficits of many types of personnel relative to established positions in polyclinics and hospitals. This resulted in the unplanned substitution of staff, queues of patients, and the reduction in average doctor consultation time. Throughout the Soviet health service shortages of medical equipment, machinery, and instruments (*see* the section below on medical technology) contributed to bottlenecks in the diagnosis and treatment of patients. The supply of medicines to patients within hospitals normally was not enough to satisfy demands. For example, in 1986 126 medicaments out of the authorized list of

825 were in deficit in the Erevan republican hospital, which as a capital city facility should have been well-supplied (Davis, 1987).

The inadequate supplies of medical services and medicines obtained by patients within the health system were primarily the result of shortages of inputs of labour, capital stock, medicines and other commodities, that were in turn caused by several factors.[8] In the case of medicaments, deficits were caused by inadequate health facility budgets as well as by the substandard work of other institutions in the health production process. The pharmacy network often: made errors in forecasting demand and determining orders for medical industry; distributed medicaments inappropriately between regions and establishments; and stored goods in substandard facilities, thereby incurring greater than planned losses. The Soviet medical industry consistently underfulfilled health system supply plans. For example, in 1986 the Ministry of Health claimed that the industry satisfied only 75–78 per cent of its undoubtedly understated demands for medicines (Davis, 1987).

These deficiencies in medical supplies could have been remedied through imports. However, foreign trade was a state monopoly and the health sector had a low priority claim on foreign currency or allocations of imports. In consequence, the volume of supplies acquired abroad was not enough to eliminate the chronic shortages of modern medicines and medical equipment in the USSR (Davis, 1987).

Although shortages existed to varying degrees in medical systems in all countries in the period 1965–85, they usually were not as pervasive and chronic as in the Soviet case. This relatively unique feature of the Soviet national health service was a function of the low priority of the health sector, failures of other institutions in the supply-constrained economy, and the tolerance by the central authorities of a fairly high intensity of shortage in the health sector (Davis, 1989a).

Rationing of medical care

Rationing of medical care usually arises in any nation which is confronted by a growing demand for medical services but sets stringent limits on health spending (Cooper, 1975). The excess demand in the medical care market results in shortages which potentially could affect the treatment of all patients. However, most societies have value systems that rank certain illness conditions (e.g. cancer, AIDS) and population groups (e.g. infants) more highly than others (e.g. arthritis, the elderly). Thus, efforts are made to ration medical care in an attempt to ensure that the most important patients receive care irrespective of general circumstances (Aaron and Schwartz, 1984).

Several rationing instruments are used in medical systems. First, closed facilities can be established that only serve pre-selected patient groups. Second, queues can be used as rationing devices because they impose time prices on patients and therefore allocate medical services to those who can afford to wait (Barzel, 1984). The advantage of the queuing instrument is that it restricts the demands of patients to manageable levels through an apparently neutral mechanism, and thereby saves medical staff from having to make unpopular decisions about whether or not each potential patient could be treated. Third, waiting lists can be employed to ration scarce medical care. Theoretical research has shown that waiting lists for medical treatment arise in an excess demand environment and have demand reduction effects similar to physical queues (Lindsay and Feigenbaum, 1984).

UK

Rationing was a pervasive practice in the UK NHS during 1965–85, due to the existence of the pre-conditions discussed above: excess demand, cost containment and shortages (Cooper, 1975; Culyer, 1976, Aaron and Schwartz, 1984; Yates, 1987). The primary instruments used were physical queuing, waiting lists and screening-out of patients. The rationing for specialized medical care appears to have had a non-egalitarian character in that there was consistent, if disguised, discrimination against elderly patients.

Physical queues existed in both GP surgeries and outpatient departments of hospitals. This obviously was the case when patients appeared at clinics unannounced and obtained treatment on a sequential basis. However, queues also existed in facilities using appointment systems. This usually was due to excessively tight booking and 'unexpected' (although quite regular) disruptions of the schedules of medical staff, especially doctors. Many patients waited 15–30 minutes after appointed times in GPs' offices and for longer in, for example, antenatal clinics in hospitals.

In Britain waiting lists frequently were used to ration in-patient treatment in hospital. From 1965 to 1985 there were increases in the numbers of patients on NHS hospital waiting lists for all departments from 567,000 to 801,000 and for acute surgical services from 519,000 to 768,000 (Office, 1987, Table 3.34). The indicator of patients on acute services waiting lists per 1000 population went up from 10.4 to 14.4. According to Aaron and Schwartz (1984, p 16) 'One-third of all admitted patients were on waiting lists for three months or more, 6 per cent for one year or more'.

This finding appears to be inconsistent with the result of a survey which showed that the mean waiting time for patients in all disease categories declined slightly from 17.5 days in 1980 to 17.1 days in 1984 (Office, 1987, Table 3.36(b)). But in that latter year the waiting time varied by disease sub-group from 1.4 days for an abortion to 36.8 days for varicose veins. These variations can be explained by the policies of dividing diseases and treatments into urgent categories (e.g. malignant neoplasms) and nonurgent ones (e.g. varicose veins, haemorrhoids), establishing different goals (less than a month of waiting for the former versus less than a year for the latter), and preferentially allocating resources to support departments offering urgent medical care (Aaron and Schwartz, 1984, p 15).

A third rationing instrument used in the NHS was that of screening from specialized diagnosis or treatment those patients with poor survival probabilities or beyond unofficial age cutoffs. This process began with GPs and was continued by district and teaching hospital staff. Aaron and Schwartz (1984, p 101) claim:

> Resource limits put doctors in a position that many of them find awkward. Trained to treat illness, they find they are unable to provide all the care from which their patients might derive some positive medical benefit . . . . Doctors gradually redefine standards of care so that they can escape the constant recognition that financial limits compel them to do less than their best. By various means, physicians and other health care providers try to make the denial of care seem routine or optimal.

Such screening practices are less prevalent, and less necessary, in countries that spend more on health. For example, Aaron and Schwartz (1984, p 34) observe that in the late 1970s new patients under the age of 45 were accepted in Britain for kidney dialysis at a rate similar to those in France, West Germany and Italy, whereas among patients 65 years and older the UK acceptance rate was only 10 per cent of those of the other countries.

USSR

In theory, the leadership in the USSR could have responded to the chronic excess demand in the market for medical services with egalitarian rationing. However, in reality an unequal approach to distribution was adopted that influenced both the organization and functioning of the health system.

One of the clearest expressions of this rationing was the division of the health service into the six subsystems described above (Davis, 1988). All of the closed facilities were relatively well-funded and supplied, so they offered their patients a higher standard of care than could the open ones. In addition, there was little referral between the three public subsystems (capital city, medium city and rural district). This meant that a differentiated allocation of resources could ensure that the important urban population groups, especially those in capital cities, received better care than residents of small towns and villages. Rationing also partly explained the organization of specialized facilities for two important population groups, pregnant women and children.

Although queuing exists in all health systems, in the USSR it had a pervasive, systemic character. In polyclinics the most frequent queue comprised patients waiting to see the doctor of first contact. Although the therapists attempted to regulate the number of patients referred for further diagnosis or specialized treatment in order to keep demand in balance with supply, many patients were still sent forward. Diagnostic departments often operated at below capacity due to equipment failures or staffing problems, so bottlenecks arose in the treatment process and patients had to wait long periods in polyclinics before they received X-ray or other diagnostic services (Davis, 1983a). The same situation obtained with respect to seeing specialist doctors within the polyclinic.

In hospitals queues existed as well, but they involved waiting in bed rather than in corridors outside offices. Again, this was caused by production bottlenecks in diagnostic and treatment departments due to deficits of technology or skilled personnel. This shortage-related bed queuing partially explains why the indicator of bed-days per patient in Soviet hospitals was considerably greater than that in British facilities.

Waiting lists were used as well in the Soviet health system to ration scarce medical care. In the case of polyclinics, a patient who could not obtain scarce diagnostic or specialist services during an initial visit was either given a future appointment or put on a waiting list. Those on waiting lists were contacted at an unspecified future date when an appointment became available. Admission to Soviet hospitals was governed by waiting lists for many non-urgent cases. The length of wait depended upon the general level of hospital provision and availability of specialized services in a region.

The existence of pervasive rationing in the Soviet health system was a predictable consequence of the chronic excess demand in the medical care market. Although Britain also was forced to ration scarce services using the instruments of queuing and waiting lists, this was not allowed to become too severe by governments because of greater popular expectations and fear of adverse feedback through the open electoral system. Due to the political and social factors identified in Table 9.1 rationing was tolerated more in the USSR. Furthermore, the Soviet Union was unusual in its practice of rationing medical care through closed subsystems within a state-financed national health service. Britain had closed facilities, especially for the military, but provided above average medical care to elite groups through privately-financed medical facilities or programmes. It appears that Soviet arrangements were made possible by the one-party political system, lack of public accountability, and censorship.

Medical technology

Over the past several decades the organization, performance and expenditures of health systems in the west have been significantly influenced by the substantial advances made in biomedical sciences, medical technology and clinical techniques. On the whole, the scientific-technological revolution in medicine has been beneficial and has raised the effectiveness of health systems in coping with illness. But it also has had numerous side effects, such as the promotion of narrow specialization of medical personnel, creation of a more alienating technocratic environment for patients, and rapid growth in the cost of medical care. In any event, it has appeared as if technological progress was an irresistible force that determined developments in all types of health systems and brought about a convergence in their characteristics. This section tests the convergence hypothesis by evaluating evidence concerning the impact of technology on the British and Soviet health services.

UK

In the UK many factors existed which exerted pressure on the NHS to raise its technological standards through the acquisition of sophisticated new instruments, machinery, equipment and supplies. Consumers became more aware of new developments in diagnosis and treatment and put pressure on the medical system through the media or the political system to provide the new services. Doctors attempted to obtain the latest technology for their establishments in order better to serve their patients and to keep up with rising standards of other nations. British medical industry was a source of considerable technological innovation and energetically marketed its products. And foreign firms were able to sell their medical technologies to potential customers, thereby maintaining competition among suppliers and a buyer's market for medical technology.

Despite this, evidence is presented in the previous section that the UK significantly lagged behind US provision levels with respect to a number of important technologies. Perhaps this is to be expected given the exceptionally high American expenditure on health. It therefore is of interest to examine the results of the comparison carried out by Stocking (1988) of the availability of sophisticated health technologies in the European Community. Table 9.2 summarises the situation for four important technologies.

It shows that on a population-adjusted basis the British NHS was considerably less endowed than were medical systems in equivalent European nations.

These international comparisons suggest that there were unique features of the British political system (e.g. ruling party discipline), society (e.g. greater passivity of the citizenry with respect to standards of medical care), health organization (e.g. the centrally controlled, publicly-financed system), and the medical profession (e.g. collegiality and salaried status of hospital doctors) which enabled the government to introduce and maintain relatively stringent

Table 9.2 A comparison of the availability of four sophisticated medical technologies in the EC and the UK in 1986

| Technology | No. per million population | | | UK as % EC Average |
	EC Highest	EC Average	UK	
Computed tomography (CT)	6.9	3.8	2.7	71
Magnetic resonance imaging	0.7	0.4	0.3	75
Megavolt therapy	6.0	3.6	3.2	89
Renal dialysis	12.5	4.8	1.2	25

Source: Stocking (1988, pp 12–14)

resource constraints on the national health service. This supports the conclusion of Aaron and Schwartz (1984, p 88) that:

> If tight budget limits endure for as long as they have in Britain, they cause significant economies in the provision of a broad range of medical services, though the effects on new technologies are disproportionate.

As in the case of shortages, though, it should be kept in mind that British NHS technological standards improved considerably during 1965–85 and were low only relative to those of medical systems in the most advanced industrial nations.

USSR

The health system in the USSR was affected by universal developments in biomedical science and technology, but to a lesser degree and in a more uneven manner than were most health services in western countries. Relative to international standards, the Soviet Union had low levels of technology and slow rates of technological progress in the health sector. This backwardness was caused by specific features of the political and economic systems that adversely affected both the demand for and supply of technology (Davis, 1983a, 1987, 1989ab).

On the demand side, the impact of consumers on medical technology acquisition was minimal due to several factors: lack of knowledge about available technologies, especially those in the west; satisfaction at receiving medical care based on relatively outdated technologies given the shortage environment; willingness to accept the explanations and decisions of medical authorities in the areas of diagnosis and treatment; and inability to influence production decisions through the market for medical care. The health system itself had a weak influence on technological progress. In the USSR medical facility managers were primarily concerned about raising the the quantity of services provided in order to reduce excess demand rather than, as in the West, constantly increasing quality on the basis of new technologies (Cullis and West, 1979). In addition, there was no pressure on doctors to engage in costly 'defensive' medicine. Staff were not worried about consumer complaints and concentrated on working competently with existing technology, even if it was outdated. Among other factors inhibiting the demand of the medical system were tight constraints on capital acquisition budgets, the low priority status of health, and ineffectiveness of price signals in a shortage environment.

Since the Soviet economy was a supply-constrained system, it follows that many of the technological problems of the health service were the result of deficiencies in distribution and production. The agency which managed wholesale trade in medical equipment and instruments, *Soyuzmedtekhnika*, was plagued by many of the same shortcomings as pharmacies: inaccurate projections of demand, inadequate storage facilities, inappropriate distribution of products between regions and institutions, and poor after-sales service and spare parts supply (Davis, 1987).

Other institutions in the health production process contributed to problems in technology supply as well. Medical industry, for example, chronically underfulfilled its plans for technology deliveries to the health system (Davis, 1987). Although the output of medical technology rose over time, industrial performance continued to be relatively substandard throughout the eighties. A report cited in Davis (1987) stated that national health service requirements for medical equipment were only 75–80 per cent satisfied and that:

> ... domestic industry did not produce a whole series of contemporary apparatuses, such as angiographic complexes, mobile photofluorographic stations, artificial blood circulation machines, biochemical analysers, and many other types of equipment.

A major cause of the deficiencies in the supply of equipment and machinery by the medical industry was the sluggishness of technological progress that was due to numerous obstacles: absence of effective incentives to innovate in industrial enterprises; lack of effective domestic or foreign competition; operation in a shortage environment so consumers would take all their output; and judgement of success by plan fulfilment rather than consumer satisfaction. In consequence, managers preferred to stick to old methods and products rather than engage in the troublesome process of introduction (*vnedrenie*) of new technology. A related obstacle was that prices of new products were determined by the bureaucracy, not the market, and often were not set high enough to compensate enterprises for the trouble of innovation.

Scientific R&D institutions in the biomedical field also were partially responsible for sluggish technological innovation. They often engaged in irrelevant projects, maximized their expenditures instead of scientific outputs, and demonstrated little interest in seeing any discoveries put into mass production.

Given the factors influencing both demand and supply in the USSR, it is not surprising that in general the level and rate of introduction of technology in its health system was low by western standards. Outside the various well-provided closed subsystems, medical establishments were short of machinery and equipment of all kinds. Public health facilities in the USSR were poorly provided with sophisticated technologies for diagnosis, such as computed tomography and magnetic resonance imaging equipment, and for treatments such as organ transplantation, kidney dialysis, coronary artery surgery, and intensive care of premature babies. Evidence of the backward technological state of the medical system can be found in the 1988 Soviet statistical yearbook, which reports the deficits of technology (on the basis of a survey of 11,000 medical facilities) shown in Table 9.3.

Furthermore, it is stated that only 2 per cent of polyclinics and 6 per cent of hospitals are able to use ultrasound technology in diagnostics.

There were shortages of more basic technologies as well, such as stethoscopes, thermometers, and syringes. Few disposable medical products or glass, plastic or paper were available either, due to shortcomings of Soviet industry. Existing equipment often was utilized in rooms that were designed for other functions and did not meet modern hygienic standards. Much of the machinery was obsolete due to low replacement rates, which were a function of 'stingy' budget norms. In addition, maintenance of existing medical technology was made difficult by shortages of engineering staff and spare parts.

The backwardness, relative to western standards, of the technological environment of the Soviet health system naturally had impacts on the behaviour of patients and staff and on the effectiveness of diagnosis and treatment. On the positive side,

Table 9.3 Shortages of medical technology in the USSR, 1988

Type of technology	% deficits of technology	
	Polyclinics	Hospitals
X-ray therapy	54	56
X-ray diagnosis	51	43
Laboratory	45	49
Physiotherapy	42	44
Electrocardiograph	38	35
Dental	35	37

Source: Gosudarstvennyy, 1989, p. 221

the low level of technology may have facilitated the development of a more relaxed doctor-patient relationship because there were lower expectations about the effectiveness of treatment and a less alienating technocratic environment. On the negative side, shortages of machinery and equipment contributed to medical service production bottlenecks, unpleasant queuing by patients, and a lower quality of medical care. In the case of staff, the lack of medical technology hindered the development or implementation of new diagnostic and curative techniques. There also was less pressure for subspecialization, since the technological support for many new Western specialities did not exist. The general deficit of equipment of all kinds, including typewriters and computers, meant that the Soviet health system was less mechanized and automated than a western one. Since middle medical personnel were in short supply too, doctors had to devote substantial amounts of time to low-level medical and administrative work.

Conclusions

In this chapter an attempt is made to carry out three general tasks. The first is to identify the universal and particular influences on the development of the Soviet and British national health services during 1965–85. A second is to compare the magnitude of a number of common challenges in the two systems and the differing responses to them. Third, an effort is made to assess changes in the health systems over time to determine whether universal forces, such as technological progress, stimulated a convergence or whether specific aspects of political, economic, social and health environments combined to maintain unique national characteristics.

The analysis of the two health services indicates that they did have some similar features because in both countries biomedical scientists made use of modern scientific theories of disease and medicine, clinicians attempted to employ internationally-recognized preventive and curative medical techniques, and the health systems function within broadly similar health production processes. Furthermore, the British and Soviet health services were influenced by common factors such as the rapid growth in the populations' demand for medical services and pressures for containment of health costs.

Despite this, the evidence presented in this chapter indicates that the profoundly different political, economic, and social environments of the health services modulated internationalizing influences. In the case of the Soviet Union, the communist political system, the socialist shortage economy, various social circumstances and cultural traits, and medical care principles based on Marxist-Leninist ideology, combined to produce a unique national health service with characteristics quite different from those of the British one, which functioned within a democratic society and capitalist economy.

The main differences between the challenges and performance of the health systems in the USSR and UK during 1965–85 in the areas studies appear to be as follows. First, the Soviet Union had a high incidence of both infectious and degenerative disease. Second, cost containment was more effective in the USSR and the health system was subjected to severe resource constraints. Third, pervasive and chronic shortages of medical service outputs and medical system inputs existed in the Soviet Union that reflected the low priority of the health sector and the failings of the supply-constrained socialist economy. Although rationing instruments (queueing, waiting lists) were used in both health services to distribute scarce medical services between population groups, a fourth difference was the Soviet practice of rationing through closed medical subsystems within the publicly-financed national health service. Fifth, technological progress had a more limited impact on the Soviet medical system than it did on the British one.

Given the importance of technology in western medical systems it is perhaps worthwhile to amplify this last point. The evidence presented in this chapter suggests that trends in the development of the British and Soviet health services were inconsistent with the convergence hypothesis. Analysis of the Soviet case shows that a combination of particular political, economic and cultural factors held back the pace of technological change and lessened its impact on the health system. Among the reasons for this retardation were the slow pace of indigenous technological innovation, problems in the domestic production of machinery and equipment for the health service, tight constraints on the medical system's budget for technology acquisition, and the barriers to international diffusion through scientific exchange and foreign trade. In consequence, the force of industrialism on medical production in the USSR was relatively weak and the Soviet health system evolved slowly and incrementally over the two decades under study. It appears likely that medical care organization and practice in the USSR in the late 1980s was as different, in relative terms, from that in Britain as it was in the 1960s. In fact, since the pace of technological change was rapid in the Britain in this period the possibility should be considered that there was a relative divergence, not a convergence, of the features of the Soviet and British national health services. In sum, the specific conclusion from this assessment appears to be that technological progress was not an irresistible force determining developments in health systems and the general finding is that there are limits to the autonomous power of technology in industrialised societies.

Notes

1   In this chapter the terms health service, medical system, health system are used interchangeably to refer to the network of facilities which provides preventive and curative medical services to the population.

2   In a forthcoming study by this author the British-Soviet comparative analysis will be extended to cover private medicine, quality of medical services, output indicators (i.e. mortality rates), and health service reform efforts in the USSR and UK.

3   The determinants of the Soviet population's health are discussed in Davis (1988). Among the demographic factors are age and sex distributions and developments in the genetic pool. The influences of consumption can be both positive (better nutrition, education, exercise) and negative (alcoholism, smoking, over-eating, vitamin deficiencies). The health environment is defined as having five dimensions: residential (housing, neighbourhood, public hygiene); family (extended family, illegitimate births, marital status, family tension); technological (mechanization, chemicalization, number of motor vehicles, safety programmes); natural (industrial, agricultural and transport pollution, protection programmes); and microbiological (viruses, bacteria, preventive medicine).

4   For informative assessments of the organization of the Soviet health service see Field (1967), Hyde (1974), Kaser (1976), Ryan (1978), George and Manning (1980), and Knaus (1982).

5   The official organizational principles of the Soviet NHS were: (1) the health system has a state socialist character, (2) qualified medical services are provided free-of-charge to all who need them, (3) the medical system is unified and develops according to a central plan, (4) the health service has a preventive orientation, (5) biomedical science and clinical practice develop in a unified manner, and (6) health service activities involve public participation (Field, 1967; Lisitsyn, 1972).

6   The factors which influenced the growing demand for medical care in the USSR included (Davis, 1989b): the rise in real per capita income (by 59 per cent from 1970 to 1984); the significant increase in educational standards; no money prices were introduced for state-provided medical services (although time prices remained substantial and money prices existed for second economy services); and the capabilities of the health system were enhanced, which contributed to the upward pressure because in the medical services market some of the demand is supplier-induced.

7   The seven features that facilitated British cost containment according to Aaron and Schwartz (1984, p 25) were: (1) the government is

formed from the majority parliamentary party, which can count on inner-party discipline and consistent support, (2) public ownership and management of the NHS is widely accepted, (3) the population has a positive assessment of the NHS, (4) the sequential referral process allows doctors to screen out cases deemed unsuitable for medical treatment, (5) the 'residue of class structure' makes UK patients willing to accept decisions of doctors, (6) the British have a more passive attitude toward combating illness than do Americans, and (7) hospital governance by salaried staff facilitates enforcement of centrally imposed budget limits.

8   First, the state plan allocated the medical system insufficient quantities of inputs, so even if everything was delivered there were shortages. Second, the planned quantity of a commodity was sufficient, but the health service received a below-plan amount because of distribution or production problems of supplying agencies. Third, in the case of labour the wages on offer were too low to attract or retain the planned number of staff.

References

The sections of this chapter concerning the USSR are based upon the analysis by this author of substantial quantities of original Soviet material. However, on the assumption that few readers are likely to examine Russian-language sources it was decided not to include them in the references. Those interested in this documentation should consult the works of the author listed below.

Aaron, H J and Schwartz, W B (1984) *The Painful Prescription: Rationing Hospital Care*. Washington DC, The Brookings Institution.
Barzel, Y (1974) A theory of rationing by waiting. *Journal of Law and Economics*, April.
Butler, J R and Vaile, M S (1984) *Health and Health Services: An Introduction to Health Care in Britain*. London, Routledge and Kegan Paul.
Cooper, M H (1975) *Rationing Health Care*. London Croom Helm.
Cooper, R and Schatzkin, A (1982) Recent trends in coronary risk factors in the USSR. *American Journal of Public Health*, 72, pp 431–40.
Cullis, J and West, P A (1979) *The Economics of Health: An Introduction*. Oxford, Martin Robertson.
Culyer, A J (1976) *Need and the National Health Service*. Oxford, Martin Robertson.
Culyer, A J (1989) Cost-containment in Europe. York, *Centre for Health Economics: Discussion Paper 62*.
Davis, C (1983a) The economics of the Soviet health system. In US Congress, Joint Economic Committee *Soviet Economy in the 1980s: Problems and Prospects*. Washington D.C., USGPO.

Davis, C (1983b) Economic problems of the Soviet health service: 1917–1930. *Soviet Studies*, XXXV, pp 343–61.

Davis, C (1987) Developments in the health sector of the Soviet economy, 1970–90. U.S. Congress, Joint Economic Committee *Gorbachev's Economic Plans*, Washington D.C., USGPO.

Davis, C (1988) The organization and performance of the contemporary Soviet health service. In G W Lapidus and G E Swanson (eds) *State and Welfare USA/USSR*. Berkeley, Institute of International Studies.

Davis, C (1989a) Priority and the shortage model: The medical system in the socialist economy. In C Davis and W Charemza (eds) *Models of Disequilibrium and Shortage in Centrally Planned Economies*. London, Chapman and Hall.

Davis, C (1989b) The Soviet health system: a national health service in a socialist society. In M G Field (ed) *Success and Crisis in National Health System: A Comparative Approach*. London, Routledge.

Davis, C and Feshbach, M (1980) *Rising Infant Mortality in the USSR in the 1970s*. Washington D.C., U.S. Bureau of the Census, Report Series P-95, No 74.

Dutton, J (1979) Changes in Soviet mortality patterns, 1959–77. *Population and Development Review*, 5, pp 267–91.

Ellman, M (1973) *Planning Problems in the USSR*. Cambridge, Cambridge University Press.

Feshbach, M (1983) Issues in health problems. In U.S. Congress, Joint Economic Committee, *Soviet Economy in the 1980s: Problems and Prospects*. Washington D.C., USGPO.

Feshbach, M (1986) Recent research on Soviet health conditions. Cambridge, Paper presented at the NASEES Annual Conference, March 1986.

Field, M (1967) *Soviet Socialized Medicine: An Introduction*. New York, The Free Press.

George, V and Manning, N (1980) *Socialism, Social Welfare and the Soviet Union*. London, Routledge and Kegan Paul.

Gosudarstvennyy Komitet SSSR po Statistike (1989) *Narodnoe Khozyaistvo SSSR v 1988 g.* Moscow, Finansy i Statistika.

Gregory, P R and Stuart, R C (1981) *Soviet Economic Structure and Performance*. New York, Harper & Row.

Hough, J F and Fainsod, M (1979) *How the Soviet Union is Governed*. Cambridge, Harvard University Press.

Hyde, G (1974) *The Soviet Health Service: A Historical and Comparative Study*. London, Lawrence and Wishart.

Kaser, M (1976) *Health Care in the Soviet Union and Eastern Europe*. London, Croom Helm.

Knaus, W (1982) *Inside Russian Medicine*. New York, Everest House.

Kornai, J (1980) *Economics of Shortage*. Amsterdam, North Holland.

Lane, D (1978) *Politics and Society in the USSR*. London, Martin Robertson.

Lindsay, C M and Feigenbaum, B (1984) Rationing by waiting lists. *The American Economic Review*, June.

Lisitsyn, Y (1972) *Health Protection in the USSR*. Moscow, Progress Publishers.

Mooney, G H (1986) *Economics, Medicine and Health Care.* Brighton, Wheatsheaf Books.

Office of Health Economics (1987) *Compendium of Health Statistics* (6th Edition). Luton, White Crescent Press.

Ryan, M (1978) *The Organisation of Soviet Medical Care.* London, Martin Robertson.

Stocking, B (1988) *Expensive Health Technologies.* Oxford, Oxford University Press.

U.S. Bureau of the Census (1984) *Statistical Abstract of the United States: 1985.* Washington D.C., USGPO.

U.S. Congress, Joint Economic Committee (1982) *USSR: Measures of Economic Growth and Development, 1950–80.* Washington D.C., USGPO

Yates, J (1987) *Why are We Waiting? An Analysis of Hospital Waiting Lists.* Oxford, Oxford University Press.

10 Workfare: Lessons from the US experience

Louie Burghes

Introduction

This chapter reviews the experience of the United States with workfare, the imposition of compulsory work for those claiming 'welfare', looks at the more broadly based work programmes of which workfare is one part and draws some points of interest for the development of policies in Britain. The chapter concludes that the policies have been neither as extensive nor as successful as is sometimes supposed. The experience of the United States is particularly pertinent now when, despite Ministers' continual assurances that programmes in this country would remain voluntary, fears that some such compulsory programme might eventually be introduced in Britain have increased with the leak of a Department of Employment paper suggesting that it is still under consideration (Harper, K, 1989).

Within the United States, policies exist which either impose an obligation on, or permit recipients of particular benefits to participate in work programmes whose components range from education and training through job clubs to work experience and 'workfare'. It often seems that the British impression is that these programmes are both common to and uniform in all states. But nothing could be further from the truth, and there is considerable diversity both in the types of programmes states have and in the components of these programmes. These differences reflect a fierce and serious social policy debate about rights and obligations and a belief in the flexibility that states should have (within statutory federal programme regulations) to determine some aspects of the programmes themselves as being the most appropriate to their state.

The history of workfare

Aid to Families with Dependent Children

The possible obligation to undertake workfare in the United States is tied to receipt of 'Aid to Families with Dependent Children' (AFDC) and Food Stamps. This chapter is concerned with the first of these.

AFDC is the major cash welfare programme for families with children. Introduced in 1935, it was designed primarily to allow widows to stay at home and look after their children rather than having to go out to work, and the cash payment was seen as a replacement for the loss of an earner in the family. It was assumed that the numbers of families needing such support would remain small.

Contrary to these expectations, almost everything about AFDC has changed. It is not now primarily a benefit for widows, and both the numbers claiming and the costs of the benefits provided have grown significantly. As other income support programmes have been developed to help widows and orphans, the AFDC programme has increasingly supported divorced, deserted or not married women and their children. Nor are working families automatically excluded. While each state determines eligibility and benefit levels, AFDC benefits are available to single-parent families with children under 18 years, whether they are working or not, providing their incomes and assets are below specified amounts.

In addition, in 1961, Congress passed legislation to allow states to extend entitlement to AFDC to two-parent families in which one parent (the principal wage earner) was unemployed. Although about a half of the states have adopted this option, known as AFDC-UP, some 90 per cent of AFDC recipients are female-headed families.

There has been a considerable increase in the numbers of families receiving AFDC. Between 1960 and 1970 their numbers rose from 800,000 to 2.2 million (Congressional Budget Office, 1987, p9) and by December 1988 to 3.7 million – a total of some 10.9 million people, of whom about 7.3 million were children (Burke, V., 1989, p2). AFDC costs rose over this time from about $1 billion to $5 billion between 1960 and 1970 – a fourfold increase allowing for inflation (Congressional Budget Office, 1987, p4 and p9) – and to $16.5 billion by 1988 (Burke, V, 1989, p2).

The early work programmes, 1962–80

The growing number of families receiving AFDC and its concurrent rising cost, coupled with the extension of the benefit to families with an unemployed father, began to give rise in the 1960s to anxieties about the possible work disincentive effects of social security benefits. A reevaluation began about who 'deserves' to receive benefit and who does not, the possible disincentive effects of benefits, encouraging 'self-sufficiency' and the rights and obligations of individuals and society. The shifts in philosophy that took place are reflected in the changes that have been made and are being made in work programmes.

The early programmes (the Community Work and Training Program – CWTP, 1967 and the Work Incentive Program – WIN, 1967) were concerned primarily with male recipients of AFDC, who were the only mandatory (non-exempt) group. Exempt groups could volunteer to enter the programme but had to have a caseworker's approval. While the 1962 legislation *allowed* states to operate such a programme, the 1967 legislation *obliged* them to do so. The WIN was intended to provide help with job placement and on-the-job training, work experience and special work projects in subsidized public or community service. The focus was on training to increase skills.

The WIN work experience was not 'workfare', indeed AFDC regulations still prohibited the programme from requiring recipients to work in exchange for their benefits. Work experience allowed short-term assignments of a maximum of thirteen weeks in public agencies and it was used almost exclusively for those with little if any recent work experience.

Because the CWTP was not thought to have been of much help to women, an attempt was made in the WIN 1967 to encourage self-sufficiency among women through the introduction of the 'working mother's budget', a set of allowances which were disregarded when entitlement to AFDC was calculated. They consisted of an earnings disregard of $30 plus one third of the remainder of monthly earnings as well as work expenses, including child care.

Despite these earnings disregards and the inclusion of child care expenses, there was a feeling that the WIN programme had not served women well and that their registration and participation in the programme were blocked by less-willing mandated male participants. As a result, amendments to the WIN legislation in 1971 brought a significant shift in emphasis to the programme with the introduction of mandatory registration and participation requirements. Registration became mandatory for all adults as a condition of eligibility for benefit except for women whose children were under six years of age (when compulsory schooling begins). Women with younger children could volunteer. Women were also advanced in the priority (after unemployed men) for the limited places available. At the same time, training and services gave way to job search assistance and immediate job placement.

In 1975, the programme was amended to strengthen work requirements and place further emphasis on job placement.

There was a reduction in emphasis on support services and those with more obstacles to employment received less of the help that they needed in getting work. The changes were criticized for encouraging 'creaming' – concentrating help on the most 'job-ready'. In response, a more 'balanced' approach was developed between 1976 and 1980 with less concentration on maximizing job placements and more on support services. These included help with job search, child care, travel to interviews and training allowances as well as counselling, training and job placement. However, this turned out to be a brief interlude and, in 1980, legislation switched the programme back towards job placement and sanctions were strengthened against those who failed to meet the programme requirements.

The Omnibus Reconciliation Act (OBRA) 1981

In 1981, the Reagan administration, which wanted both to reduce the numbers of benefit recipients and to move beneficiaries off the rolls as quickly as possible, introduced legislation which would have obliged states to replace the existing work programmes with a mandatory work requirement for those receiving AFDC. Congress opposed this attempt at a blanket imposition in part because they were 'uncertain about the feasibility, effectiveness and cost implications of mandatory workfare nationwide' (Gueron, M, 1986, p3). What they did enact increased the range of work-related programmes which states could operate, of which one was known as 'workfare', the Community Work Experience Programme (CWEP). This legislation continued to allow states to design their own programmes in such a way as to produce quite considerable differences between them. Perhaps most significantly, they could choose whether or not to have a workfare programme.

Under CWEP, AFDC recipients could be required to participate in it in order to receive benefit and, if so required, would be obliged to work in unpaid public service jobs. The number of hours to be worked was calculated by dividing their AFDC grant by the minimum wage. (The federal minimum wage is $3.35 an hour. In some states a higher minimum applies.) Participants had either to be provided with transport and child care or be reimbursed for their costs.

While it may appear as if there is little difference between the public service employment under the earlier WIN programme and that introduced by the OBRA 1981, the intention of the programme was quite different. The primary purpose of the earlier work experience was to improve the longer term employment prospects of participants by providing them with employment experience of no more than thirteen weeks. The primary purpose of CWEP was quite different; it was to 'work off' their welfare benefits, and no time limit on their participation in the programme had to be set.

The other major activity under this legislation was a job search component. AFDC recipients could be required to take part in a job search programme for a period of eight weeks, beginning as early as the time of application for benefit, and they could also be required to repeat it for a second time within the first year and again once in each year that they were receiving AFDC.

One recommendation of the Reagan administration that was accepted by Congress was a reduction in the financial help given through the 'working mother's budget'. While on the one hand the administration wanted to encourage 'self-sufficiency', on the other it maintained that the work incentives had not done so and that it discriminated against other low income workers who, if they were not receiving AFDC, could not get this financial help. Some of the reductions in help were eased by the Deficit Reconciliation Act 1984, but despite these changes, the rules were still stricter than before.

The Family Support Act (FSA) 1988

In 1987, a number of work/welfare reform bills were introduced into Congress, of which one was the Reagan administration's proposal, Greater Opportunities through Work (GROW) programme. This bill proposed that all employable adults, except mothers of children under six months (*sic*) of age, should be required to take part in work related activities chosen by the state. These included workfare, job search, education and training.

Once again, the Reagan administration's proposals were not enacted. But the legislation that was passed by Congress in 1988 did alter work and training requirements for AFDC recipients with the aim of ensuring that 'needy families with children obtain education, training and employment that will help them avoid long-term welfare dependence' (Committee on Ways and Means 1989, p9). In doing so, Congress was thought to be accepting, at least implicitly, that 'the purpose of AFDC is not to furnish long-term income support but rather to provide short-term assistance to enable recipients to manage on their own'. (Focus, Winter 1988–89).

There are a number of significant elements to this legislation:
i) compulsory participation has been extended to women with children between three and six years of age, although only where

child care is provided and for a maximum of twenty hours a week. States can also apply to impose a participation requirement on those whose children are only one year old;

ii) states must offer educational activities and compulsory education can be required for parents under twenty years old who did not complete high school;

iii) all states must offer AFDC to needy unemployed families (for at least a limited period);

iv) participants can be required to accept jobs providing that they do not reduce the net income of their family;

v) lack of child care is deemed to be a good reason for not participating in the programme or for refusing employment.

Under this new legislation, WIN was repealed and replaced with the Job Opportunities and Basic Skills Training (JOBS) Program. States must offer at least two of a number of components including job search, on-the-job training, workfare or other work experience. Once again, therefore, while a state may choose to operate a compulsory workfare programme, it does not have to do so and even in states that do, not all participants will necessarily be forced onto workfare.

For each participant, states are required to undertake an assessment of (i) their education, child care and support service needs; (ii) their work experience and employment skills; and (iii) each individual's family circumstances and the needs of the children. An 'employability plan' must be developed in consultation with the participant describing both the programme activities they are required to do and the services that are to be provided for them. States may require each participant to negotiate and enter into an agreement with the agency that specifies such matters as the participant's obligations, duration of participation and activities and services to be provided by the state. But it is not clear how much say a participant really has either in the choice of activity or the alternatives within any activity. For example, they will not presumably be able to refuse to be assigned to workfare. Similarly, while participants' circumstances are to be taken into account in allocating them to work assignments, this would seem to be an area of discretion and it is not clear at what point participants might be said to have failed to comply and become subject to some sanction. Similarly, since states do not have to offer every possible programme component, their choice will limit what participants can choose to do, as may lack of funding which can restrict both the range of activities and the number of places in any activity.

However the legislation does specify certain standards for work assignments. For example, the state agency has to ensure that an assignment takes into account the physical capacity, skills, experience, health and safety, family responsibilities and place of residence of those taking part. Individuals must not be discriminated against, the conditions of their participation must be 'reasonable' and they may not be required to travel 'unreasonable' distances from home. Under CWEP (workfare) the number of hours of work required will be calculated for the first nine months by dividing the AFDC benefit by the higher of the state or federal minimum wage. After nine months in a CWEP position, the number of hours of work required is then based on the rate of pay of individuals employed in the same or similar positions by the same employer.

The concern in the US with long-term welfare dependency is reflected in this recent legislation with the imposition of targeting. States are required to target JOBS funds on those families who are considered to be most at risk of remaining dependent on AFDC for long periods. These groups are: (i) parents who are under 24 years old who have either not completed high school or who have little or no recent work experience; (ii) families in which the youngest child is within two years of being ineligible for benefit because of age, and (iii) families who have received assistance for more than 36 months in the preceding 60-month period. Within these groups, volunteers are to have priority. The legislation has also established general participation rates for the nonexempt AFDC population which each state must meet to receive full federal funding. The rates rise from 7 per cent in 1990 to 20 per cent in 1995. Required participation rates for the AFDC-UP group are set at 40 per cent by 1994 and 75 per cent by 1997/98.

However, there is a contradiction between the requirement that volunteers are served first by the programme and that certain groups are targeted and participation rates met. Targeting on groups 'at risk' may well distort the programme in terms of serving volunteers versus mandatory groups and in terms of what programme activities can be offered, particularly if the numbers of people that the programme has to serve is very large.

'Participation' is defined in the legislation. To be counted towards these rates, participants must be active in the programme for a specified number of hours per week: for on-the-job training the specified requirement is full-time work; for job search and workfare, 20 hours a week. As not all participation counts towards meeting the participation rate quotas, the needs and priorities of some volunteers could be undermined since they will not assist the state in meeting these quotas. If this interpretation is correct then, for example, a non-mandatory parent of a young child might be turned down if she wanted to receive training of only fifteen hours a week.

To make the programme compulsory, sanctions are specified that must be applied to nonexempt participants if they fail or refuse to take part in the programme, 'without good cause'. When a sanction is applied, no benefit is paid for that participant, or in a two-parent family for both adults, although other members of the family will still receive it. The length of the sanction varies, and for the first offence it is applied until the failure to comply ceases; for a third offence, a similar sanction or a six-month loss of benefit whichever is the longer is imposed.

The philosophical debate

The general debate

The history of AFDC and its relationship with work programmes

> reflects a changing, and often controversial, set of goals, expectations and priorities. Debates have raged, not only about the most effective ways to link welfare and employment, but also about the appropriateness and fairness of any kind of requirement for women receiving AFDC
>
> (Champion, H, 1985, p8).

This seems an entirely appropriate view of the earlier summary of the changing work/welfare legislation of the last 30 years which suggests that the changes introduced over time reflect swings in conflicting philosophies about rights versus obligations, incentives versus disincentives, dependence versus barriers to self-sufficiency.

Much of the rising anxiety about these conflicting issues seems to have been due, as already mentioned, to the increasing number of claimants and costs of AFDC. This plus the extension of the benefit to two-parent unemployed families gave rise to critics seeing AFDC as increasingly undermining the work ethic and creating dependence on benefit.

The case for compulsory workfare is generally put on a number of inter-related arguments arising from these and similar issues, including

a   that people who can should support themselves;
b   that it is an effective test of need – those who do not really need welfare help will be deterred from claiming by the work requirement;
c   that it can reduce welfare costs;
d   that it can maintain labour market attachment, preserve or improve work skills and instil a sense of responsibility and 'work ethic';
e   that it makes welfare more equitable between those in and out of employment.

Supporters also suggest that useful public services could be performed in mandatory public jobs and that workfare will reduce public hostility and increase public support for welfare.

Those opposed to workfare argue that:

a   the community should support those who cannot support
     themselves;
b   workfare is bound, in some cases, to impose a work require-
     ment on people for whom such a requirement is inappropri-
     ate;
c   there will be undue pressure even on those who are not
     mandated to workfare to undertake it;
d   workfare is stigmatizing and contrary to traditional forms of
     support which have developed systems of universal income
     support like negative income tax;
e   mandatory workfare would be difficult to implement on a large
     scale, requiring large numbers of jobs that provide skills devel-
     opment without displacement of existing potential employees.

Workfare opponents also reject the 'needs test' argument because
AFDC is in any case paid only to those with either no income or
a very low income and in many cases they are already obliged
to undertake a mandatory job search. The skills argument can
only hold true where there are relevant job opportunities. It is
not thought that this is widely the case. The equity argument is
thought to be unconvincing because job losses are almost invariably
beyond an individual's control and few people could be shown
to be willingly staying on welfare rather than taking employment.
Compulsory participation in a programme may also interfere with
an individual's job hunting which may be more efficient. Critics
also argue that voluntary, non-mandatory work programmes have
an advantage over compulsory programmes because volunteers
increase their self-esteem by being able to do so. Conversely,
mandatory participation often ignores individual circumstances and
can cause resentment.

   Nevertheless, the belief that women heading single families may
be 'trapped' on welfare is one reason for growing support for
compulsory workfare, which is seen as the first step for these
women to come off welfare and into financially self-supporting
employment. The implicit if not explicit attitude would seem to
have turned full-circle since 1935 when AFDC was introduced
specifically so that women (mostly widows) with young children
would not have to go out to work and would be able to stay at
home and look after them. The fact that many women with children
do now go out to work is used to argue the obligation to do so on
other single women. While it may be true that more mothers work
now than did in 1935, the prevailing attitude may stem also from a
notion that these single mothers are 'less deserving' than were those
– the widows – whom the AFDC was originally designed to serve.
Indeed, Joel Handler has suggested that the attitude that welfare
mothers should work is not new and that it can be traced back
to the time when they were first allowed to claim a benefit from

which they were previously excluded. He comments of the 1967 legislation that it

> marked the start of the counterchange in AFDC, but not because attitudes towards mothers had changed; rather, to reflect constant attitudes. In 1967 the program started its long process of reasserting social control (Handler, J, 1988, p30).

States and mandatory participation

Despite the obligation on states to have a work/welfare programme and on those who wish to receive AFDC to register and participate in the programme, there is in practice ambiguity about the concept, and states operate these regulations in different ways. The result, in practice, is to make the programmes voluntary in some states but compulsory in others. For example, registration may be mandatory but participation effectively voluntary. This can occur for a variety of reasons. For example, some states are sensitive to the difficulties that people face with child care or travel from rural areas, or they may be excused participation because of their own ill health or that of a family member. Or compulsion may be limited by allowing participants to choose between various activities, or they may not in fact be sanctioned for failing to take part. Where programme places are limited, priority may be given to volunteers.

Attitudes to workfare

Little information is available about the views of those obliged to undertake workfare. A number of the evaluations of work programmes by the Manpower Demonstration Research Corporation (MRDC) have studied participants' attitudes and report that many thought that the work requirement was 'fair' but that the employer 'got the better end of the deal'. MDRC suggested that because they believed that most of the states they had studied did not implement workfare with a punitive intent, this might explain why fewer participants than might have been expected viewed the short-term work obligation as unfair. Of course, that the work requirement was mostly short-term may have had a lot to do with it. On the other hand, in West Virginia, where the obligation to undertake workfare lasted as long as welfare receipt, the particularly poor labour market conditions which made their chances of finding employment unlikely, may have similarly made people less hostile.

There are other possible explanations for participants' views. In a society critical of welfare and with a strong sense of the work ethic, they may well feel that working improves their status, limits harrassment and get critics off their backs. The MDRC has suggested that their findings show that 'the poor want to work and are eager to take advantage of opportunities to do so . . . .These workfare programmes did not create the work ethic, they found it . . .' (Gueron, J M, 1986, p14).

However, researchers caution against the generalization of attitudes towards workfare. They point out that those interviewed are only a small proportion of participants and that they may not turn out to be representative of the total mandatory population. Those not included in the programme for one reason or another, including those who were screened out or sanctioned for failure to participate, might have quite different attitudes. Nor would the same attitudes necessarily be found if the programmes were differently designed, extended to a wider population or of longer duration. The results may also arise where states serve volunteers first. The very method by which the attitudes were obtained might itself need investigating. In my view, the data reviewed is so limited that it seems very likely that only one aspect of this issue has been uncovered. It seems strange to find such limited hostility. It may well be that such information is more difficult to come by and might only come from local campaigning groups.

Sanctions

The data on the use of sanctions suggests that the findings on attitudes towards workfare might have been somewhat different if the views of those who had been sanctioned had been investigated.

The GAO's 1985 study found that about 5 per cent of participants (in 39 programmes) were sanctioned (General Accounting Office, 1987, p62). However, there are considerable variations between states in their use of sanctions and within states between the different components of state programmes. The range between states in the GAO study was between zero and 29 per cent of participants. The GAO found twelve programmes in which more than 10 per cent of the participants had been sanctioned and that CWEPs (workfare programmes) 'tended to sanction more than other programmes' and that it was in the CWEP programmes that the highest percentage of participants sanctioned were found (General Accounting Office, 1987, p62).

The use of sanctions is thought to be restricted for a number of reasons. First, under the WIN programme a period of 30 days had to be spent trying to reconcile the dispute before sanctions were applied. Second, the administrative paperwork is thought to have been cumbersome and the process time consuming and costly. Some states that have switched from mandatory to voluntary programmes (such as Massachusetts) have done so in part to concentrate their limited resources on those who want to participate in the programme.

Extent of participation by different states

Although it is often thought that workfare is a universal programme operating uniformly throughout the US, this is not the case. Workfare is merely one component that states may choose to include in their work programmes.[2] Data for 1987 collected by the General Accounting Office (GAO) showed that of the 42 states with a WIN work programme, only 27 were operating a CWEP (workfare), 25 had job search programmes, 26 had extended AFDC entitlement to two-parent families and 8 had waivers allowing them to mandate participation of parents with children under 6 years (Congressional Budget Office, 1987, p25 and Nightingale, D.S. and Burbridge, L.C. 1987 pp44–9). Even where states do have workfare programmes they are unlikely to operate throughout the state. In 1985, of 22 states with CWEPs, only two operated statewide (General Accounting Office, 1987). Data collected at the same time also showed that participation is limited – to about a fifth of the adult AFDC population at that time – and this is generally attributed to restricted funding and the exemption of women with children under six years of age.

Just as restricted funding has limited the number of people who can take part in a programme, so too it has limited the sort of activities that the programmes can offer. The GAO obtained detailed information on the activities in work programmes of just under 500,000 of the total of some 700,000 participants. The vast majority of them were involved in individual or group job search (about 80 per cent). The CWEP accounted for only 20,000 participants of whom some 18,000 were involved in workfare. In addition, there were another 24,000 involved in work experience or on-the-job training under the WIN Demonstration programme. Neither of these, however, is identical to workfare. Even if those on workfare and work experience are combined they account for only a small proportion of those in work programmes. Participation in other activities was much more limited. Most significant is the large number of programmes that in theory offer education and training while in practice they accounted for only about 10 per cent of activities. Indeed, the Urban Institute concluded that in 1986 there were only four states in which the work-welfare programmes were providing a full range of employment and training services to more than a limited number of participants. These states were Massachusetts, New York, Ohio and Vermont. In seven other states a significant amount of training and education is provided with special state funds through vocational and educational agencies.

The dominance of job search activities places certain groups at a great disadvantage, namely those who need further skills if they are to get work. They may well also be more likely to need support services, help with child care or travel costs, which also makes them more costly to help. All these factors work against the participation of those with the greatest barriers to employment and in favour of those who would in any case have the best chance of finding work on their own. For these reasons the programmes have been accused of 'creaming' and failing to help those who are most at risk of remaining dependent on benefit, about whom there is most political anxiety. The new legislation may address some of these problems with its insistence on the provision of education and child care. It has also considerably increased the amounts of money that will be available. In 1988, the final year of the WIN programme, total funding was $93 million; the allocation under the FSA 1988 is $600 million for 1989 of a total of $3 billion over five years. However commentators are still uncertain that funding will be sufficient to provide a great deal of quality training, given that the states have to meet certain targets in terms of the proportions of the potentially eligible population that they serve.

Results from state programmes

Assessing the success of workfare and the wider work programmes is difficult for a number of reasons. First, what is 'success'? Politicians have wanted to see a reduction in the numbers dependent on benefit and to cut costs through a reduction in benefits paid. This is often linked to a concern with generating self-sufficiency. Self-sufficiency may be linked to aims to reduce poverty. But this is not necessarily the case. For example, costs could be cut without relieving poverty; programmes designed to produce one result might not necessarily produce the other.

The success of the programmes is also difficult to measure both because there are few nationally comparable statistics about the state programmes and because the programmes themselves are very different from one another. Moreover, where programmes do have workfare as well as other components, it may be very difficult to isolate its effects.

Some general information about the programmes was collected by the GAO in their 1985 enquiry. Information from 55 programmes found that the median 'placement' rate – the proportion of programme participants finding employment – was 30 per cent. A quarter of the programmes had placed less than 20 per cent; another quarter more than 40 per cent. Different programmes produced very similar placement rates (General Accounting Office, 1987, p99). But placement rates are not in themselves a measure of success. They do not take account of other influences, for instance, that some participants would have found work without the help of the programme; that clients vary in their qualification and work experience and therefore the ease with which they will find work; that states may avoid or aim their programmes at those with greatest barriers to employment, and that labour markets differ and that this effects the results that states can achieve.

The MDRC have undertaken a number of studies of state work/welfare programmes using control groups to allow them to assess the effectiveness of the programmes. These compare the employment and earnings of participants in the programmes (the experimental group) with a control group who have either not taken part in the programme or have taken part in some but not all of it.

In general the studies have shown no more than relatively small gains by the experimental participants over the control group for 'employment gains' – work found. Indeed, in some states there have been no gains of one group over the other. For example, statistically significant employment gains ranged in four states studied between three and eight percentage points. In two states there was no statistically significant difference between the two groups.

There was more variation in the earnings gain, from one state in which the average earnings of the control and experimental group were 'almost identical' to a 23 per cent gain (over a five quarter follow-up period) in another. This is an average earnings gain for the group, a combination of more women working than had done before, longer hours of work as well as better paying jobs.

The labour market is frequently cited as a critical factor. For example, in West Virginia, where unemployment is very high, programme planners did not expect there to be great employment or earnings gains and none were made. On the other hand, the highest employment gains found by the MDRC studies occurred in California, and they are thought to be associated with a less disadvantaged welfare population and an increasingly buoyant labour market.

But earnings gains from work programmes may also come from a relatively low base. The GAO found from their 1985 survey that (in 45 programmes) the average wage of those who found employment was $4.14 an hour – compared to a federal minimum wage of $3.35 an hour. While there was little difference in hourly rates between the different types of programmes, workfare had a slightly lower median hourly rate of $3.98 (General Accounting Office, 1987, p104). A further study by the GAO in 1986 found that of four work programmes, the highest hourly earnings gained were $5.45 an hour, by those who had graduated from the Massachusetts

Employment and Training Choices programme; this is thought to be due to the much higher expenditure in the ET programme and greater use of education and training.

The generally low level of earnings is thought to reflect the fact that where programmes have not helped people to improve their skills, they are most likely to find jobs in the clerical and service fields traditionally occupied by women at entry level and low wages. On the other hand, programmes that manage to train and place women in traditionally male occupations have had more success at increasing their earnings.

Similarly the programmes are of least benefit for those with the most skills and recent work experience. Conversely those with the least skills and work experience gained most, that is they tended to achieve greater employment and earnings gains when compared with a similarly inexperienced control group who did not take part in the programme. This is not to say that this group had a higher employment rate or greater earnings than those with work experience, but that compared to their own control group, their gains were much greater than were the gains experienced by a better skilled and more experienced group.

In general, states have only made relatively small savings through welfare reductions, since many of those who find work are still eligible for AFDC although to a reduced extent. Indeed, initially there are no financial gains since there is a time lag between the outlay required at the beginning and the start of any eventual savings. The MDRC predicts that, in the states that they investigated, the outlay should be usually more than offset by savings over a two- to five- year period, but it remains to be seen whether this can be achieved.

Prospects for future programmes

The conclusions drawn by researchers range from those who view the results as being so limited as to be useless and an unjustified imposition on benefit recipients, to those who see the gains as small but 'useful'. But even for those who see them as having some value, the catch word is 'modest' and there is an underlying anxiety that the programmes should not be oversold in terms of what they can achieve.

Moreover, the researchers are also anxious to point out that there is no reason to assume that these results can be replicated elsewhere. They emphasize that the findings relate to specific participants in particular programmes, the best of their kind, often in areas with highly motivated and skilled planners and staff, in particular economic conditions (*see* for example, Focus, 1988; General Accounting Office, 1984 and 1985; Greenstein, 1987).

Workfare and poverty

Work and poverty

The second possible criterion mentioned for the 'success' of workfare and work programmes is a reduction in poverty. Workfare alone is of no help against this, since it only imposes a work obligation in return for the benefit but does not produce an increase in income and, as shown earlier, the average earnings of those leaving work programmes are generally low (General Accounting Office, 1987 and 1988). If this remains the case today, participants are likely to be doing not much more than swopping poverty out of work for poverty in work, especially once they have met their work expenses, in particular those of child care and health insurance.

The labour market

Chances for 'above the poverty line' employment will also depend on the labour market. In general the prognosis of recent years has not been very good as better paying jobs have been lost from manufacturing and gained in lower paying service industries. The number of working poor has also been increasing and the value of the minimum wage falling. While in the 1960s and 1970s someone in full-time employment would have had an income roughly equal to the poverty line for a three-person family, this is no longer the case. By 1989, a person in full-time work earning the minimum wage produced an income 30 per cent short of the poverty line for a family of three (Shapiro, I and Greenstein, R, 1989). If the minimum wage is not increased, it will produce annual earnings equal to only 60 per cent of the poverty line for the same size family by 1992 (Shapiro, I and Greenstein, R, 1989).

Lessons for the UK

This review of the evidence suggests a number of findings worth considering in the development of employment and training policies. First, programmes must be designed to meet specific goals; no matter what their respective merits, reducing the number of benefit claimants, reducing costs, combating dependency, encouraging self-sufficiency and fighting poverty are not necessarily compatible goals which could be the aim of any single programme. Indeed, each term in itself could be defined in a number of ways.

Second, to be successful, account has to be taken of the fact that the programmes do not operate in isolation and external factors have to be considered. These include, for example, the labour market –

availability and duration of jobs and rates of pay; availability and cost of child care; effects of compulsory participation on children; work associated costs.

In the United States there seems also to be a recognition that significant results cannot be got on the cheap and that, even at their best, programme results are likely to be 'modest'. Programme funding was increased markedly in the 1988 legislation, but Congress seemed aware that there could be no swift or great expectations of savings from the increased self-sufficiency that the legislation hoped to achieve.

The government have always maintained that they do not intend to introduce mandatory workfare in Britain and that adult training and employment schemes, such as Employment Training, Jobclubs and Restart, will not be made compulsory. But there are now doubts about this, first because of the introduction in 1989 of regulations which require unemployed claimants to show that they are 'actively seeking work'. Attendance at one of these employment or training schemes would count as 'actively seeking work' while not doing so is likely to lead to a further examination of the adequacy of the claimant's job search. While these are not strictly 'compulsory' schemes, claimants may feel themselves to be pressed to participate. Second, a leaked paper from the Department of Employment is reported to show that the possibility of compulsory training is still being considered, that it might be politically feasible in 1990 and would allow sanctions to be applied selectively to un-cooperative clients (Harper, K, 1989).

Notes

1 Certain groups of AFDC recipients have traditionally been exempt from compulsory participation. They include those who are ill, incapacitated, aged, geographically remote from a project, full-time students and those caring at home full-time for an ill or incapacitated member of their household.

2 All the evidence relates to work/welfare programmes implemented according to pre-1988 legislation.

References

Burke, V (1989) *Welfare.* Issue Brief, Education and Public Welfare Division, Congressional Research Service, The Library of Congress, Washington DC, USA.

Champion, H (1985) Evidence by the Former US Secretary of the Department of Health and Human Services to the Committee on Government Operations, *Opportunities for Self-Sufficiency for Women in*

Poverty. United States Government Printing Office, 99–459, Washington DC, USA.

Committee on Ways and Means (1989) *General explanation of the Family Support Act 1988*. United States House of Representatives, H.R. 1720, 100th Congress, Public Law 100–485. Washington DC, USA.

Congressional Budget Office (1987) *Work-Related Programs for Welfare Recipients*. Congress of the United States, Washington DC, USA.

The Economist (1988) *America's Shrinking Middle*, Schools Brief.

Focus (Spring 1988) Special Issue, *Welfare Reform and Poverty*. Institute for Research on Poverty, University of Wisconsin-Madison, USA.

Focus (Winter 1988–1989) *The Family Support Act of 1988*. Institute for Research on Poverty, University of Wisconsin-Madison, USA.

General Accounting Office (1984) *CWEP's Implementation Results to Date Raise Questions About the Administration's Proposed Mandatory Work Program*, GAO/PEMD–84–2, Washington DC, USA.

General Accounting Office (1985) Report to the Subcommittee on Intergovernmental Relations and Human Resources, House Committee on Government Operations, *Evidence is Insufficient to Support Administration's Proposed Changes to AFDC Work Programs*. GAO/HRD–85–92, Washington DC, USA.

General Accounting Office (1987) *Work and Welfare. Current AFDC Programs and Implications for Federal Policy*, GAO/HRD–87–34, Washington DC, USA.

General Accounting Office (1988) *Work and Welfare. Analysis of AFDC Employment Programs in Four States*. Fact Sheet for the Committee on Finance, U.S. Senate, GAO/HRD–88–33FS, Washington DC, USA.

Greenstein, R (1987) *Statement before the Senate Finance Committee*. Center on Budget and Policy Priorities, Washington, USA.

Gueron, J M (1986) *Work Initiatives for Welfare Recipients*. Manpower Demonstration Research Corporation, New York, USA.

Handler, J (1988) 'Consensus on redirection - which direction?' *Focus*, Spring Issue, Institute for Research on Poverty, University of Wisconsin-Madison, USA.

Harper, K (1989) 'Jobless may be forced to train.' *The Guardian*.

Nightingale, D S and Burbridge, L C (1987) *The Status of Work-Welfare Programs in 1986: Implications for Welfare Reform*. The Urban Institute, Washington DC, USA.

Shapiro, I and Greenstein, R (1989) *Making Work Pay: A New Agenda for Poverty Policies*. Center on Budget and Policy Priorities, Washington DC, USA.

11 Reforming family income support; reforming labour markets: pursuing social justice in Australia in the 1980s

Bettina Cass

Introduction: social justice and fiscal restraint: the structure of ambiguity

How can principles of social justice be placed on social policy agendas and implemented in some policy arenas, in a period when a government is imposing tight fiscal restraint, when the official priorities of economic policy involve significant restraint and real reduction in public expenditure with the objective of turning the Commonwealth government's budget deficit to a surplus, and then further reducing public expenditure as a proportion of Gross Domestic Product. Under what conditions did the Labor Prime Minister of a capitalist welfare state, whose government's priorities include controlling inflation, a wages and incomes Accord with the organized union movement to maintain wage restraint and generate job growth, controlling a burgeoning current account deficit and overseas trade imbalance, consolidating the processes of consultative corporatism between the government and the peak organizations of private industry and the trade unions, also promise to eradicate child poverty within three years?

To pose the question in this way is to connote a scepticism which is not my intention. Rather the intention is to connote contradiction, the contradiction between a Prime Ministerial pledge made in the context of an election campaign in July 1987 — 'By 1990 no Australian child will live in poverty' – with other government rhetoric emphasizing the importance of substantial reduction in the 'size of government' through the reduction of budget outlays as a proportion of Gross Domestic Product (Keating, 1989).

In pointing out this contradiction it is required that I declare my own interests. As Consultant Director of the Social Security Review established by the Minister for Social Security Brian Howe in 1986, I carried out for three years a Review of five areas of social security policy: income support payments for children, policies for sole parents, income support and labour market programs for the unemployed and for people with disabilities, and retirement incomes policy.

At this stage with six Issues Papers (Cass, 1986, 1988; Cass, Gibson, Tito, 1988; Crompton, 1987; Foster, 1988; Raymond, 1987) and 31 Research Papers published and distributed, consultations with interest groups held in relation to each Issues Paper, submissions received and analysed, several major social policy reforms implemented in the areas of family income support, retirement incomes policy, labour market programs for sole parents and the long-term unemployed, other matters currently on the political agenda, in particular policies for people with disabilities, and some major matters yet to be elevated to that position, I have returned to the *relatively* safer waters of university life to complete the Final Report.

I returned to academic life after three years of engagement in a highly interactive and public process of social policy debate, research, policy analysis, consultation and the formulation of policy reforms. In the process, there were periods of elation when key recommendations of the Review, requiring significant expansion of social expenditure and redistributive allocations, were incorporated into government policy, and periods of deep disappointment when other recommendations were overcome or displaced by the policies of fiscal restraint.

To be engaged in a process of social security reform in a period of fiscal restraint which has characterized Australian social policy and that of most other OECD countries since the mid 1970s, and to be concerned with the role of social security in combating poverty and reducing inequality, is to locate oneself in the interstices of contradiction, while remaining optimistic that the fundamental aim of the project is to keep principles of social justice on the political agenda, and to mobilize sufficient support for them to prevail. Second, to be engaged in a process of social security reform sitting more or less comfortably or uncomfortably both 'inside' and 'outside' Government is to take on all the contradictions of the 'stranger' (Simmel, 1950) subject to being 'in' but not 'part of' the administrative bureaucracy and outside its patterns of authority and management structure, yet, paradoxically, with the opportunity to have a clarity of purpose, a longer-term view and an autonomy denied to most of those bound to the day-to-day constraints of government and the political process.

The reference to 'social justice' in the question posed at the beginning of this paper is based on a particular application of that notion. By social justice I mean the use of a coordinated set of tax and benefit policies, collectively provided community services, education and labour market programmes, housing and health policies to intervene in market processes so as to redress the inequalities of income, wealth and resources generated by unregulated markets and the structure of gender relationships. This concept of social justice relies upon both horizontal and vertical equity principles (i.e. cross-class and life-cycle redistributions), embodied in 'social wage' provisions and tax policies, to guide the allocation of resources in those periods of life when age, illness or disability or obligations to care for others, preclude or limit labour force participation, or when the same constraints are imposed by adverse labour market conditions. In the light of these principles, Social Security Review publications stated from the outset that social security reform must resolve the apparent (in fact ideologically constructed) conflict between equity and efficiency criteria by addressing fully three major issues:

- *Redistribution or equity in allocation.*
- *Adequacy and uniformity of payments*, i.e. transferring a basic income sufficient to meet needs, to provide the conditions to live in dignity and to maintain or renew participation in economic and social life.
- *The making of links between income support and other programmes*, in particular education, training and job placement, and the services like childcare required to sustain economic activity, so as to restructure those conditions which create the traps of poverty, long-term unemployment and labour force marginality.

To expect that the tax/benefit system, community services and labour market programme will be the major bearers of equity principles is to sit within a social democratic tradition. However, the onset of recessionary periods in most of the capitalist welfare states since the mid-1970s, associated with high rates of unemployment and joblessness, high rates of inflation and the entrenchment in the 1980s of long-term unemployment and joblessness persisting even in the context of renewed economic growth, in conjunction with the imposition of tight fiscal restraint by many governments in the OECD area, demands a differently framed welfare debate,

G

envisioning more extensive and effective public policy and more democratic processes of representation (Mishra, 1984). First, it is held that the principles of social democracy or democratic socialism need to be reformulated to apply to those allocative institutions and areas of negotiation which they previously rarely entered. According to theories of corporatism, vigorous government intervention into labour market processes is imperative to achieve public and private sector employment growth, requiring the adoption of a full employment objective, with the associated public investment in active labour market programmes, as the old industrial structures change, and skills are made redundant (Korpi, 1989; Rowthorn, forthcoming; Sinfield, 1983). Such labour market interventions in conjunction with measures to reduce high wage dispersions are as central to a social justice approach as is reliance on redistribution through the tax/transfer system and through social services. To do otherwise is to rely on the belief that equity principles can prevail through a reformed social security system and through improved health and welfare provisions, leaving the market to embody only efficiency principles.

However, as has been shown in Australian research on wage fixation, the theoretical dichotomy between equity and efficiency in the market is questionable, because efficiency can be defined only with reference to desired ends. The definition of such ends might well include the breaking down of labour market segmentation and reduction in wage inequalities, since both rigid segmentation and high wage inequalities contribute to rigidities in the efficiency of labour market functioning (Gill, 1989). Further, Bob Rowthorn (forthcoming) has shown, in a cross-national study of various OECD countries, the various ways in which less unequal wage distributions, a more generous social security system and high employment rates interact to produce more egalitarian outcomes in the Nordic welfare states. This study points to the strength of a dual strategy which pursues equity principles both through the redistributions of the tax/benefit system, and through primary distribution from waged work, using public investment and government regulation to increase public and private sector job growth, dismantle the impediments to skills acquisition which confront those who would otherwise enter and remain in the secondary labour market and to improve the relative income position of the low paid.

Such a dual strategy requires the development of relatively egalitarian corporatist institutions, in which a well organized and strong labour movement is prepared to negotiate and has the institutionalized power to negotiate not only about the market wage and industrial conditions, but about training and skills acquisition and responses to unemployment (Cameron, 1984; Mishra, 1985). A further condition is a willingness of government and the unions to integrate wages policy and social wage provisions, to provide net advances in living standards through reduced unemployment, strong job growth, education and training programmes, childcare provision, adequate levels of social security payments and other forms of income support, industrial legislation recognising the parental responsibilities of employees, and labour market reforms which address the discriminations which confront women, ethnic and racial minorities and people with disabilities. The social policy literature identifies the Nordic welfare states and Austria as having some, but certainly not all elements of such corporatist models, which vary considerably in their levels of egalitarianism (Borchost and Siim, 1987; Jangenas, 1985; Korpi, 1987; Mishra, 1984; Rowthorn, forthcoming; Wadensjo, 1987).

It would appear from the recent comparative literature on social security provision that a strong labour movement, able to protect and improve the position of low paid workers, is also critical to the project of social security reform. Without these institutionalized protections, the punitive and exclusionary policies of libertarian and market welfare exponents are more likely to be successful in promoting and enforcing concepts of 'less eligibility', legitimating reductions in the real value of benefits so as not to create 'disincentives' to take low paid work. In addition, the coercive aspects of 'workfare programmes', like those mandated for lone mothers in AFDC programmes in several of the states of the United States, are able to go unchallenged, i.e. compulsory work in return for very low 'benefits' is able to be enforced, precisely because there is no strong union organization able to protect the wages and conditions of low paid work (Handler, 1987).

Recent developments in Australian social policy under the Labor government since 1983 have occurred in a developing corporatist structure. This follows an agreement between the government and the peak union body, the Australian Council of Trade Unions, negotiated prior to 1983 before the Labor Party was elected to office, and subject since then to continual 'bargaining' and renegotiation, that compliance with wage restraint under the wages and incomes Accord would be accompanied by increased provision of non-wage benefits and services, including universal health insurance, the more equitable coverage of occupational superannuation, childcare provision, paid and unpaid maternity leave, parental leave, and the use of tax and transfer policies to direct benefits to low and middle income earners with children. Such a log of 'social wage' claims, linked with wage negotiations, is unprecedented in post-war Australian trade union politics. A study of the corporatist negotiation processes in Sweden and Austria influenced the publication by the ACTU of *Australia Reconstructed*, following a much publicized visit to Northern Europe in 1987. This document noted the success of Sweden and Austria in achieving low inflation, low levels of unemployment, and strong job growth

through formal and informal processes of cooperation and negotiation between government, unions and business. The Australian
union officials proposed a very active role for the unions in industry
restructuring and industrial democracy, strong government and
business investment in training and retraining, and measures to
break down labour market segmentation (Australian Council of
Trade Unions/Trade Development Council, 1987).

The issue of the 'social wage' received much less attention, but
earlier Accord statements had put the case for universal health
provision and superannuation. These latter two have been major
achievements of this log of claims, through the re-introduction
of a universal health insurance scheme (Medicare) and an improved and somewhat more equitable coverage of occupational
superannuation. Subsequent developments in 1987–89 saw links
made between wages policy and family income support through
reforms of the tax/transfer system, in which the trade union movement played a key role in negotiation with the Commonwealth
Government over a wages/tax/benefits 'package'. In addition, in
early 1989 the ACTU announced its intention to use Australia's
currently highly centralized and regulated wages system to press
for substantial improvements in the relative position of low wage
earners, an initiative which, if implemented, will have implications
for reducing wage inequalities and for social security reform.

Australia's recent tentative moves in the direction of corporatism
do not involve only the traditional tripartite 'social partners' of
business, unions and government. Although there is little public
debate on this point, the tripartite arrangement holds the dangers
of entrenching the power of very strong elites, while excluding
those relatively powerless groups without the material or the
organizational resources to be even considered as participants
in the politics of corporatism. The feminist critique developed
by Borchost and Siim of the processes of political representation
in the social democratic, corporatist welfare states of Denmark and
Sweden shows women's low representation in formal state power
structures, the continuing sex segmentation of the labour market and
women's continuing responsibilities in non-market forms of caring
work (Borchost and Siim, 1987). In Australia, where the processes of
corporatism are much less developed than in Sweden or Denmark,
not only is there no specific representation of women's groups in the
key advisory bodies, but there is little explicit political discussion that
this might constitute an issue. It is expected that women's interests
are either subsumed within the interests of the 'key players,' or that
any separate interests will be represented, in particular by union
officials.

In the Economic Planning and Advisory Council, however, where
labour, capital and government discuss major fiscal, industry and
tax issues, there is representation from the peak Australian welfare

body, the Australian Council of Social Service (ACOSS), legiti-
mately placed in a context where the opportunities exist for the
non-government welfare sector to make strategic alliances. It would
be misguided in the extreme to believe that the very poorly funded
Australian welfare sector is in a position to prevail over the claims
made by unions and business and the fiscal restraint of government.
Nevertheless, an institutional base was forged in recent years for the
welfare sector to make public claims, and to have a public voice
not only on social wage issues, which is its traditional field, but on
other central economic, industry and tax policies (Disney, 1987). In
addition, some women's groups have a strong voice in the peak
organization of the welfare sector, and attempt to bring women's
issues and policies which would redress gender-based inequalities
into debate and advocacy. Welfare policy in Australia in 1983–1989
has been placed explicitly in the arena of wages and tax policy, a
placement recognized as such by the key participants.

This is the institutional context of the Prime Minister's child
poverty pledge.

The situation to be addressed: family poverty in Australia: 1972–73 to 1985–86

To answer the questions which I posed at the outset, this chapter
will outline the economic and social conditions and public policies
which placed *family poverty* centrally on the political agenda in
1987; the social security and labour market measures introduced
by the Hawke Labor government from 1987–89 in response to the
promise to mitigate poverty; other matters which have impinged
on economic welfare; evaluations which have been made of the
tax/transfer reforms; and then sketch briefly a longer-term view of
the policies and processes required to sustain reductions in poverty
and inequality. This chapter examines developments in Australian
family policy in the 1980s, defining family policy broadly to include
tax/transfer measures for dependent children, job growth and labour
market programmes to redress the workforce disadvantages of unemployed and jobless parents, and to expand their opportunities to
find secure work.

The end of 'full employment' in Australia from 1974–75, which
ushered in a period of reduced levels of economic growth, increased
rates of inflation, increased rates and durations of unemployment
and joblessness, followed by the recessions of 1978–79 and
1982–83 (when unemployment rates reached almost 10 per
cent), brought, by the early 1980s, recognition that rates of
poverty had increased considerably, and that households with
children were more likely than in the earlier post-war years to

be in poverty (Bradbury, Encel, and Vipond, 1988; Cass, 1988; Gallagher 1985; King, 1988; Social Welfare Policy Secretariat, 1981; Vipond, Bradbury and Encel, 1986).

Reporting in 1975, but basing its analysis on data collected in 1972–73 before the recessionary changes, the Commission of Inquiry into Poverty concluded that the *ability* of the household head to work was the dominant factor determining poverty. At that time, three-quarters of the poor were outside the workforce because of old age, sickness, disability or single parenthood or, in a very small proportion of instances because of unemployment as officially defined (which accounted at that time for only 3.4 per cent of all poor income units) (Commission of Inquiry into Poverty, 1985, p16). With the end of full employment, the dominant factor became the chances of adults in the household to *find* paid work, or to combine wage earning with childcare responsibilities.

Poverty has been measured in Australia since 1972–73 using the poverty lines constructed by the Henderson Poverty Commission. Although contention of both a scientific and a political nature surrounds the continued use of these measures, and the concept of a 'poverty line' has not been officially adopted in Australia, nevertheless this measure of poverty has provided academic researchers and welfare advocates with a powerful tool for mapping changes over time in the rate of poverty. Even more importantly, it has provided a means for identifying changes in the demographic composition of people in poverty (Gallagher, 1985; Saunders and Whiteford, 1989).

A government report on poverty measurement, published in 1981 and based on 1978–79 income distribution data, noted that it was not only the absence of paid employment which was associated with a high risk of poverty. The intensiveness of labour force participation also mattered: full-year full-time employment offered greater protection than part-time or part-year employment; two adults in employment, at least one full-time, provided the greatest protection; while the long-term unemployed and sole parents (the majority of whom were reliant on social security for their principal source of income) were among the poorest groups in Australian society (Social Welfare Policy Secretariat, 1981).

Again, analyses of Australian Bureau of Statistics Income and Housing distribution data for 1981–82 (before the major recession of 1982–83) emphasised the importance of paid employment in preventing poverty, finding that the key labour force characteristics associated with increased risk of poverty were long periods of unemployment or long durations spent outside the labour force, because of illness, disability or single parenthood (Gallagher, 1985; Vipond, Bradbury aand Encel, 1986).

Using the ABS Income and Housing Survey for 1985–86, King found an increase in the rate of poverty between 1981–82 and

1985–86, measured after taking housing costs into account. The household types which had experienced a significant increase in poverty were sole parent families (with 43 per cent in poverty in 1985–86) and larger two-parent families with three or more children, where about one in five were poor. This is attributed to the increased rate of unemployment (which rose from 6.2 per cent in 1981–82 to almost 10 per cent in 1983, falling to 7.9 per cent in 1985–86) and more particularly, to the increased median duration of unemployment (Table 11.1).

In summary, Australian poverty research from 1972–73 to 1985–86 has identified a strong association between labour market circumstances and poverty, citing increases in the incidence and duration of unemployment as the key explanation of both increased levels of poverty and the changing composition of people in poverty – namely, the increased share of poverty borne by people of workforce age caring for dependent children. While explanations tend to have focused on officially recorded unemployment, recessionary changes since 1974 also resulted in a significant increase in labour force withdrawal by people of workforce age, when illness or disability exacerbated labour force marginality (Cass, Gibson, and Tito, 1988), or when sole parenthood created significant barriers to women's labour force participation (Raymond, 1987). It was not only the increased incidence and duration of *unemployment*, but also the increased incidence and duration of *joblessness* which had a significant impact on the economic welfare of families. In 1972–73 households with dependent children comprised 28 per cent of all poor households; by 1981–82 this had increased considerably to 46 per cent. By 1985–86 the proportion had dropped slightly to 43 per cent, suggesting that conditions producing labour force marginality for family breadwinners had at least not worsened. Nevertheless, in 1985–86 poverty rates for large two-parent families were considerably higher than the aggregate rate for all income units, and the poverty rate for single parent families at 47.3 per cent was almost 4 times higher than the rate for all income units.

The rate for single parent families, in aggregating male and female sole parents, in fact obscures the much higher rates of poverty for women-headed families. However, since about 87 per cent of sole parents are women, it is not too blunt an index of the vulnerability of this family type. What is different about the period since the mid-1970s is the increased recorded incidence of sole parent families (currently comprising about 15 per cent of all families with children), largely resulting from an increase in separation and divorce, and the 'visibility' of women's poverty, which has been placed on the political agenda in Australia predominantly through feminist scholarship (Baldock and Cass, 1988).

Table 11.1 A comparison of the extent of poverty in Australia: 1981–82 and 1985–86[1]

| | No. of income units ('000s) | | Per cent of income units below poverty line | | | |
| | | | before housing costs | | after housing costs | |
	1981–82	1985–86	1981–82	1985–86	1981–82	1985–86
Married couple income units with no dependents						
head aged < 65	902.9	996.5	4.2	6.0	3.8	6.0
head aged > 65	411.0	485.6	5.1	4.8	3.1	3.8
Married couple income units with dependents						
1 dependent	473.3	492.9	6.2	6.3	6.7	6.8
2 dependents	656.0	659.9	7.2	8.1	7.3	7.8
3 dependents	284.1	276.1	10.5	19.0	8.9	20.1
4 or more dependents	96.6	94.1	26.6	23.9	23.9	21.3
Single parent income units	211.9	249.7	43.4	47.3	37.6	43.2
Single person income units						
aged 15–24	377.1	367.0	16.0	15.1	20.8	17.2
aged 25–64	855.8	962.0	11.9	16.2	11.8	10.9
aged > 65	576.0	600.2	7.2	13.7	4.6	4.5
All income units	4844.7	5184.2	10.1	12.6	9.5	10.4

Source: Estimates based on unit record data from the ABS 1981–82 *Income and Housing Survey* and ABS 1986 *Income Distribution Survey*.
Excludes income units with self-employment as principal source of income and income units who were children of the household head.

The convergence of two trends, usually treated as separate, resulted in the increased share of poverty borne by families with children. The first was the increased rate and duration of unemployment affecting family breadwinners, both male and female. Between 1974 and 1983 the number of two-parent families where the father was unemployed increased by 340 per cent (from 25,000 to 110,100 families), but then fell considerably with the reduction in unemployment from 1983. Further, there is a strong association between husbands' unemployment and wives' unemployment or low labour force participation: the wives of unemployed men have markedly higher unemployment rates and considerably lower labour force participation rates than do the wives of employed men. In 1988, wives with unemployed husbands had an unemployment rate which was eight times higher than the rate for wives with employed husbands and a labour force participation rate which was only half that of wives whose husbands were in work: unemployment rates of 43.8 per cent and 5.3 per cent respectively; participation rates of 29.4 per cent and 59.8 per cent respectively (Table 11.2).

The second trend was an increase of 87 per cent in the number of sole parent families in the period 1974 to 1988, in at least 80–85 per cent of instances formed following the end of a marriage or cohabitation relationship. But, of much greater consequence for the number of families experiencing financial hardship is the increase in the number of sole parent families where the parent is not employed, an increase of 110 per cent over the period (Table 11.3). It is of interest that the labour force participation rate of female sole parents which declined substantially between 1974 and 1983 (from 45.2 to 38.8 per cent) saw a steady increase since that time, reaching 47.0 per cent in 1988. However, a significant proportion of this more vigorous labour supply is composed of yet unsuccessful job search, reflected in a high unemployment rate. Nevertheless the considerable increase in sole parents' employment rate since 1983 suggests a process of redefinition of the possibilities of combining parenting and wage earning, in a climate of job growth.

Despite the tendency of Australian poverty research to categorize the poor according to family type, essentially similar labour market conditions, parents' unemployment, labour market marginality and joblessness in a period of industrial restructuring constitute the core explanation. Family composition *is* important because sole parents face not only scarce resources of income but scarce resources of time, having to provide children's care as well as augment or provide the principal source of family income, if they can overcome existing barriers to workforce participation (Jordan, 1989). But poor two-parent families also contain low-income mothers, highly likely to be jobless or unemployed, and highly likely to experience formidable barriers to labour force participation, which appear to

Table 11.2 Married couples with dependent children: labour force status of wives in relation to husband's employment status 1980–1988

	1980	1981	1982	1983	1984	1985	1986	1987	1988
Wives with husbands employed									
1 Number ('000)	1737.3	1740.1	1726.4	1679.0	1708.4	1708.7	1698.6	1691.3	1738.3
2 Labour force participation rate %	47.6	47.1	47.9	48.5	49.4	53.1	56.7	59.1	59.8
3 Unemployment rate %	4.5	4.6	5.3	7.0	5.4	5.6	5.6	5.1	5.3
Wives with husbands unemployed									
1 Number ('000)	43.2	42.6	57.0	110.1	87.6	80.7	83.1	88.4	82.3
2 Labour force participation rate %	25.2	31.7	24.6	29.0	25.9	25.3	24.5	27.6	24.9
3 Unemployment rate %	39.5	40.7	32.9	51.7	56.8	52.9	58.3	46.7	43.8

Sources: Austrailian bureau of statistics *labour force status and other characteristics of families,* various years 1974–88. Cat.No 6224.0.

Table 11.3 Sole parents with dependent children: employment status 1974–88

	1974	1979	1980	1981	1982	1983	1984	1985	1986	1987	1988
Women sole parents											
1 Number ('000)	157.8	224.6	229.5	236.8	260.9	258.7	274.2	279.0	279.6	306.7	300.0
2 No. employed ('000)	68.5	85.0	86.8	89.0	91.2	83.0	93.4	98.7	109.3	118.0	117.7
3 Employment to population ratio %	43.4	37.8	37.8	37.6	35.0	32.1	34.1	35.4	39.1	38.5	39.2
4 Labour force participation rate %	45.2	43.4	42.8	41.2	39.3	38.8	40.5	40.8	45.2	44.1	47.0
5 Unemployment rate %	4.1	12.7	11.5	8.8	11.1	17.3	15.9	13.3	13.5	12.8	16.5
Male sole parents											
1 Number ('000)	24.7	45.5	40.6	45.3	45.5	36.6	39.5	37.4	40.3	41.6	42.6
2 No. employed ('000)	22.4	37.4	30.2	37.4	34.1	24.1	27.5	27.8	26.8	28.8	32.5
3 Employed to population ratio %	90.7	82.4	74.4	82.6	74.9	65.8	70.0	74.3	66.5	69.2	76.3
4 Labour force participation rate %	94.7	87.0	78.6	87.9	83.5	79.7	77.4	78.9	76.7	76.7	83.3
5 Unemployment rate %	4.3	5.3	5.3	6.3	10.3	17.5	—	—	15.7	9.7	8.5

Sources: Australian bureau of statistics *labour force status and other characteristics of families*, various years 1974–88. Cat.No. 6224.0.

be as entrenched as those confronting sole mothers (Donnelly and McClelland, 1989). As Jane Millar (1987) notes, using British data, it is the underlying *similarities* and *continuities* in the disadvantaged labour market circumstances of both single-parent and two-parent families in poverty and of women in particular, which are of greater importance in explanatory terms and for policy formulation than is a more narrow consideration of family composition.

Statistical and survey studies of people in poverty were published in Australia through the period 1981–87, a process of research and advocacy on which the Social Security Review drew and to which it contributed. Issues Paper No 1 of the Social Security Review on *Income Support for Families*, published in 1986, recommended that immediate priority in social security reform be given to providing adequate and indexed levels of income support for children in low-income families, both those outside the workforce and those in low-paid work. In addition, *Issues Papers* 3, 4 and 5 of the Review recommended active labour market programmes to improve parents' employability and earning capacity. Access to education and better levels of support while in education, training, retraining and job creation programmes, and childcare provision were identified as the public policies required to provide parents (in two-parent and single-parent families) with the resources to enter the workforce, and maintain job security. Strong and concerted lobbying from welfare organizations constituted an independent source of advocacy, usually supportive of the general position adopted in Review papers, but also critical when various groups considered that Review recommendations were not strong enough, particularly in terms of adequacy of payments, and liberalization of social security conditions (ACOSS, 1986, 1987, 1988; McClelland and Sheen, 1988).

Family policies: 1976–89

Apart from increased rates of unemployment and joblessness, another major cause of increased family poverty in the period under review was the failure of the social security system to protect family payments by indexation in a period of high inflation. It was an extraordinary anomaly of the Australian social security system, a situation analogous with other Anglophone countries (Britain, Canada and New Zealand), that children's payments had no protective mechanisms of indexation. Although all pensions and some benefits for adults were protected by indexation from 1976, both the universal family allowance payment and the income-tested additional payments for the children of pensioners and beneficiaries were not indexed and were increased only on an *ad-hoc* and irregular basis. As a result, the real value of family allowances had fallen by almost one quarter between their introduction in 1976 and 1983. In combination with the declining real value of the additional payments for children in pensioner and beneficiary families, the total real value of child-related payments for the poorest families fell by more than 17 per cent over this period (Cass and Whiteford, 1989).

Family Income Supplement (FIS) was introduced in 1983, a tightly income-tested payment for low-income working families with children, paid, like family allowances, to mothers. By June 1987 this payment was made to about 93,000 children in 31,000 very low income families, comprising about 2 per cent of dependent children. When the programme was introduced it was publicized as a work incentive measure, to ensure that low-paid workers with children would be better off in employment than receiving benefit. But since no real effort was made to publicize it, the take-up was estimated as very low, probably between 30–50 per cent of eligible families, although those who received it strongly endorsed its importance in augmenting low family income (Pech, 1986).

The Family Income Supplement and the additional payments for the children of pensioners and beneficiaries (the latter received by about 791,200 children in 420,000 families in 1987, comprising almost 20 per cent of dependent children) were increased several times by the Hawke Labor government from 1983, as part of an overall social security policy of 'targeting' increases in income support. Increases in payments for children in low income families were identified as a priority in a period of restraint, while the universal family allowance payment continued to erode in real value. As a result, a significant shift in the allocation of family payments occurred, giving much greater priority to income-tested payments in line with the objective of vertical equity. In a context of fiscal stringency and of poverty research demonstrating increased financial need in families, the debate about the relative weight to be given to universal assistance for all children or to poverty alleviation shifted inexorably both in public opinion and in government policy.

It was in this context that the Social Security Review's First Issues Paper *Income Support for Families with Children* was published and became the focus of widespread community consultation, carried out by both the Review and the Australian Council of Social Service. In addition, the Paper spearheaded negotiations between the ACTU and the government about the importance of family payments in a period of wage restraint.

The Social Security Review Paper went somewhat against the trend in recommending strongly that family allowances should be retained, increased and indexed as a universal payment to mothers to recognise the increased costs which child rearing incurs, but that priority should be given to substantial increases in the income-tested payments for low-income families. The Paper argued that there is no fundamental contradiction between horizontal and vertical equity measures for family income support: they fulfil somewhat different but overlapping objectives, in both cases providing mothers as principal carers with additional (sometimes their only source) of income to augment resources for their caring work.

Nevertheless, debate if not conflict about the relative merits of horizontal and vertical· equity instruments became a strong· one, given the government's defined fiscal imperatives. There were some on both the Right and the Left in Australia who dubbed universal family allowances 'middle-class welfare', presumably because the recipients were women in households where the *combined* parental income did not classify them as poor. The debate even reached the letters pages of the *Australian Financial Review*, couched in terms of the alleviation of poverty or tax equity for families as competing priorities for scarce social security expenditure. This debate gained great urgency in the 1986–87 climate of severe fiscal stringency and government determination to reduce the budget deficit. Into this volatile mix of politics and economics came the Prime Minister's statement that his government would, if re-elected, fight family poverty, and that 'by 1990 no Australian child would be living in poverty.'

Policy changes were introduced in two stages. In the May Economic Statement of 1987 the Treasurer announced the decision to income-test family allowances in the context of a package of cuts in social security expenditure designed substantially to reduce the budget deficit. The income test was set at $50,000 of joint parental income, where there was one child, with steps of $2500 for each additional child, and the abatement rate was set at 25 cents in every dollar by which joint parental income exceeded the relevant threshold. This income-test is indexed annually in line with increases in the Consumer Price Index and in late 1989 stood at $53,000 where there is one child, with steps of $2678 for each additional child. It is estimated that about one tenth of families with dependent children lost their entitlement to family allowances as a result of the income test.

The announcement was received, as would be expected from the public debates which preceded it, with approval from those organizations, particularly in business and industry, advocating tighter targeting of social security and severe reduction in public expenditure. It also received approval from some trade union and Labor Party members interested in the greater redirection of resources to low income families. A number of groups, dubbed by one Financial Review columnist as an 'unholy alliance' of the women's movement, the Catholic Social Welfare Commission and ACOSS, were critical of this major change in family policy for a variety of reasons: because of the erosion of the concept of universality in family support and because the removal of the payment from some mothers was based on the contestable premise that 'parental income' adequately reflected the woman's own access to income within the family.

The next step in the restructuring of family support payments was introduced in the budget of 1987/88, with the announcement of the 'Family Assistance Package' providing a significant increase in expenditure on income-tested payments for children in families receiving pension or benefit and in low paid working families. The Family Allowance Supplement was introduced, replacing FIS, and the totality of new measures represented a very significant restructuring of the overall system of family support, with about 63 per cent of all family assistance payments directed to 27 per cent of families in the lowest income groups. The Family Allowance Supplement built substantially on previous measures by:

- providing an increased payment in two tiers, the first tier for children aged 0–13, with a higher payment for children over 13 to recognise the increased costs of teenagers;
- promising to increase payments in stages to achieve benchmarks of 15 per cent for younger children and 20 per cent for older children of the married rate of pension, and then effectively to index the payment. These benchmarks were reached in July 1989;
- providing rent assistance for family allowance supplement recipients in private rental housing, a particular innovation for low paid workers who had not previously been eligible for rent assistance;
- directing the payment to mothers as the parent primarily responsible for children's care;
- increasing the income threshold at which the family allowance supplement can be received to $300 per week of parental income for a one child family, plus $12 a week for each additional child, thus bringing eligibility to receive the allowance further up the income distribution. Since December 1988 the income test has been based on the parents' combined taxable income for the financial year ending in the previous calendar year. In mid-1989 Family Allowance Supplement was received by about 10 per cent of families; in the main, these are families where only one parent is in the workforce as a low wage earner, or in a minority of cases, where a parent is a student or a trainee.

In an economic period characterized by marked fiscal restraint, this substantial additional expenditure on family payments ($500 million in a full year with additional increases in 1989/90 to reach the promised benchmarks and the commitment to indexation increases), together with the restructuring of the system of payments, represented a significant measure of redistribution. The ACTU, ACOSS and various women's groups welcomed the measures because of their redistributive impact, and because equity concerns could re-emerge in the prevailing atmosphere of expenditure restraint.

Taken together, the income-testing of family allowances and the introduction of the family allowance supplement reflect the demise of universality in current social security provisions, and the dominance of vertical equity over horizontal equity concerns. About one tenth of mothers lost, and a substantial proportion of low income mothers, about 29 per cent, gained an increase in payments for their children and the promise of a much improved and indexed payment for the future.

Turning briefly to the other side of the tax/transfer coin, the dependent spouse rebate, providing tax relief for taxpayers with a dependent spouse of whom a considerable number, but by no means all have dependent children (65 per cent), was much more rarely depicted as 'middle class welfare' during these debates, and in the climate of expenditure restraint escaped income-testing. Since men comprise 96 per cent of recipients of the dependent spouse rebate (comprising a cost to revenue of $1.01 billion in 1985/86), and because there is no income-test limiting the eligibility of taxpayers to receive the rebate, it could be said that horizontal equity is much less embattled in the tax system and in application to men's entitlements, in comparison with women's entitlements.

The final step in the reshaping of Australian family policy to date occurred in the April Economic Statement of 1989, when, in the context of a major statement about the restructuring of the income tax scales to reduce the tax liabilities of all tax payers (but to provide greater proportional relief to low and middle income earners), the Treasurer announced substantial increases in family allowances (the first increase since 1982–83) and increases in the rate of family allowance supplement. In addition, the Treasurer stated that from 1990 all child-related payments (including family allowance, family allowance supplement, child disability allowance, the additional payments received by pensioners and beneficiaries with children, the dependent spouse tax rebate and the sole parent tax rebate) would be indexed (Keating, 1989).

It could well be said that indexation is an 'act of historic justice' (to borrow a phrase from Hilary Land (1975), writing about family allowances in Britain). For the first time in the history of the Australian social security system a successful concerted effort was made to improve the adequacy of children's payments for low income families and to introduce indexation mechanisms to protect the real value of all children's payments. As a result of the various increases between 1983–89, the real value of total family payments for children under 13 increased by 41 per cent and by 84 per cent for children aged 13–15. In terms of structural change, it is held by various organizations concerned with family welfare (in particular the Australian Institute of Family Studies) that the principle of indexation provides the conditions which enforce the claim of children in low income families to a guaranteed minimum income.

It is critical to this analysis that these family income support reforms were announced in the context of a major political statement about taxation and wages policy. This signifies recognition by the government, the ACTU and the welfare sector (through ACOSS) that family living standards are composed of the net effects of the market wage, tax liability and transfer payments. This recognition clarifies the central role of family payments. They are instruments of tax equity; they are instruments which recognize that the wages structure cannot take account of family responsibilities, *and* they redistribute to women, who have major responsibility for children.

However, the question remains: is such a set of family policy reforms *sufficient* to the task of combating children's poverty, or does it provide a *necessary* base on which to build other programmes essential to altering the conditions of parents' labour force marginality? It is clear from the earlier analysis that sustained job growth, active labour market policies, and wage restructuring are also required, and this point has been made by various commentators (Australian Institute of Family Studies, 1989; Cass, 1989; Saunders and Whiteford, 1987, 1989). But at this point it is necessary to assess the impact of these policy changes on families' economic welfare.

Assessments of the impact of family policy changes

Analysis by Saunders and Whiteford of the impact of the 1987 measures showed a reduction in child poverty of about 20 per cent (bringing the number in poverty to about 400,000 children, or 10 per cent of all dependent children), with a substantial reduction in the poverty gap (of about 45 per cent) for other poor families (Saunders and Whiteford, 1987). The increases which took effect in July 1989 are expected to further reduce poverty; however this effect cannot be taken out of the context of the reduction in unemployment of family breadwinners and the increased participation rates of sole parents. Saunders and Whiteford noted that sole parent families and larger two-parent families with high housing costs, particularly those in private rental housing, were most likely to remain poor, indicating that a co-ordinated housing policy and an active labour market policy were required to complement the social security reforms.

The Australian Institute of Family Studies' assessment of the family policy reforms 1987–89 noted that the changes had redressed the losses in families' disposable income which had occurred over the 1980s, and provided substantial increases in the real value of children's payments (Australian Institute of Family Studies, 1989). This report identified two other matters relating not to the tax/transfer system but to employment growth and wage fixation, which have had, or are expected to have a significant impact on the economic welfare of families. The first is the general increase in employment, decline in unemployment rates and increase in labour force participation of married mothers and lone mothers since 1983. The second is the ACTU/government agreement to increase low wages through supplementary payments, 'broad-banding' of awards and through training while in employment. It is estimated that such attempts at a more egalitarian wages policy could benefit about 300,000 families with children.

To look first at employment growth: between 1983 and 1988 the proportion of two parent families with at least one parent employed remained constant at about 90.6 per cent, while the proportion with both parents employed increased from 40.4 pr cent to 50.9 per cent. In addition, the labour force participation and employment rates of sole parents moved strongly upwards. These trends are welcome signs of a reversal of the conditions which contributed strongly to the high levels of poverty measured in the period 1981/82–1985/86. They also indicate that an active labour market policy is required to create job opportunities for those who have not benefited from the period of growth.

While the numbers of two-parent families with the father un-employed and the mother not in employment fell considerably between 1983 and 1988 (from about 95,000 to 69,000 families), the concentration of unemployment is a key issue for social security reform and for the provision of active labour market programmes. Such reforms must recognize that there are two adults who might become income earners, if benefit conditions and labour market programmes were appropriate.

In addition, barriers remain to sole parents' labour force par-ticipation: lack of formal job qualifications; scarcity of appropriate childcare services; lack of English language fluency for migrant sole parents; problems of access to efficient transport services; reduced self confidence and self esteem. The Jobs Education and Training Program (JET), (to be discussed below), introduced for sole parents in February 1989, is designed to address a number of these barriers, particularly in the areas of training and job placement. However, the many interlocking dimensions of sole parents' labour market, financial, housing, and locational disadvantages require full recognition in public policy responses (Jordan, 1989).

Finally, the campaign of wage restructuring to improve the actual and relative position of low paid workers has the potential to benefit female sole parents and those who have left spells of long-term unemployment. Gaining a job is not sufficient in itself to ensure a long-term, secure employment history for those with few formally recognized skills, likely to move into low paid jobs in the secondary labour market. Measures to break down labour market segmentation and to reduce high wage dispersion are therefore a necessary counterpart to social security reform and job growth.

What are the likely effects of a programme like family allowance supplement on the welfare/employment transition? This payment is not only a measure for increasing the disposable income of low-income families with children, in particular low-income mothers, it is also a measure which might enable parents to enter and remain in the workforce with greater economic and psychological security. Although no systematic survey research has yet been completed on the effects of family allowance supplement on jobless parents' perceptions of their opportunities to enter the workforce, two studies carried out by the Social Security Review prior to the introduction of FAS shed some light on this question.

The first is a study of recipients of family income supplement which documented respondents' perception that the additional payment for children increased their net rewards from paid work and tipped the balance in favour of workforce participation (Pech, 1986). The second is the study of the barriers to employment faced by unemployed couples with children carried out in 1987, when family income supplement was still in force. There appeared to be very limited knowledge about this payment amongst the respondents, of whom a considerable proportion may have been eligible to receive it on entering the workforce. This study concluded that respondents perceived financial disincentives to entering low paid work, and in so doing losing the children's payments which beneficiaries receive, disincentives which would have been lessened by receipt of family allowance supplement, requiring of course knowledge of their entitlement (Donnelly and McClelland, 1989). Family allowance supplement is structured to better ensure that payments for children continue to be made in the period of labour force transition, while workforce earnings remain low in relation to family size.

Between June 1987 and June 1989 the numbers of two-parent families receiving family allowance supplement (compared with those receiving FIS) increased more than four-fold (from 31,000 to 143,500 families), with an even larger twenty-one fold increase for female sole parents (from only 924 to 19,600 families) (Table 11.4).

Table 11.4 Number of family allowance supplement recipients
compared with family income support recipients

June 1987–June 1989

	June 1987 FIS	June 1988 FAS	June 1989 FAS
2 Parent families N	31,016	128,631	143,552
increase	–	–	× 4.6
June 1987 – June 1989			
Female sole parents N	924	10,816	19,640
increase	–	–	× 21.3
Male sole parents N	192	1,519	2,28
increase	–	–	× 11.9
Total N	32,132	140,966	165,479
increase	–	–	× 5.2
Receiving rent assistance N		27,544	36,410
% of all FAS recipients	NA	20%	22%

Source: Department of Social Security administrative statistics

This is attributable first to the eased income test and eased income-
testing conditions compared with FIS, and second to increased
knowledge of the payment through more widespread government
publicity and information. It is clear that such a programme can be
of considerable importance in supporting workforce transition in a
period of job growth. The substantially increased receipt by sole
parents suggests that the supplement is seen as a complement to
workforce participation, supporting increased economic activity.

What does this analysis suggest about the role of expanded
and increased family income support in augmenting earnings
and supporting workforce participation? It suggests that there
are considerable benefits in programmes which, while certainly
not universal, cast their net much more widely than those which
are so narrowly 'targeted' that they include only those on very
low incomes, and particularly only those outside the workforce.
It is essential that such programmes avoid the risk of residualism,
and hence of marginalizing recipients. They are able to dissolve
the dichotomy between 'work' and 'welfare' and to establish a
more innovative arrangement of market wage and social wage,
as suggested in a recent OECD (1988) publication on the *Future
of Social Protection*. Where trade unions have bargaining strength
in political arrangements, such family payments are least likely to be
used to legitimate low pay. Their progressive role lies in providing

transfers to carers facing the increased costs of child rearing, while family income is relatively low in relation to family needs. Where trade unions continue to have the institutionalized power to protect and improve the position of low paid workers, the progressive role of such family payments will also be protected.

Labour market programmes

In 1988 the Commonwealth government responded to some of the recommendations of the Social Security Review by introducing two labour market programmes designed to redress the labour market disadvantages of the long-term unemployed (NEWSTART) and of sole parents (Jobs, Education and Training, JET). The significance of both is that linkages are made between receipt of income support and labour market programmes, so as to move the Australian system of social security for people of workforce age further down the 'active labour market' path pursued successfully by Sweden and some other Nordic countries; and to improve the skills and job chances of disadvantaged job seekers. The JET programme for sole parents is a major initiative, in that 'joblessness' is given a priority in access to training and job placement programmes previously reserved largely for those officially defined as unemployed. In other words, JET is a programme for women with sole responsibility for children, providing sole parents, on a *voluntary* basis, with individual assistance, information and support, access to labour market and educational programmes, job placement and subsidized childcare. Since the programme has been in operation only for several months, it is too early to make assessments about its efficacy. But at this stage there are signs that JET is meeting a considerable well-spring of demand for such assistance, tapping and supporting sole parents' struggle to combine caring with wage earning, which they are better able to do when the supports of childcare and family payments bastion their dual responsibility.

Even with these measures, Australia's armoury of labour market programmes has a major deficiency in the absence of public sector job creation (the very effective Community Employment Program was abolished in 1987) and in the relative lack of emphasis given to subsidized private sector employment programmes, since major emphasis is placed on training. There is evidence that such job expansion programmes in the private and public sectors are of importance in many OECD countries in breaking the nexus of labour force marginality faced by highly disadvantaged job seekers (OECD, 1987). Finally, re-instating full employment as a priority in both economic and social policy is essential if sustained improvements in economic welfare are to be consolidated.

Conclusions

To return to the question posed at the outset: 'How can principles of social justice be placed on social policy agendas and implemented in some policy arenas, in a period of fiscal restraint?' A partial answer lies in linking three claims: claims to re-instate a full employment objective, which requires realization through strong job growth and active labour market programmes; claims to a much more equitable combination of market wage and family income support than the old 'family wage' concept ever encompassed; and claims by the unions to reduce wage inequalities to improve the position of low-paid workers. There is a recognition in this tripartite strategy that reform of income support arrangements, reform of labour market programmes, increased job growth and a more egalitarian wages policy must be linked and coordinated. This Australian study of changes in family policy has shown that the directions have been mapped and foundations established, but a great deal of work remains, linking social policy with economic policy.

But social democratic policies for reducing poverty and inequality are not the only potential responses. Waiting in the political wings are libertarian and market welfare exponents whose responses, as now stated, would include labour market deregulation; withdrawing central government support from a range of labour market programmes; substantially reducing social expenditures; placing various health and welfare services in the market sector, where purchase would be bastioned by regressive tax concessions; tightening the eligibility for unemployment benefit while also reducing social investment in the components of an active labour market policy; and allocating very large amounts of expenditure for families through tax rebates, which would redistribute regressively (Freebairn, Porter and Walsh, 1987; Hendrie and Porter, 1987; James, 1989; The Liberal and National Parties, 1989).

This is the point at which the political debate stands in January 1990.

References

ACOSS (1986) *National Community Sector Consultation Conference on Income Support for Families with Children*, A Report on Proceedings. ACOSS, Sydney.

ACOSS (1987) *Assistance for Families*. ACOSS submission to the Social Security Review, ACOSS, Sydney.

ACOSS (1988) *Income Support and Unemployment*. ACOSS response to the Social Security Review Issues Paper, ACOSS, Sydney.

Australian Council of Trade Unions/Trade Development Council (1987) *Australia Reconstructed*. AGPS, Canberra.

Australian Institute of Family Studies (1989) *Families and the Tax Package*. AIFS, Melbourne.

Baldock, C and Cass, B, eds (1988) *Women, Social Welfare and the State*. Allen and Unwin (Australia).

Borchost, A and Siim B (1987) Women and the Advanced Welfare State – a new kind of patriarchal power? In Sassoon, A Showstack (ed) *Women and the State*. Hutchinson.

Bradbury, B, Encel, D, and Vipond, J (1988) *Poverty and the Workforce*. Social Welfare Research Centre, R&P. No 72, University of New South Wales.

Cameron, D R (1984) Social Democracy, Corporatism, Labour Quiesence and the Representation of Economic Interest in Advanced Capitalist Society. In Goldthorpe, J H (ed) *Order and Conflict in Contemporary Capitalism*. Clarendon Press.

Cass, B (1986) *Income Support for Families with Children*. Issues Paper 1, Social Security Review, AGPS, Canberra.

Cass, B (1988) *Income Support for the Unemployed: Towards a More Active System*. Issues Paper 4, Social Security Review, AGPS, Canberra.

Cass, B (1988) The Feminisation of Poverty. In Caine, B, Grosz, E and de Lepervanch, M (eds) *Crossing Boundaries*. Allen and Unwin (Australia).

Cass, B (1989) Expanding the Commitment to Children: An Integrated Response. In *Policy Issues Forum*, Victorian Council of Social Service, Melbourne.

Cass, B, Gibson, F, Tito, F (1988) *Towards Enabling Policies. Income Support for People with Disabilities*. Issues Paper 5, Social Security Review, AGPS, Canberra.

Cass, B and Whiteford, P (1989) Social Policies. In Head, B and Patience, A (eds) *From Fraser to Hawke*. Longman Cheshire, Melbourne.

Commission of Inquiry into Poverty (1985) *First Main Report*. AGPS, Canberra.

Crompton, C (1987) *Too Old for a Job, Too Young For a Pension*. Issues Paper 2, Social Security Review, AGPS, Canberra.

Disney, J (1987) Poverty, Welfare and Tax Reform, *Canberra Bulletin of Public Administration*, 51 (May).

Donnelly, C and McClelland, J (1989) *My Family is Depending on Me: A Study of the Barriers to Employment Faced by Unemployed Couples with Children*. Social Security Review, Background/Discussion Paper 29, Department of Social Security, Canberra.

Freebairn, J, Porter, M and Walsh, C (1987) *Spending and Taxing*. Allen and Unwin, Sydney.

Foster, C (1988) *Towards a National Retirement Incomes Policy*. Issues Paper 6, Social Security Review, AGPS, Canberra.

Gallagher, P (1985) Targetting Welfare Expenditures on the Poor: Work in Progress on Poverty in Australia 1981–82. *Social Security Journal* (December).

Gill, F (1989) Labour Market Flexibility and the Trade Cycle: Who Benefits? Paper presented at the National Social Policy Conference, University of New South Wales.

Handler, J (1987) Consensus on Redirection – Which Direction? *Focus*, 11, No 1 (Spring). Journal of the Wisconsin-Madison Institute for Research on Poverty.

Hendrie, D and Porter, M (1987) The Capture of the Welfare State. *Canberra Bulletin of Public Administration*, 51 (May).

James, M, (ed) (1989) *The Welfare State: Foundations and Alternatives.* Centre for Independent Studies, Sydney.

Jangenas, B (1985) *The Swedish Approach to Labour Market Policy.* The Swedish Institute, Uppsala.

Jordan, A (1989) *Lone Parent and Wage-Earner? Employment Prospects of Sole-Parents Pensioners.* Social Security Review, Background/Discussion Paper 31, Department of Social Security, Canberra.

Keating, P J (1989) *Economic Statement April 1989.* AGPS, Canberra.

King, A (1988) The extent of poverty in Australia, 1981–82 and 1985–86, *Social Policy Research Unit Newsletter*, National Institute of Economic and Industry Research (November).

Korpi, W (1989) Can We Afford to Work? In Bulmer, M, Lewis, J, and Piachaud, D (eds) *The Goals of Social Policy.* Unwin Hyman.

Land, H (1975) The Introduction of Family Allowances: An Act of Historic Justice. In Hall P, Land, H, Parker, R and Webb, A *Change, Choice and Conflict in Social Policy.* Heinemann.

McClelland, A and Sheen, V (1988) *Unemployment and the Reform of Benefits and Training.* Brotherhood of St. Laurence, Melbourne.

Millar, J (1987) Lone Mothers. In Millar, J and Glendinning C (eds), *Women and Poverty in Britain.* Wheatsheaf.

Mishra, R (1984) *The Welfare State in Crisis.* Harvester Press.

Mishra, R (1985) Rethinking the Welfare State: After the New Right. Unpublished paper.

OECD (1988) *The Future of Social Protection.* OECD, Paris.

OECD (1987) *Employment Outlook.* OECD, Paris.

Pech, J (1986) *The Greatest Asset Since Child Endowment? A Study of Families Receiving Family Income Supplement* Social Security Review, Background/Discussion Paper 9, Department of Social Security, Canberra.

Raymond J (1987) *Bringing up Children Alone: Policies for Sole Parents.* Issues Paper 3, Social Security Review, AGPS, Canberra.

Rowthorn, B (Forthcoming) Corporatism, Wage Dispersion, and Equality, In Pekarrinnen, J and Pohjola, M (eds) *Coping with the Crisis: Lessons from the Corporatist Experience.*

Saunders, P and Whiteford, P (1987) *Ending Child Poverty: An Assessment of the Government's Family Package* SWRC R&P, 69, University of New South Wales.

Saunders, P and Whiteford, P (1989) *Measuring Poverty: A Review of the Issues.* EPAC, Canberra.

Simmel, G (1950) The Stranger. In Wolff, K (ed) *The Sociology of George Simmel*, Free Press.

Sinfield, A, (1983) The Necessity for Full Employment. In Glennerster, H (ed) *The Future of the Welfare State; Remaking Social Policy.* Gower.

Social Welfare Policy Secretariat (1981) *Report on Poverty Measurement.* AGPS, Canberra.

The Liberal and National Parties (1989) *Economic Action Plan* (October). Outline of Liberal-National Parties' Economic and Tax Policies.

Vipond, J, Bradbury, B and Encel D (1986) Unemployment and Poverty: Measures of Association. *Australian Bulletin of Labour Vol. 13, No. 3 (June), pp179–91.*

Wadensjo, E (1987) Labour Market Policy and Employment Growth in Sweden. *Review of Labour Economics and Industrial Relations* Florence, 1, No 3 (Winter).

12 Women and 1992: opportunity or disaster?

Gill Whitting

Introduction

The drive to achieve full economic and monetary union within the European Community (EC) brings to the forefront those issues historically at the centre of Common Market debates. In the past, the question of sovereignty has dominated the negotiations; to different degrees Member States have been wary of what they consider unwarranted intrusions into national affairs. Moreover, the economic thrust of the Treaty of Rome has prompted at least two major questions: first, will *economic* union bring benefits to *all*, or will it result in additional benefits to those countries, regions and individuals that already enjoy a relatively high level of social and economic integration and prosperity? Second, to what extent does the Treaty of Rome allow for policies that can inject a social dimension to reduce existing irregularities and counter some of the additional 'costs' of an economic-oriented Internal Market?

With regard to the second question, the development of equal treatment legislation is one of the most significant in the evolution of a European social policy. Indeed the promotion of women's rights has been assisted by Article 129 of the Treaty of Rome which imposes a firm legal obligation to implement a policy of 'equal pay for equal work'. And complementary to this chapter, Directives have been passed on equal pay, equal treatment and social security (Szyszczak 1986/7; Meehan, 1987; Docksey, 1987). Nevertheless, there are considerable obstacles to the progress of equal treatment between men and women throughout the EC, not the least of which is the attitude of the UK government which has seriously affected European policy, regarding, for example, parental leave and the conditions of part-time work. This attitude of the UK government draws attention to the most fundamental criticism of existing legislation, that is the restriction of equal rights to the sphere of work.

Even the more radical EC policies are focusing on a rather narrow set of issues that obscure the fact that many women cannot compete equally in the labour market. Women's roles in the family affect their employment experiences, not only in terms of access to work in general, but also in terms of the type of work into which they are channelled and the pay that they receive. Equal value campaigns emphasize this point that women's work is badly paid because the paid work they do is analogous to household employment and undervalued in the market because domestic labour is unpaid (Meehan and Whitting 1989).

The general issues that question the role of Europe and the prospects of economic and social integration are highly visible in the public debates surrounding 1992, the year set to complete the Internal Market. The more specific issues that identify the roles of and consequences for women, either as workers or as citizens with basic 'rights', are less visible. The Commission of the European Communities is however actively encouraging research and debate at a European level on the consequences for women (Moss, 1988, CEC, 1989). In the UK, the Equal Opportunities Commission (EOC) views 1992 as an opportunity to bring 'equal opportunities into the mainstream of British life'. The British government is being asked by the EOC to back its verbal commitment to equal opportunities with tangible support for new initiatives. The EOC strategy calls for measures enabling men and women to take an equal share in work and the family; an equal chance for women to have training; a narrowing of the pay gap between the sexes; better protection for part-time workers and greater protection in tax and pensions. It is important for this discussion to note the EOC emphasis on policies at the interface between *social and economic* problems in the relations between men and women.

The purpose of this chapter is to discuss some of the *social and economic* consequences of 1992 for women. It argues that the Single European Act is significant for women in the way that proposals interact with existing socio-economic structures and trends. For example, if economic integration is success-ful in its demands for a flexible workforce, the precarious position which women currently occupy in the labour market could intensify; women may remain unequal when compared to men as regards pay, conditions and career prospects; and the reform of the Structural Funds (main EC funds for re-gional development and training) may reduce rather than en-hance the visibility of women in EC expenditure, planning and resource allocation. On the other hand, the Single Euro-pean Act may provide opportunities for women to enhance their economic position, as European wide social policies are introduced, sometimes over the heads of reluctant national governments.

The Single European Act

Aims and objectives

The Single European Act (the Act) aims to remove all remaining barriers to free trade between the 12 Member States of the EC in order to achieve economic integration on a scale that would allow the European market to compete more effectively with its Japanese and American counterparts. Some 280 legislative measures are proposed to free the movement of capital, goods, services and labour and to remove a number of fiscal barriers. Monetary union is a further aim of the Act. A change from unanimity to qualified majority voting in the council of Ministers has assisted the agreement (of those representing heads of Member States) to some two-thirds of the Internal Market proposals. Unanimity still applies however for measures concerning the movement of individuals, employee rights and fiscal policy (Cmnd. 372, 1988).

The Act is primarily concerned with economic and monetary change. References to social policy and other sectors specify the health and safety of workers, recognizing the need to harmonize conditions across the EC, and the promotion of the dialogue between management and labour at the European level. Social cohesion features within the spirit of the Act. This relates to the strengthening of economic and social cohesion within the Community and, in particular, to the reduction of regional inequalities. For this purpose the Act specifies reforms to the way in which the Structural Funds are allocated and managed. Developments in research and technology are also encouraged in the interests of European and international competitiveness and a number of environmental actions are also recommended.

Social policy and social dimension

The Internal Market programme raises wider issues of social policy than those included in the Act. Social policies are required, first, to assist the operation of a European-wide market on the scale intended and, second, to meet the economic and social costs of consolidating the Internal Market. The role of social policy is well documented by the Commission of the European Communities (the Commission) (CEC [1988] 1148, September 1988). The Commission recognizes that the social implications of the Internal Market require the active participation of both national authorities and Community institutions. A number of priorities have been identified, for example, the social policy contribution to establishing a single European *labour* market; the scope and financial cost of providing *social security*; action in the field of *education, training and job creation*; and legislation relating to *working conditions and industrial relations.* The Commission makes reference to existing high levels of unemployment, growing inequalities in income distribution, the appearance of new forms of poverty and the processes by which particular groups in the population become marginalized and excluded (*see* Room, Lawson and Laczko, 1989, for a discussion of 'new' poverty).

The social implications of the Internal Market and the more concrete measures that may come forward from the Commission as part of the Social Charter have generated considerable controversy. The UK in particular has a reputation for opposing virtually all forms of EC social legislation. Although the 1989 European elections resulted in a balance of power perhaps more favourable to the development of a 'Social Europe', Mrs Thatcher is still strongly opposed to a social Europe because, in her view, this would hinder rather than assist the operation of a free, European-wide market. In Thatcherist terms, an EC Social Charter is legitimate only in as far as it deals with job creation and this in turn is viewed as a consequence of wealth creation. Other social policies are perceived as the sole and proper responsibility of Member State governments; therefore Mrs Thatcher strongly objects to the 'imposition' of legislation and the breaching of sovereignty with respect to existing or future EC legislation that deals with equal treatment, social security, workers' rights, and so on. However, it is interesting to note that one of the radical proposals coming from Europe concerns the introduction of a 'guaranteed minimum income' across the EC (O'Higgins, 1988). Although in its infancy, this proposal is allowing a debate to take place that would not otherwise be present in the UK given the social, economic and political preoccupations of the current administration.

Key issues

Any assessment of 1992, however preliminary, raises a number of issues. First there is the question of time-scale. The current debate places too great an emphasis on the 31st December 1992 as the date by which it is anticipated that European integration will be completed. Some of the changes are taking place in advance of 1992: this includes the issuing of new guidelines that determine the allocation and management of the European Social Fund, a fund providing essential resources for vocational training initiatives. Many of the the less controversial Directives have also been approved. These include for example the removal of technical barriers to trade of different kinds. By contrast, the more controversial legislation relating, for example, to the free movement of people is less likely to be on the statute books by the end of 1992. Realistically, the changes envisaged are likely to be effected far into the next century.

Second, each Member State is unique in terms of existing economic and social laws and policies, the traditions that underpin them, the institutions empowered to enforce or implement them. For example, different countries have different approaches to providing social security and any assessment of the effects of a more competitive job market will need to consider the social security implications and the differences between countries in their ability to respond.

Third, the aims and objectives of the Internal Market will interact with an existing socio-economic and political context. This context includes for example trends across the EC in demographic change, unemployment and employment patterns and, in consequence, their challenge to policy makers in the Member States.

The context for implementing the Single European Act

The most significant factors for the future operation of the Internal Market are the numbers, skills, location and 'flexibility' of workers. Demographic change in the EC will increasingly put pressure on the availability of younger workers. The service sector will continue to expand while the manufacturing sector shrinks and the skills required by employers will continue to change. It is anticipated that companies may relocate their operations as the opportunities within the wider European market become more visible; this relocation may be determined by the presence of a suitably skilled work force and/or it may have relocation consequences for workers seeking employment. (One of the fears voiced by the trade union organisations is that relocation decisions may be based on perceptions of geographical areas where trade union organization is weak or partial and/or where wage rates are low (Labour Research, November 1988).) But if new technology predictions are any indication of future work organization, the location of the worker may be less important as computer operatives can increasingly work from home. Nevertheless the trend is for employment to be more varied with an increasing number of part-time jobs, jobs undertaken by self-employed workers and jobs that are temporary.

It is anticipated that these changes to the location and nature of work will generate economic and social costs which will fall upon particular geographical areas and population groups. For example, the Commission warns that progress towards the single market is likely to involve new patterns of 'social exclusion and marginalisation' (CEC [88] 1148, September 1988). Over 40 million people in the EC are currently in poverty (O'Higgins and Jenkins, 1989) and approximately 10 per cent of an EC total population of 320 million are currently unemployed (Labour Force Survey, 1988). It is difficult to be precise as to how the Internal Market will affect the labour market; there is however no evidence to suggest that those who are vulnerable now will fare any differently after 1992. One assessment of the effects of the Act suggests that in the short term jobs will be lost; in the medium term an increase of 1.8 million jobs is forecast; in the long term the forecast is 5 million new jobs created (Cecchini, 1988). But these are rather sweeping figures based on rather controversial and questionable assumptions about the EC economy and the gains from market integration.

The detail of social policies vary from country to country but there are nevertheless common problems. Taking social security as an example, three problems arise (Com (87) 230 Final): the financing of current or projected needs in terms of social protection expenditure; the implications of demographic trends for public expenditure and labour costs; and the problem of marginalization affecting a considerable number of people in the Member States. Social security financing is affected by the growth in expenditure resulting from persistent high-level unemployment and pressure on old-age and sickness insurance sectors, and by a slowing down of incoming revenue. As the population ages, there are increasing demands on public expenditure, particularly on health for older people. The ageing of the working population also has consequences for the cost of labour; geographical and vocational mobility is likely to decline amongst older workers and a sharp drop is anticipated in the rate at which the active population is renewed. There may be a need for a migration policy to encourage labour mobility in the more distant future.

The consequences of the Act for women

The possible consequences for women arise, first, from their economic and social position within the EC labour market as it currently operates and, second, from the prediction that a more competitive and European-wide market will demand a more flexible response from its future work force.

Recent trends in the European labour market appear, superficially, to benefit women. Certainly between 1975 and 1985 participation rates for women have increased in all the Member State countries (*see* Table 12.1). Except for Ireland, where male activity has continued to show a major increase, women have been the chief agents in the 82 per cent growth in the active population in the EC as a whole. This change derives essentially from the rise in the relative number of women seeking work, especially married women who increasingly form an important part of those participating in the

Table 12.1 Women in the active population

Country	Mean annual growth rates of active female population	Contribution of active female population to growth in total active population (%)	Rates of female activity	
	1975–1985	1975–1985	1975	1985
Belgium	1.9	145	44.0	50.5
Denmark	2.3	75	63.5	74.5
West Germany	0.7	75	49.6	50.4
Greece (77–85)	4.0	66	–	41.8
France	1.8	106	51.0	55.0
Ireland	2.0	49	34.5	36.6
Italy	2.6	79	34.6	41.0
Luxembourg	2.0	200	38.3	43.2
Netherlands	3.9	76	31.0	41.2
Portugal	2.1	71	51.5	57.2
Spain (76–85)	1.1	104	32.4	33.6
UK	1.4	84	55.1	60.1
EEC – Twelve	1.6	82		

Sources: EUROSTAT and OECD. Employment prospects. Compiled by Daniele Meulders, *"Employment"*, Paper given at a Conference on Evaluation of Commuity Policy on Equal Opportunities, Toledo, April 1989.

labour market (Meulders, 1989). An expansion of the service sector has also contributed to the reorganization of female work patterns. However, further analysis suggests that the position of the female workforce has not markedly improved. For example:

– Women are not an homogeneous group: age, and other socio-economic factors determine their position and future opportunities in the labour market. Lone mothers and migrant women are two groups which are particularly vulnerable. Older women are also precarious given that their socio-economic position depends on previous work histories and current social protection (especially pension) rights.
– Women face considerable problems arising from long-term unemployment: with the exception of Ireland and the UK, the numbers of women unemployed – according to official statistics – is higher than the numbers of men unemployed (Table 12.2).

Table 12.2 Women out of work

| Country | Overall unemployment rates | | | |
| | 1976 | | 1986 | |
	M	W	M	W
Belgium	4.5	10.2	8.9	17.9
Denmark	5.1	5.2	5.7	9.8
West Germany	3.5	4.9	7.2	9.5
France	3.3	5.7	9.6	12.4
Ireland	10.4	6.6	19.2	16.8
Italy	5.2	6.6	11.2	18.6
Luxembourg	0.3	0.4	1.2	1.9
Netherlands	5.8	5.1	12.2	12.7
UK	6.0	3.1	14.0	9.3

Source: EUROSTAT; Meulders (1989).

- Throughout the EC, women tend to be confined to certain professions and, despite the Equal Pay legislation, are still likely to earn less pay than men.
- Women's jobs are typified by part-time, temporary and precarious work of many kinds; in the more developed countries part-time work is seen as a major characteristic of the service sector. In Italy, Greece and Portugal part-time work is a feature of the agricultural sector (Table 12.3).

It is argued that this current experience may intensify post – 1992. Completing the Internal Market places emphasis on 'flexibility'. For the employer, an existing workforce appears more flexible if workers can be moved from job to job by downgrading skills, contracts and shift patterns; a new workforce is more flexible to the employer if it is part-time, temporary, free-lance, home-based, subcontracting, and so on. Many Member States are indeed developing new forms of employment which differ from more 'traditional' jobs: the differences include working days, duration of contracts, hours, workplaces, mode of payment, and so on, preferred because of the advantages they offer to employers. Women's jobs are particularly affected by these developments (Huws, 1989).

Demographic and other future changes are likely to result in fewer people of the appropriate age to participate in the labour force. There are therefore considerable opportunities for women from all socio-economic groups to continue to take up work. These issues however raise policy questions. Although circumstances differ between different groups of women depending on their socio-economic characteristics, the demands of the Internal Market highlight the need for training – to ensure that *all* women can take

Table 12.3 Part-time work – data from the 1986 *Labour Force Survey*

	Part-timers as % of total persons employed	Women part-timers as % of employed women	Main sector	Main status
Under 10%				
Italy	5.02	9.51	00 Agriculture	Employees
Greece	5.78	10.33	00 Agriculture	S–employed Employees
Portugal	6.04	9.98	00 Agriculture	S–employed Employees
Ireland	6.14	14.29	9–6 Services and trade	Employee
Luxembourg	6.71	15.69	9–6 Services and trade	Employees
Belgium	9.37	22.64	9–6 Services and trade	Employees
From 10 to 20%				
France	11.71	23.05	9–6 Services and trade	Employees
West Germany	12.91	29.77	9–6 Services and trade	Employees
Over 20%				
Denmark	23.67	41.88	9–6 Services and trade	Employees
UK	21.36	44.51	9–6 Services and trade	Employees

Source: EUROSTAT (1986); Meulders (1989).

advantage of new work opportunities, especially in new technology industries and non-traditional occupations and for social protection to ensure that the unintended but perhaps inevitable consequences of integration are met.

Challenge for social policy

Social policies are required, first, to assist the operation of an European Community integrated market and, second, to meet the economic and social costs arising from economic integration. Policies are required that recognize that women overall require special treatment that will enable them to compete equally with men; however, policies should also consider the differences between women that require differential and not equal treatment. If women are to take advantage of new work opportunities, social policy needs to consider employment barriers, incentives and disincentives. Policies could encourage, for example: the availability of secure and well-paid jobs that can be filled by those with domestic responsibilities; the provision of good quality, affordable and accessible child-care; the provision of training to ensure that women have the skills required; the removal of financial disincentives created by the level and structure of social security benefits (Millar, 1989). To what extent are these issues addressed by EC policies?

Equal treatment

Equal treatment between men and women is addressed by the EC through its equal opportunities legislation and action programmes. The EC's commitment to equality between men and women goes back to Article 119 of the Treaty establishing the EEC, with subsequent legislation based on the Social Action Programme of 1974. The aim was to achieve 'equality between men and women as regards access to employment and vocational training and advancement as regards working conditions, including pay . . . and to ensure that the family responsibilities of all concerned may be reconciled with job aspirations' (Council Resolution 21.2.74).

In legal terms, the EC's commitment to equal opportunities is founded upon three main equality Directives (Docksey, 1987): the Equal Pay Directive adopted in 1975 designed to implement the principle of equal pay for men and women; the Equal Treatment Directive adopted in 1976 guarantees the principle of equal treatment for men and women in access to employment, vocational training and promotion, and working conditions; the 1978 Directive concerns the progressive implementation of the principle of equal treatment for men and women in statutory social security schemes. Two further Directives were adopted in 1986: to extend the principle of equal treatment to occupational social security schemes, and to men and women in self-employed occupations including agriculture, and the protection of self-employed women during pregnancy and maternity. The Commission has also drafted a Directive on Parental Leave and Leave for Family Reasons which is presently before the Council of Ministers; this has not been adopted owing mainly to the opposition of the UK government. There is also a proposal for a Directive on the burden of proof in the area of equal pay and equal treatment for women and men (Com (88) 269 Final). Once again, this has not been adopted due to opposition from the UK. In addition, the Commission has been asked to prepare a directive on the prevention of sexual harassment at work which would have as its aim protecting workers against the risk of sexual harassment and encouraging employers to establish and maintain working environments free of sexual harassment.

The Commission monitors existing legislation and develops existing policy through the establishment of Community Action Programmes on the Promotion of Equal opportunities for Women. There are also networks of independent experts from all Member States which monitor the practical and legal implementation of Directives, and note obstacles and cases of discrimination. There are now five networks covering: the application of the equality Directives, women in the labour force, the diversification of vocational choices, child-care, and women in local employment initiatives.

The challenge for social policy is, first, to continue to develop equal opportunity legislation and action at the level of the Community and, second, to assist the full implementation of these Directives and Programmes within Member States. The implementation of equal opportunities legislation relies primarily on the powers which the EC has to influence practices in the Member States. This is particularly so for policy areas, e.g. income maintenance, which remain the responsibility for national governments. Where legislation exists, as is the case for equal treatment between men and women, the EC is able to exert greater influence over Member States primarily through the work of the European Court of Justice. But even with this assistance, implementation is a complex, slow and frustrating process. 1992 presents a prime opportunity to review the scope of legislation and the content of plans and to expand policies and programmes to counter discrimination on the grounds of sex.

Unequal treatment

Social policy needs also to address the implications of 1992 for women who, on their own or with children, migrate to an EC country, either from within or outside the existing EC (Prondzynski, 1989). With the completion of the Internal Market, migration is a key area of concern. The situation for migrant women is complicated by at least three factors. First, persons migrating within the Community are provided for under the Treaty of Rome and subsequent legislation, conferring rights in employment, pay and conditions, and social security. In contrast, those persons emigrating from outside the EC are not affected by the Treaty (Sivanandan, 1988); their situation is governed by numerous national laws which differ from one Member State to another. Second, the majority of women enter the country of immigration as dependants, and not as workers in their own right. Third, migrant women are also a heterogeneous group. There are women who migrate alone or with their husbands and who seek employment in the receiving country. Women may join their already emigrated husbands and, in this case, the continuation of residence in the new country often depends on the husband's work and the marriage relationship. There are migrant women who choose not to work but who face problems of social and cultural isolation in the new environment. Women who marry migrants face problems arising from cross-cultural marriages and new problems are added if the migrant decides to return to his home country. Migration also leads to women being left behind with the responsibility for supporting and caring for children.

Migrant women pose a particular challenge for employment and training policies; typically, migrant women are in low paid, insecure employment with little opportunity to gain access to training schemes. Without sufficient attention to these issues, increased mobility in the 1990s and into the twenty-first century may intensify the situation for certain groups of migrant women who, at least initially, are restricted in their independence.

Training

The provision of training will play a vital role in the success of the new, enlarged market; the rate of women's participation in the more secure and better paid jobs will depend on their ability to acquire the necessary skills. Within the EC the major resource for funding vocational training is the European Social Fund (ESF), one of the EC Structural Funds recently doubled in size to support the Internal Market programme. In the past, these resources have been used in the UK to create and sustain local labour market strategies for vulnerable workers, including women, and to lever other financial resources from government and from the private sector (Whitting and Quinn, 1989).

The allocation of ESF funds has now moved away from priorities determined by eligible population groups on the basis of submitted *projects*. Priorities are now determined at the level of regions on the basis of *programmes* that specify labour market priorities. Because the successful training schemes run by or for women are often small-scale and local organisations, it is feared that the interests of women will be bypassed in the new allocation arrangements. The challenge for social policy is to ensure that area-based programmes filter down to those in the community most in need. In the UK at least it is proposed to prepare a separate women's training opera-tional plan. Other countries, especially the new members of the EC, are less experienced in getting European funds. The organization and development of women's groups also varies between countries;

not all Member States have women's organizations which can initiate and sustain training that is geared to women's needs. One of the results from the EC's Second Programme to Combat Poverty demonstrated how projects successfully met the training needs of lone mothers (Whitting, 1988). In many countries, the projects had initiated training schemes that were tailor-made to the life style of the lone parent family. For example, schemes provided childcare for participants and they were sensitive to the restrictions on a lone mother's time. But more than this. The approach to training and the organization and direction of courses required careful thinking to avoid a situation where women felt 'put off' or unable to participate, or even to feel a 'failure'. The example of training also emphasizes the need for proper monitoring and evaluation of social policy so that initiatives, particularly of the innovative kind referred to here, can be evaluated so that other organizations and future policies benefit from the experience.

Child Care

The European Child Care Network, established as part of the second European Equal Opportunities Programme, has undertaken a study of childcare policy and provision throughout the Community, and has made proposals for action to the Commission which in turn is committed to put forward its own proposals for action. The Childcare Network proposals envisage a three part European Strategy consisting of legislation, with Directives on Childcare Services and Employment Rights for Parents, funding for the development of services, primarily in less developed regions, possibly through the use of the Structural Funds; and a European Action Programme on Childcare, involving collaboration and exchanges between Member States. The Coordinator of the Network emphasized (Moss, 1988) that the issue of childcare, and more broadly, the issue of reconciling work-family responsibilities, is assuming greater importance in the Commission. This reflects an increasing realization that discussions of the implementation of the Internal Market have been gender-blind. For example, the free movement of labour needs a uniform and high level of childcare services and parental employment rights in all countries, if it is to fully benefit women with children. Although there is a serious lack of childcare provision in the majority of the Member States, a number of Member States are responding innovatively to the new opportunities for women and the labour market. In the UK, however, the position is far from favourable; current developments in childcare which consist entirely of exhortations to employers may well fail to address adequately a labour market opportunity of major social and economic significance.

Conclusions

It is virtually impossible to predict the outcomes of 1992; essential legislation has yet to be passed. Moreover, the scale of the operation suggests change far into the next century. However, for many in the UK the EC presents a political agenda far more progressive than the current, national policy agenda. In the field of social policy, debates are taking place in Britain which continue to reflect a more collectivist ideology; these are supported in Europe and are currently a challenge to the market-oriented and individualist stance of the Thatcher administration. Nevertheless, these more radical social policies are not enshrined in the Single European Act. It remains to be seen to what extent the social dimension of the Internal Market can be translated into legislation and more concrete and robust programmes of action. 1992 is essentially about trade: trade within Europe and between Europe and other world markets. The future of social Europe depends on the decisions of Member State leaders and their commitment to address existing and future inequalities within their own countries. In the UK the responsibility falls on political activists and commentators of many kinds to lobby and campaign for social and economic policies to address the issue of increasing inequality.

As far as women are concerned, the major impact of 1992 will arise from the demands of economic integration on labour markets. Although different issues will arise for different countries, the changes envisaged may reinforce rather than reduce the precarious and exploitative situation that typifies women's employment in Member State countries. But at the same time, 1992 presents an opportunity to raise and resolve issues that effect women's employment opportunities and outcomes. Social policies are required to ensure equal treatment between men and women and to recognise the *differences* in socio-economic circumstances and needs of different groups of women. In particular, migration is a key area of concern for 1992 and it is migrant women who are particularly *vulnerable* when it comes to the question of rights, protection and citizenship.

Note

An earlier version of this paper was presented at the Social Policy Association Annual Conference, Bath, 1989. At that time the author was employed by the University of Bath as a Research Fellow. She is now a Senior Researcher at ECOTEC Research and Consulting Ltd in Birmingham. The views expressed in this paper are those of the author and not necessarily those of the European Commission or other Community Institution.

References

CEC (1988) 1148, *The Social Dimension of the Internal Market*. September.

CEC (1989) Conference Report on Evaluation of Community Policy on Equal Opportunities. Toledo, April 1989.

Cecchini, P (1988) *1992: The Benefits of a Single Market*. Wildwood House.

Cmnd. 372 (1988) *The Single European Act*. HMSO.

Com (87) 230 Final, 'Problems of Social Security - Common Interests in the Member State'.

Docksey, C (1987) 'The European Community and the Promotion of Equality'. In McCrudden (ed.) *Women, Employment and European Equality Law*. Eclipse.

Huws, K (1989) 'Danger: Women at Work'. *New Society*, 17th March.

Labour Research (1988): 'Are Europe's unions United?'

Meehan, E and Whitting, G (1989) 'Gender and Public Policy: European law and British Equal Opportunity Policies'. Special issue of *Policy and Politics*, 17, no 4.

Meehan, E (1987) 'Women's Equality and the European Community' in Ashton and Whitting (ed.) *Feminist Theory and Practical Policies*. Occasional Paper 29, School for Advanced Urban Studies.

Millar, J (1989) 'Employment for disadvantaged groups: Single Parents'. Paper given at a Conference on Evaluation of Community Policy on Equal Opportunities in Toledo, April, 1989.

Moss, P (1988) *Consolidated Report of the European Childcare Network*. CEC.

Moss, P (1989) 'Childcare and Employment'. Paper given to the Annual Conference of the Social Policy Association, University of Bath, 1989.

Meulders, D (1989) Employment Paper given at a Conference on Evaluation of Community Policy on Equal Opportunities in Toledo, April, 1989.

O'Higgins, M and Jenkins, S (1989) 'Poverty in Europe'. Paper presented at EUROSTAT Seminar on poverty statistics, Nordwijk-an-Zee, Netherlands, October.

O'Higgins, M (1988) 'Horizon 1992 and the Guarantee of a Minimum Income'. Paper to a European Seminar CRESGE/EEC, Tilques, October.

Prondzynski, I (1989) 'The Social Situation and Employment of Women in the European Community'. In *Policy and Politics, op. cit.*

Room, G, Lawson, R and Laczko, F (1989) 'New Poverty in the European Community'. *Policy and Politics*, April 1989.

Sivanandan (1988) 'The New Racism'. *New Society*, November 4.

Szyszczak, E (1987) 'The Future of Women's Rights: the role of Community Law'. In *Year Book of Social Policy 1986/7*, Longman.

Whitting, G (1988) 'Women and poverty in Europe: experiences and action from the 2nd EC Programme to Combat Poverty'. Paper to the European Network of Women's Tribunal, Brussels, November 1988.

Whitting G, and Quinn, J (1989) 'Women and work: preparing for an independent furture'. In *Policy and Politics, op. cit.*

13 Alcohol and drug policies in Sweden and the UK: a study of two counties

Arthur Gould

This study was financed by the Nuffield Foundation

Introduction

This chapter was written because it was felt there was a need to compare alcohol and drug policies at a local level in Britain and Sweden. There is already a body of literature which outlines the national policy frameworks of both countries[1], but in the field of substance misuse[2] there has been hardly any attempt to see how policies are interpreted and implemented locally. It is widely recognized in policy analysis that to focus on the national level is misleading, given the variations that can exist between different local authorities and agencies. Moreover, the further from the centre a policy travels, the greater can be the impact of particular local welfare professionals and administrators, as well as local pressure group activity. While such an argument is taken for granted within one's own country, there is a tendency in comparative work to remain restricted to the level of national programmes, policies and legislation.

The choice of Örebro (Län) county and Leicestershire was partly a matter of convenience, since I work in the British county and had already had some research experience in Örebro (Gould 1988, chs 5 and 7). But of greater importance was the fact that each of the two counties seemed to represent an approach which *typified* a certain national tendency. I shall describe these later as a 'restrictive' tendency in Sweden and a 'liberal' one in Britain. Note that I am not suggesting that the two are *typical*. Rather they each represent 'ideal types' in each country which one would be unlikely to find in the other.

Both Örebro and Leicestershire are prosperous midlands counties with low unemployment rates. Although Örebro Län is four to five times the geographical size of Leicestershire, Leicestershire has a population of 860,000, over three times the size of Örebro Län's 270,000 (both these facts need to be borne in mind throughout the chapter, particularly when resources and problems are being discussed). However, neither could be described as including large conurbations.

Interviews were carried out with a variety of local professionals and officers in statutory and voluntary services in both counties, their 'capital' cities of Örebro (pop.120,000) and Leicester (280,000), and the small towns of Karlskoga (35,000) and Loughborough (55,000). The modest scale of the study made it impossible to interview all those concerned with substance misuse, but an attempt was made to interview those involved in the provision of specialist services, particularly those employed by health and social services, the education authority, the police and voluntary agencies. A similar range of non-specialists was also interviewed. This was felt to be important since their knowledge of, perception of, and referrals to specialist services were often crucial to the latter's effectiveness.

The questions concerned the substance misuse problems they faced, their respective policy rationales, the resources they had at their disposal, the degree to which they cooperated with other agencies, what difficulties they faced and what policy changes they would like to see. It was hoped in this way to elicit a broad picture of how the problem of substance misuse was treated in the two counties. The interviews were supplemented by annual reports and other documentation. The results of this survey are presented and compared after the next section.

Background

Swedes freely admit that their society lacks a 'pub' or café culture. What they mean by this is that for decades they have followed a policy which seeks to discourage alcohol consumption. Strict regulations ensure that establishments which do not provide restaurant facilities are not granted a licence to sell alcoholic drinks. As a result pubs are few and far between. Only state-run off-licences are allowed to sell wine, spirits and beer beyond a minimal strength. Moreover, Sweden's temperance movement, which has always had strong links with the ruling social-democratic party, has ensured that social policies generally have been influenced by temperance values. In particular, in the early part of this century, adult alcohol consumption was regulated by ration books, and the possibility of taking misusers into compulsory care has existed under various temperance laws since 1913. While the ration book system was abolished in 1955, compulsory care persists not only for those with an alcohol problem but also for misusers of drugs (since 1982) and volatile solvents (since 1988) (Gould 1988 and 1989).

It is illustrative in this context to note that whereas Sweden is regarded as a very liberal country on many social and sexual matters, on drink and drugs it is restrictive. Consequently, Swedish policies towards AIDS and homosexuals are considered quite progressive, but as far as the risks of the HIV virus being transmitted by intravenous drug users is concerned, needle exchanges are not permitted by national policy. Yet while the British have quite a reactionary reputation on social and sexual matters, and at central government level illegal drugs are frowned upon, needle exchanges have been encouraged as part of the policy to combat the spread of AIDS.

Even more liberal of course is British society's acceptance of alcohol. In 1979, the Central Policy Review, a central government think tank, produced a report which argued that alcohol problems were reaching dangerous and costly levels and recommended, amongst other things, that the government should seek to reduce overall levels of consumption. The Report was never published, let alone discussed publicly. Since that time alcohol prices have continued to fall, consumption has risen, the number of retail outlets has grown and licensing hours have been extended. In Sweden, on the other hand, central and local governments are committed to reduce Sweden's already low per capita consumption of alcohol by 25 per cent, in accordance with the guidelines laid down by the World Health Organization. Moreover there is much pressure upon the Swedish government to introduce a nil alcohol limit for car drivers. Another interesting contrast between the two countries is that, whereas in Swedish public debate 'drug liberal' is an effective term of abuse, in the UK, it is possible for major public figures to call for the legalization of drugs[3].

In both countries, attempts are being made to reduce the medical emphasis on drug and alcohol problems. This entails cooperation between, and the coordination of, medical and social services, to ensure that people are offered a wide variety of community-based services from information, advice and counselling to detoxification, psycho- and behaviour therapy. Moreover, the recognition that many people have a range of alcohol and drug problems has led to services being less preoccupied with 'alcoholics' and 'addicts'. This wider definition of the 'problem' population has led in turn to a greater recognition of the need to coordinate the efforts of other statutory agencies – such as education, housing and the police – and those of voluntary agencies.

In Sweden, collaboration between health care and social services is made a little easier by the fact that county councils are responsible for health care delivery, while the local kommuns (boroughs or districts) within the county are responsible for social services. In Britain, the National Health Service (NHS) is responsible for health care and the counties are responsible for social services. It is rarely the case that the boundaries of the NHS' district health authorities (DHAs) are coterminous with those of a county but this happens to be the case in Leicestershire, which means that cooperation between the DHA and Leicestershire's social services should also be somewhat easier.

In contrast it must be said that social services in Sweden have had greater experience in dealing with, and responsibility for, alcohol and drug problems. Apart from the temperance legislation referred to above, each of Sweden's major pieces of social services legislation imposes clear and explicit obligations upon the kommuns to deal with those who have such problems[4]. No such obligations have been imposed upon British social services departments. Moreover Swedish social workers, unlike their British counterparts, have traditionally been responsible for the administration of social assistance. This has widened the scope for intervention into the lives of those who misuse alcohol and drugs and are dependent upon the kommun for financial support.

Örebo Län

Rationale

Örebro's policy towards drug use has been heavily influenced by the pressure group FMN (*Föräldrar Mot Narkotika*, Parents against drugs) which is well organized both locally and nationally. This group sees the problem as an epidemic which will spread unless society takes drastic action. As alcohol has become culturally acceptable, so might drugs. Experimentation with soft drugs by the young is likely to lead to a progression to harder drugs and a career which will result in serious damage to health if not death. It therefore follows that all drug use is dangerous, and that early intervention by the authorities is essential. Preventative work must be vigorously carried out in a high-profile campaigning style to prevent the young from experimenting in the first place; and the compulsory care and treatment of young addicts in particular is seen as necessary because addiction, by its very nature, prevents those affected from seeking care on a voluntary basis. The health and lives of young people must be protected by the coordination of the efforts of parents, social workers, teachers, doctors and the police. Early detection and intervention inevitably demand vigilance and close supervision of young people's lives and activities (Örebro Län 1986a).

This evangelical approach is not reflected to the same degree as far as alcohol is concerned, although a recent campaign by the local temperance association called for county councillors to make a public declaration of their intention to abstain from alcohol for three months as an example to the young. The responses (mainly assenting) were published in the local press underneath photographs of the local politicians (Sundell 1989).

Organization, staff and resources

The division of tasks between the Län and the kommuns is a complex and changing one. Often the administration of a particular service is in the hands of one, but is partly paid for in the form of grants and fees by the other. Consequently there is a need for the joint planning of some resources. One can say that the Landsting's (county council's) health department has responsibility for the institutional treatment of misusers and detoxification services, while the kommuns provide out-patient clinical and counselling services as well as access to various forms of accommodation.

At the present time the county authorities have responsibility for three homes, each with about 40 places (Örebro Län 1986b), one of which employs about 60 people, half of whom are medical and social work professionals[5]. Since 1982 the county has also provided a special drug unit (50 per cent funded by the City council) solely to help young people. It employs seven full-time and three part-time staff, including a doctor, a psychologist and five social workers. The county's general psychiatric hospital has a special drying-out unit with thirteen places and a detoxification unit with 28 places (Örebro Län 1988).

Örebro City, a kommun divided into fifteen districts, employs three people to run an alcohol clinic (including a part-time doctor and two nurses), nine in a unit for adult drug misusers (including five social workers, a psycholgist and a psychiatrist from the Län's health department), three in an alcohol information and advice centre, six in a treatment unit, seven who run one short-stay hostels (21 places), twelve in two long-stay hostels (21 places each), and others who supervise accommodation in various flats – a total of 50 (Örebro Kommun 1988). Other kommuns, such as Karlskoga, Lindesberg, Hallefors and Kopparberg, also have advice and/or treatment centres as well as special accommodation for misusers. Even some of Örebro City's districts like Varberga and Vivalla-Lundby also employ specialist social workers and assistants to counsel misusers and supervise them in their accommodation on poorer estates. Substantial grants are also given to voluntary temperance organizations in the kommuns to provide drop-in centres, recreational facilities, counselling and support. Lastly, the county's police force employs ten criminal inspectors in its drugs squad.

Local problems: actual and estimated

Drug and alcohol problems are notoriously difficult to estimate, and a distinction has to be made between those people who come to the attention of various agencies and are helped or treated by them and estimates of the far wider range of people who do not seek help.

The agencies in Örebro Län were only too willing to provide estimates of the wider problems that existed. No prevalence survey was ever quoted but there was substantial agreement amongst informants. Alcohol dependency in the county was considered to be no different from the rest of Sweden; figures of one in ten of the adult population were often quoted. There was concern that women were drinking more than in the past but alcohol problems were considered to affect a wide cross-section of age and status groups. There was clearly a big problem with what were usually referred to as social rejects or outcasts (*utslagna*), often single men above the age of 35, with a spirits problem. With more certainty Örebro kommun's information and advice bureau was able to say that there were 6000 people who were dependent upon alcohol, by medical definition.

Estimates of the drug problem ranged between 2-5000 for the city of Örebro. The higher figure was often attributed to an estimation by misusers themselves. Most of those affected in the county were thought to be young men between the ages of 18 and 35, although an increasing number of young women were turning to drugs. It was also said that amongst young people there were more likely to be problems of mixed misuse (i.e. alcohol and drugs). There was particular concern that drugs were moving up the social scale. Whereas, in the past, it had been those who were without jobs and homes that were taking to drugs, more and more people with an established way of life were now doing so people with decent jobs and a secure way of life. Nobody thought that there were many cases of heroin or cocaine being taken. Cannabis and amphetamines were the chief cause for concern.

While the police claimed that 1250 individuals were on various local registers in the city as having a drug problem, the adult drug unit claimed that 500 individuals were known to other agencies. The latter, at any one time, was dealing with about 50 cases, while the county's drug unit for young people has reported an average number of new cases each year of about 30. During 1988 there were almost 400 visits to the latter unit by young people (half of them female), and almost 200 visits to the homes of young people by staff. In addition over 300 visits were made to other agencies concerning patients and 260 visits of a 'general preventative' nature (Örebro Län's Narkotikaenheten 1988)[6].

The city's alcohol clinic reported 447 people visiting them in 1988, three-quarters of whom were men and a quarter women. In total they made 2574 visits to the doctor to discuss alcohol and related problems. In addition 10,595 visits were made for medical treatment. This refers largely to visits made to the clinic by drinkers to obtain antabuse, a medicine which has the effect of making people vomit if they consume alcohol. This form of aversion therapy, common in Sweden, is hardly used in Britain.

In Karlskoga's Alcohol and Drug Unit, medical personnel tended to deal with alcohol problems and the treatment counsellors with those on drugs or a mixture of drugs and alcohol. Between 1984 and 1987, the counsellors dealt with 109 cases, 30 of whom were female. During the same four-year period 44 people were placed in treatment homes for periods of up to a year, while twelve were placed in foster homes (Socialtjäansten i Karlskoga 1989). In 1987 over 6000 visits were made to the nurses in the unit (mostly to obtain antabuse) and 155 visits were made to people's homes. Visits to the doctor amounted to just under 400. Fifty-two people were placed in treatment homes (Socialtjänsten i Karlskoga 1989).

Cooperation and coordination

Many of the respondents recognised a need for cooperation between various agencies over alcohol and drug problems. Many were also part of one coordinating group or another. Rarely were other agencies cited as being uncooperative, but psychiatric services consistently came in for criticism[7]. There is a statutory obligation for representatives of the county health authorities and the kommuns' social services departments to form a group to make decisions about resource planning for community and institutional care, Vårdresursplanering (VRP). There also exist advisory working parties set up at county, city and kommun level which aim to provide a forum for various agencies, statutory and voluntary. All of these deal with substance misuse to a greater or lesser extent.

VRP consists of a group of local politicians, backed by a working party of administrators. VRP functions with some difficulty since there are a wide range of interests to satisfy. There are often differences between the county representatives and those representing the kommuns; and between the larger and the smaller kommuns. A current problem besetting VRP concerns treatment homes for misusers. For some years places were being closed down because of the liberalizing laws of 1982[8]. The lengthening of compulsory care under the new 1988 LVM law[9] has created a problem. More places may be needed in the future but who will pay for them? The county has the responsibility to provide and manage such institutions but the kommuns have to pay the fees of those who receive treatment in them. Moreover the county wishes to retain an emphasis upon institutional care whereas the kommuns would prefer to provide more community care. In the absence of state funding and with the pressure upon local budgets to cut expenditure, decisions about institutional care are not easy. Another recent problem concerns the provision of drying-out and detoxification facilities. These at present exist within the city but there is a demand for such facilities within some of the kommuns. Agreement exists on the need for provision but not on which authorities should pay.

A different problem persists in the county *narkotikagrupp*. This has no decision-making powers or command over resources, but in 1984 it produced a policy programme for the county which by and large reflected the philosohy of FMN. This was subsequently watered down because of opposition from some of the kommuns, notably Karlskoga, where the social services department took a much more liberal line over drug problems. That tension still persists although in some ways it has mellowed. One of the intentions of the *narkotikagrupp's* drug programme was that each district of the city and every kommun in the county should have its own coordinating group to handle drug problems (Örebro Län 1986a). In reality such groups often find that they have insufficient drug problems to occupy their time and take on a wider brief, that of dealing with the problems of young people as a whole[10].

Cooperation between agencies is often made easier on those estates and in those areas where local agencies have actually been sited in the same group of buildings. In Vivalla-Lundby, a district of the city, the modern estate has many of its own public services located close by each other. This makes cooperation between social services, the school, and the medical centre a relatively easy matter. The same applies to the west district of Karlskoga and many others. Whether meetings are formal or informal, directly or indirectly concerned with misuse problems, cooperation between different services is enhanced by sharing the same or adjacent sites.

Changes required

Many respondents, including those in favour of compulsory institutional treatment, called for a greater emphasis upon preventative work, community care and smaller treatment homes, and some, particularly those in social services and in Karlskoga, were critical of the new law concerning misusers (LVM 1988: *see* notes 8 and 9). Others were well satisfied with the opportunities that extended compulsory care gave them but also wanted the consumption of drugs to be an imprisonable offence.

Although some, particularly the police, called for increased resources in dealing with the drug problem[11], there were many others who felt that the level of resources was satisfactory, including, interestingly, FMN supporters. The latter seemed to think that changes in attitudes were of greater importance and called for greater cohesion and commitment in the fight against drugs. Others were critical of resource planning and considered the present arrangements unsatisfactory. Greater cooperation and coordination were also often mentioned, but whereas some were concerned with tackling problems more effectively in a general way and preserving the confidentiality of individuals, others clearly saw a need for less confidentiality and a greater willingness to disseminate information concerning individuals.

The latter view was particularly common amongst those who saw the problem of drugs increasing. One respondent expressed the view that the scale and cost of the drug problem in the future would threaten the whole fabric of democracy in Sweden. While many estimated substance misuse in the future as stable or a matter of fluctuating cycles, others were clearly perturbed by what they saw as the drug problem's scale. A respondent concerned with the alcohol problem also raised the prospect of the welfare state crumbling under the weight of the cost of alcohol problems, claiming that it needed to be reduced in order that the money could be spent for more useful purposes. Others who considered alcohol to be the greater of the substance misuse problems, doctors in the main, thought that a return to the ration book system was justified.

Leicestershire

Rationale

If there is a dominant approach to drug and alcohol problems in Leicestershire then it is one that has been heavily influenced by the community drugs and alcohol services (see below). These clearly reject a disease model of such problems and steer clear of such terms as *alcoholism* and *addiction*. The prevailing rationale seems to be that we have to accept that we live in a drug-taking society. People take drugs in a variety of forms (including alcohol) and do so because they do something positive for them: give them pleasure, help them relax, make life bearable, help them to cope with other problems. Most people will be able to manage their particular drug in a way that does little harm, but in those cases where drugs are mishandled and begin to add to their problems, it is important that they have someone to turn to for information, advice, help or treatment. The job of these services is to *minimize the dangers* inherent in drug-taking. *Risk-reduction* is another way in which this philosophy is expressed (Cameron *et al.* 1981 pp 1-4 and Christie *et al.* 1989 pp 7-8). The concept of an inevitable 'drug' career has less of a place here. The experimentation with substances, which some young people indulge in, is seen as normal and in most cases, unproblematic; a phase which most pass through, relatively undamaged. Problems of misuse can take place at any time in a person's life and follow no particular pattern. What is important is that problems are responded to quickly, effectively, with minimal intervention and in the least stigmatizing way possible. Those who support this approach are usually critical of the kind of high profile campaigns that central government promotes.

Organization, staff and resources

The principal specialist services in Leicestershire are the result of cooperation between the district health authority and the county's social services department and the voluntary sector. The different parts of the Community Alcohol Service (CAS) were established towards the end of the 1970s while the Community Drugs Service was established in 1986. There are no specialized detoxification units in the county, apart from a few beds in a hospital for the mentally ill. What detoxification takes place occurs largely in people's homes.

The Alcohol Advice Centre and the Drug Advice Centre are voluntary agencies. Thus individuals seeking advice for themselves or relatives do not have to present themselves or reveal their identities to a statutory agency. Should further help or treatment be required, then people are referred to either the Community Alcohol Team or the Community Drug Team. Each of these consists of specialist medical and social services personnel.

The Alcohol Advice Centre consists of a director, a counsellor/administrator, a clerical assistant and a receptionist. Although it is a *voluntary* agency it is largely funded by Social Services with the receptionist paid for out of the Inner Area Programme (75 per cent central government, 25 per cent City Council). The Alcohol Team consists of nine people: a consultant psychiatrist, a psychologist, six community psychiatric nurses, a social worker and two secretaries. An important facility which the services make use of and are used by is Hastings Hostel, a registered charity, which has sixteen self-catering units for those with serious drink problems. Although no alcohol is allowed on the premises, it is not necessary for residents to abstain from alcohol. However, residents, who come to the hostel on a voluntary basis, must be motivated to do something about their problems. Through arrangements with a local housing association four further units provide nineteen places for people with alcohol-related problems. Altogether this core-cluster scheme, as it is called, is staffed by a team of twelve paid for by Social Services.

The Drug Advice Centre is also operated by a voluntary agency, Leicester Action for Youth Trust (LAYT) which is concerned with a number of problems faced by young people, drugs being one of them. It is financed by the DHA (70 per cent) and Social Services (30 per cent). An assistant director of LAYT is in charge of the Drug Advice Centre, which employs eight people: a county development worker, a drug-line volunteer coordinator, a risk reduction worker (part of whose job it is to operate a needle exchange scheme in the City), a hostel development worker, 1.5 social workers and two secretaries. The Drug Team consists of eight staff, including: a clinical psychologist, a consultant psychiatrist, clinical nurse manager, two community psychiatric nurses, two secretaries and a psychology technician (the clinical psychologist, clinical psychiatrist, the nurse manager, the psychology technician and one of the secretaries are shared with the Alcohol Team).

In addition the Health Promotion Unit employs a health promotion officer, concerned principally with drug and alcohol problems, and until recently the County Council's Education Department employed an adviser to schools on drug and alcohol misuse. Social services are currently about to appoint four additional social workers to work closely with two of the county's major hospitals on HIV and drug-related matters. The drug squad in Leicestershire Constabulary consists of thirteen officers.

Local problems: actual and estimated

No respondent was able to hazard a guess as to the numerical size of either the county's alcohol or drug problems. Although some thought alcohol problems were quite severe, Leicestershire was thought to have moderate problems in terms of alcohol and a minor one in terms of drugs. The police were particularly concerned with alcohol where it resulted in public disorder and drunken driving. The drug squad claimed that although Leicester was a centre for the wholesale supply of heroin, there was little evidence of heroin or cocaine consumption within the county. As in Örebro, the principal illegal drugs consumed were cannabis, cannabis resin, and amphetamines. Another worrying problem amongst young people still at school was glue-sniffing.

The Drug Services annual report for the year ending April 1988 shows that there were 878 responses by the service but only 317

(36.1 per cent) were contacts with drug users themselves and 125 of these were telephone contact only. The majority of contacts were contacts with third parties (friends, relatives and agencies) concerning drug users and general preventative contacts, visits and teaching sessions (Christie 1989 p20)[12]. The increasing use being made of the service is indicated by the fact that total initial contacts by the service were running at 30 a month in April 1987, but were over 100 by March 1988.

A different pattern of services response emerges from the Alcohol Advice Centre (Alcohol Advice Centre 1988)[13]. The higher number of responses, 1444, consisted of 621 (43 per cent) contacts with alcohol users of which less than 60 were by telephone (4 per cent). The remaining responses were third party contacts and preventative contacts, visits and teaching sessions. Total responses rose for the following year by 70 per cent to 2455 but the actual number of problem drinkers dealt with rose by only 8 per cent from 760 in 1987-88 to 822 in 1988-9. People with alcohol problems had a mean age of 40, while those presenting with drug problems had a mean age of 30. Of the problem drinkers 66.7 per cent were men. Of the DACs all known drug users 58 per cent were men, but of those assessed for long-term treatment 74 per cent were men.

Cooperation and coordination

While most agencies were regarded as cooperative by various respondents where it concerned substance misuse, general practitoners were most often cited as being out of touch, having a stereotypical view of drug problems, being isolated and unwilling or too busy to find out about what is available in the county. Yet while it was clear that agencies made use of the Health Promotion Unit, the Alcohol Services and the Drug Services, there seemed little evidence of local groups of professionals coming together at a local level to deal with substance abuse. However, a number of respondents had recently received a circular from the ministerial group on alcohol misuse, encouraging the formation of local groups to tackle alcohol problems in their area. The circular suggests how this may be done and the kind of work that such groups might undertake (Department of Health 1989).

However, at a county/DHA level a number of coordinating mechanisms already exist. With the increasing emphasis upon reducing the occupancy of hospital beds and upon community care, the mechanisms for making decisions about resources in Leicestershire are the two Joint Consultative Committees one for the DHA and the County Council and one for the DHA and the District Brough Councils. Each body consists of equal members of the DHA and the Councils, with a smaller number of representatives from the voluntary agencies. It is to the JCCs' sub-committees of Health Education and Mental Health that those making demands for resources for drug and alcohol services would have to apply.

By and large such applications, when they concern substance abuse, come from two other coordinating bodies – LACDM (Leicestershire Advisory Council on Drug Misuse) and LCA (Leicestershire Council on Alcoholism). LACDM was set up after DHSS Ministers asked every DHA to set up a Drug Advisory Committee in 1985. The membership of the Committee was to include representatives from the health service, social services, the police, the probation service, the local education authority and the voluntary sector. Many of those interviewed about the work of LACDM seemed to think that it had been effective in terms of getting resources out of joint planning/finance machinery and from other central and local government initiatives, but that it lacked a coherent strategy for the future. Some of its problems were seen to arise from the fact that it was heavily influenced by health service professionals, most of whom were involved in the management of the service. What had originally given LACDM its cohesion seemed to becoming a source of disadvantage, dissension and confusion.

When difficulties arose they were as likely to be between different elements within the health service as between health and non-health agencies. There was also concern about the under-representation of ethnic minority customers using the drug services. In part, it was felt that this arose because there was no ethnic minority representation; little contact with minority groups; and a general lack of outreach work in their direction. This was linked in the minds of some with the medical influence referred to earlier.

The same principal criticism was made of the county-wide coordinating body for alcohol problems, the Leicestershire Council on Alcoholism (a voluntary body and therefore different in purpose and status to LACDM). This body was not thought to function as well as LACDM and it was hoped that, with the possible future move to house the two services in the same building, one coordinating body could deal with both drug and alcohol problems. In particular there seemed to be a difference between those who preferred a medical approach based upon a reactive individual-oriented appointment-based system and those who favoured a pro-active, community-oriented, outreach service.

Despite these differences many respondents were proud of what the two services and their coordinating bodies had achieved in terms of a common philosophy, good practice and cooperation. It was said, more than once, that the alcohol service reached more than any other similar service in the country and there would seemed some strong comparative local data to support its claim to effectiveness (Cameron 1986).

Changes required

The possible amalgamation of alcohol and drug services in the same building was welcomed by those who preferred to see substance misuse as the principal focus of their work; as was the hope that this would lead to a unified management structure and coordinating committee. It was hoped too that this would lead to a better use of resources, a better way of tackling problems and a new sense of direction.

Within the health promotion unit it was felt that a more explicit acceptance by non-specialist agencies of substance misuse, and policies, personnel and resources to go with it were important. But although one respondent suggested that in-service training for social workers on drug and alcohol problems might come about (particularly where it concerned the well-being of children in families), generally-speaking, in non-specialist agencies, there seemed little concern with substance misuse as a specific problem. There seemed to be some evidence for the allegation that in social services and probation there was a lack of concern about such problems at a middle-management level. This was re-inforced by the non-specialists' claim that they did not need their own specialist personnel to deal with substance abuse. Indeed, in the case of the Education Department, it had recently chosen not to continue with the post of an advisory teacher with specific responsibility for substance abuse and instead to make it a part of the responsibility of a number of non-specialists.

Both non-specialists and specialists alike thought that there ought to be more resources for specialist services. One proposal was that the County, like the City, needed a risk reduction worker and the City, like the County, needed a development officer. The Alcohol Advisory Service needed an additional administrator to free the counsellor for counselling work, and a number of respondents pointed to the need for new staff to develop work with specific groups, such as ethnic minorities and women. Different respondents pointed to needs that were certainly met in Örebro such as drop-in centres, supervised housing arrangements and detoxication facilities (though on the latter there was some disagreement), as home detoxification and mental hospital detoxification were considered to be insufficient.

There seemed, amongst many non-specialists, a rather weak feeling that they should know more about substance abuse and that they should be doing more. This was reinforced by the many specialists who saw a real need to train, educate and inform primary workers about the problems. In addition, amongst both specialists and non-specialists there was the suggestion that collaborative work was what was required – agencies and workers working together on the same cases. Again both the police and the alcohol service could see the need for more collaboration over licensed premises. Criticism too was aimed at those services, like schools, local social work offices and general practitioners, that seemed to operate in isolation from others.

Concerning the prognosis of drug problems in the future, many would not hazard a guess and most thought that problems were likely to remain stable. Alcohol problems were likely to grow, it was thought, as long as the price remained low. As far as policy changes for the future were concerned, there was substantial agreement that the government's high-profile scare tactics on the drugs issue were misplaced and counter-productive. The greater problem of alcohol should be tackled centrally and locally in a variety of ways. Suggestions included further limitations on advertising, raising alcohol duties and lowering the alcohol limit for drivers. Many called for greater supervision and control over licensed premises and the 'drinking environment'. But always the emphasis was upon risk management rather than encouraging abstention. One respondent said drugs should be legalized, but in a controlled way; others said that liberal licensing hours were no problem, but that the drinking environment needed to be controlled. These were not arguments against control as such but for a different approach to the idea of control.

A comparison

The contrast between the way in which the practioners in the two counties perceived substance abuse problems and dealt with them was considerable. In Örebro there was a view amongst many that alcohol- and drug taking were abnormal and life-threatening to individuals and to society itself. The aim was a drug-free society to be achieved through high profile campaigns and early, pro-active intervention. This approach was promoted by pressure from the traditional temperance associations coupled with the modern equivalent in terms of drugs - FMN. The conflict played out at a national level between the restrictive and liberal camps over substance use and misuse (Gould 1988 and 1989) was reflected in both the formulation and implementation of policies in Örebro Län. Even the outcome was much the same with a compromise between the two camps in which the emphasis remained on the restrictive side.

In Leicestershire, alcohol- and drug-taking were regarded as a normal and acceptable part of human life, but with dangers that required prompt intervention. Intervention was largely reactive and scare tactics were avoided. There was no evidence of particularly influential pressure-group activity but a group of liberally-minded health care professionals seemed to have had considerable influence upon local policies. Whereas at a national level the government's moralistic approach to drug problems stood in marked contrast to its soft-pedalling on alcohol issues, in the County a more consistent attitude towards substance misuse as a whole led to a more tolerant and more understanding attitude towards the use of illegal drugs.

It may therefore be that in Sweden the strength of local pressure groups is an important factor in the formulation and implementation of local substance misuse policies. In Britain, where the existence of such groups is either weaker or non-existent, it may be (given the NHS's greater responsibilities for drug and alcohol problems) that the attitudes of local medical professionals are crucial.

In comparing the scale of both service provision and the problems they were designed to meet, it must be borne in mind that Leicestershire has three times the population of Örebro Län. Services in Leicestershire were heavily influenced by the medical profession and were centrally-based in the city of Leicester. The more locally-situated social services offices were not required by law to see substance misuse as a primary problem, nor did they. Although some work had been done to increase the awareness of primary workers in a variety of services, there was no line management pressure upon them to do so. In Örebro Län, social services were the responsibility of every kommun and were required by law to actively provide information and advice about alcohol and drugs, provide help and support to those with problems, and, together with the Län health authority, see that there were adequate institutions providing residential treatment for those adult and young misusers taken into care voluntarily and compulsorily. There were three such institutions within the Län, each with around 40 beds, but there was only one in Leicestershire, with sixteen places.

Örebro Kommun employed almost as many specialists to deal with substance abuse as the whole of Leicestershire County (about 50 people). Yet, while both counties had advice and treatment centres, many of the kommuns in Örebro county also provided such services. Accommodation for those with substance abuse problems was also more widely available in various kommuns. In Örebro city alone there were hostels with 50 places, while in Leicestershire there were, in addition to Hastings Hostel, only 19. Although detoxification took place within hospitals and people's homes in both counties the emphasis was on specialized medical units in Örebro and on home detoxification in Leicestershire. Moreover there is pressure at the present time for more locally-based detoxification centres in the kommuns; and while no-one in Leicestershire wanted to put the emphasis on large detoxification units, there were those who felt that detoxification facilities were lacking.

It is difficult to compare the statistics concerning caseloads throughout the two counties but it would seem that the work of the drug unit for young people *alone* in Örebro Län (over 1100 'visits') is similar to that handled by the drug team and advice centre in Leicestershire (less than 900 'responses'). In addition a number of kommuns including the one for adults in Örebro town, dealt with drug cases. As for alcohol problems, the number of problem drinkers receiving advice and treatment in Örebro Län's clinic (447) and Karlskoga's (approximately 250) would seem to come pretty close to the cases dealt with by Leicestershire's alcohol services (822). But in addition, there were literally thousands of visits to nurses in the Örebro and Karlskoga units, many of which were for antabuse tablets, a corollary of which simply does not exist in Leicestershire.

Both in terms of resources and caseloads then, the figures in Örebro Län would seem to be similar to, if not greater than, than those of Leicestershire in spite of the fact that the latter county has three times the population of the former. This greater service response in Örebro would seem to be directly related to the perception of the problem in the Län. Many of those interviewed considered that the problem they were facing was of damaging proportions and they were able to quantify its scale, whereas in Leicestershire the wide problems were seen as moderate and no-one could put a figure on them. While there was talk in Örebro of society and the welfare state collapsing under the weight of such problems, there was no such talk in Leicestershire. It is very difficult to know what to make of these contrasting perceptions. Can it be that in *the* welfare state, where unemployment is below 2 per cent and material poverty is almost invisible; where housing, health care, recreation facilities and public transport are all of such a high quality; and where general living standards for the mass of the population are as high as in the US, that substance misuse problems are higher than in a country plagued by unemployment, poverty and a generally low standard of public services? Or are the problems in Örebro exaggerated by a temperance tradition which still sees alcohol as a moral evil and an anti-drug movement which defines *all* drug use as misuse and imagines it is possible to have a drug-free society? The converse may certainly be true, that in British counties, the extent of alcohol and drug problems are under-stated; the awareness of the problems by non-specialist agencies, minimal; and the amount of resources and pro-active work necessary to adequately deal with the problems greatly underestimated.

Both counties recognised the need for cooperation and coordination and those involved in the various bodies seemed satisfied with the way they worked. Difficulties arose in both, between social services and health authorities, over the degree of community-based activity, but in Örebro there were significant differences over the allocation of resources and the financing of services. Here the differences were more between those who favoured a reactive apointment-based system and those who wanted more outreach work and community involvement. Although both LACDM and Örebro's *narkotikagrupp* could claim a clear cut philosophy, the latter's consensus had only been achieved after considerable conflict and debate, with many practitioners and some kommuns favouring a more liberal, less restrictive approach. Coordination at a local level seemed more a matter of course for the Swedes, although much of this was not concerned directly with substance abuse. There is evidence however that such coordination between agencies is being encouraged at a local level in Britain.

As to future needs, in both counties there were many who wanted to see more proactive outreach work and community-based work. Many would also like to see the price of alcohol increased. However there were also those in Örebro who also wished to see a return to the ration book system and a punishment of imprisonment for drug-users. In Leicestershire, the controls favoured for alcohol were less in terms of individual restrictions and more in terms of regulating drinking behaviour through controlling the drinking environment.

Conclusion

Two conclusions could be drawn from the above:

1   *That in Örebro they recognize the serious nature of substance misuse problems and make generous provision to deal with them and that in Leicestershire, problems are underestimated and neglected and services under-resourced.* Our tolerance of alcohol, it could be argued, is largely the result of the economic and political power of the brewing industry; a power that governments are unwilling to tackle. Moreover it would be politically difficult to restrict the ordinary citizen's drinking rights in a country where easy access to alcohol in pubs and supermarkets is seen as normal. It may also be that toleration of one serious drug, alcohol, makes it more difficult to be restrictive about other drugs.

2   *That in Örebro, the Swedes have got such problems out of proportion, over-react to them and as a result, exacerbate and even cause them, whereas in Leicestershire, minimal but effective intervention ensure that problems are dealt with in a humane and understanding way.* In trying to aim for a drug-free society and to prevent young people from indulging in experimentation, even in alcohol, Swedish temperance attitudes encourage the very behaviour they seek to repress. The lack of access to

a pub or cafe culture promotes a sub-culture which indulges in both alcohol and drugs to excess as a reaction against an over-bearing authority. Evidence for this can be seen in the drunken behaviour of school students when term finishes, the exams are over, or on the occasions of certain national festivals – a pattern of behaviour often referred to by those involved in local coordinating groups.

Only a definitive study of the estimates of alcohol and drug problems in both countries could satisfactorily show which conclusion is the correct one. My own feeling is, quite genuinely, that the answer lies somewhere in between. The Swedes probably exaggerate the scale of the problems they have to deal with but respond to them generously; whereas we underestimate alcohol problems in particular and provide inadequately for them.

A more relativistic argument might suggest that the two countries have historically and culturally determined problems to which they have responded in the way best suited to their own systems and practices. If that is the case then there is little to be learnt from their respective problems and policies. But is the only conclusion a culturally-bound one which argues that different problems demand different responses? On the contrary, the evidence of this chapter would suggest that there is strong meeting ground for those genuinely concerned with problems of substance misuse in both countries. There is much to be learnt from Sweden in terms of mobilizing resources and generating widespread commitment to deal with serious social problems. Equally there is much to be learnt from the British example in terms of recognizing the pleasures and needs which different *drugs* satisfy; the positive and rational side to such behaviour; and the complex and subtle ways in which risks and damage can be limited. Similarly, it is possible to see how a 'restrictive' approach can so easily degenerate into a paternalistic repression, while a 'liberal' approach can so easily become the basis for benign neglect.

How to mobilize resources and commitment without generating a moralistic panic, on the one hand; and how to deal effectively with the problems of substance misuse in a way that respects the integrity and rights of individuals are two questions that many practitioners in Sweden and Britain could usefully cooperate over in the search for solutions.

Notes

1 *See* Davies,P and Walsh,D (1983) *Alcohol Problems and Alcohol Control in Europe*, Croom Helm; Baggott,R Alcohol, Politics and Social Policy in *Journal of Social Policy* 15 4 pp 467-488; Stimson,

G V British Drug Policies in the 1980s in *British Journal of Addiction* 1987 82 pp 477-488; Smart,C Social Policy and Drug Addiction in *British Journal of Addiction* 1984 79 pp31-9; Gould,A 1988 ch, 7 and Gould,A 1989 (details below).

2   I have sometime used the term substance misuse throughout to avoid constantly having to refer to drugs and alcohol.

3   For example Professor Patrick Minford, an economic adviser to Margaret Thatcher, Jonathan Guinness and Auberon Waugh.

4   The 1982 Social Services Law (SoL), the law concerning the Care of Young People (LVU), as well as the Law on the Care of Misusers (LVM), all refer in their early sections to reponsibilities with regard to substance misuse problems.

5   Sweden had more than 50 such residential institutions in 1986 providing more than 2000 places (Swedish Institute 1986; CAN 1982). In 1981, there were 13 residential homes in Great Britain with less than 270 places (DHSS 1982); while in 1986 in the UK there were 78 catering primarily for those with alcohol problems with less than 1250 places. A significant difference when one compares the Swedish population of 8 million with the UK's 55 million.

6   Table 13.1 indicates in greater detail some of the activities of the drug unit including outreach work.

Table 13.1   The activities of Örebro Country's drug unit for young people February 1986–December 1988

		Feb 86–Mar 87	Mar 87–Feb 88	Feb 88–Dec 88
Visit to the unit	Boys	107	91	191
	Girls	50	92	197
	Total	157	183	388
Home visits	Boys	144	86	104
	Girls	74	63	83
	Total	218	149	187
New patients		31	27	37
Visits to other agencies concerning patients		332	198	306
General preventative visits		226	239	260

(Source: Örebro Läns Narkotikaenheten – verksamhetsberättlse 1986–88)

7   Partly because, it was alleged, that such services failed to see individual problems in a social context, and partly because they sought to offload difficult mental cases to agencies primarily concerned with alcohol and drug problems.

8   SoL, LVU and LVM (see above) were each an attempt to reduce the element of compulsion in Swedish welfare legislation. LVM in particular reduced the length of time an adult misuser could be taken into care compulsorily to a maximum of four months.

9   The new LVM (1988) increased the length of compulsory care for adults to six months.
10   These would include deciding what to do on those occasions during the year that school students would embark on bouts of heavy drinking eg the Santa Lucia festival, end of term and after examinations.
11   The drug squads in both counties felt that a major need was a greater range of cars, since the limited ones they had soon became recognisable by drug dealers and users.
12   Details are as follows: 14.2 per cent telephone counselling for drug users; 6.8 per cent advice sessions for users (short-term); 11.0 per cent drug users assessesd for long tem treatment; 3.9 per cent drug users referred to other agencies; 0.2 per cent assessed inappropriate; 36.1 per cent (320) total concerned with drug users; 22.8 per cent telephone counselling for third party (agencies, family, friends etc.); 1.8 per cent advice sessions for third party; 34.0 per cent teaching sessions, visits, projects, service information only; 1.0 per cent not known; 4.2 per cent appointment not attended; 63.8 per cent total other responses.
13   Details are as follows: 4.0 per cent telephone counselling for alcohol user; 8.0 per cent advice for user (short-term); 30.0 per cent user allocated to prime therapist; 1.0 per cent user referred to other agencies; 43.0 per cent total concerned with alcohol users; 9.0 per cent telephone counselling third party; 3.0 per cent advice third party; 28.0 per cent teaching session, visits, projects, service information only; 17.0 per cent appointment not attended; 57.0 per cent total other response.

References

Alcohol Advice Centre (1988) *Annual Report 1987-8.* Leicestershire Alcohol Advisory Service.

Alcohol Concern (1986) *Alcohol Services a directory for England and Wales.*

Cameron,D (1986) *Indirect Indices of Alcohol Problems.* Leicestershire Community Alcohol Services

Cameron,D, Hopley,M, Coope,G (1981) *Leicestershire Community Alcohol Services.* Paper presented at the Fifth Annual Conference on Alcohol Related Problems, University of Liverpool.

CAN (1982) *Alcohol Policy in Sweden.* Stockholm.

Christie,M and Arrindell,T *Annual Report 1987-88.* Leicestershire Community Drug Services.

Department of Health (1989) *Circular on Alcohol Misuse HN(89)4*

DHSS (1982) *Treatment and Rehabilitation.* Report of the Advisory Council on the Misuse of Drugs, HMSO.

Gould,A (1988) *Conflict and Control in Welfare Policy: the Swedish Experience.* Longman.

Gould,A (1989) Cleaning the People's Home: recent developments in Sweden's addiction policy. In *British Journal of Addiction* 84 pp731-41.

Leicestershire Community Alcohol Services (nd) Information Leaflet.

Örebro Län (1986a) *Narkotikapolitiskt Program*. Örebro.

Örebro Län (1986b) *Värdresursplan för Örebro Län 1987-9*. Örebro.

Örebro Län (1988) *Av och Till: enöversun av tillnyktrings- och avgiftningsvården i Örebro Län*. Örebro.

Örebro Läns Narkotikaenheten (1986-8) *Verksamhetsaberättlese*. Örebro.

Socialtjänsten i Karlskoga (1989) *Alkohol- och Narkotikaenheten: uppfölining från starten 1984*. Karlskoga Kommun.

Swedish Institute (1986) *Alcohol and Drug Abuse in Sweden*. Fact Sheets on Sweden, Stockholm.

Sundell,G (1989) Nio nykterister i kommunstyrelsen. In *Kuriren* 18th April 1989, Örebro.